Contested Classrooms

Education, Globalization, and Democracy in Alberta

Contested
Classrooms

Education, Globalization, and Democracy in Alberta

edited by Trevor W. Harrison and Jerrold L. Kachur

The University of Alberta Press
and Parkland Institute

First published by
The University of Alberta Press
Ring House 2
Edmonton, Alberta   T6G 2E1

and

Parkland Institute
11045 Saskatchewan Drive
Edmonton, Alberta   T6C oW3

Copyright © 1999 The University of Alberta Press
First edition, forth printing 2012.
Printed and bound in Canada by Blitzprnt Inc., Calgary, Alberta.

LIBRARY AND ARCHIVES CANADA CATALOUGING IN PUBLICATION

Main entry under title:
Contested classrooms

Copublished by: Parkland Institute.
Includes bibliographical references.
ISBN 0–88864–315–2

1. Education–Government policy—Alberta. 2. Politics and education—Alberta.
3. Education and state—Alberta. I. Harrison, Trevor, 1952– II. Kachur, Jerrold L. (Jerrold Lyne),
1955– III. Parkland Institute

LC91.2.A4C66 1999   379.7123   C99–910031–9

The University of Alberta Press acknowledges the financial support of the Government of Canada
through the Book Publishing Industry Development Program for its publishing activities. The
Press also gratefully acknowledges the support received for its program from the Canada Council
for the Arts.

To Kelli and Nik,
Jayna and Keenan,
and the rest of Alberta's children.

Contents

Acknowledgements

This book began as a passing conversation, gathered steam at an actual meeting in February 1997, and finally crystallized in the fall of the same year. Like any other project of this sort, it could not have been put together without the efforts of a great many people. First and foremost, of course, are the contributors themselves. Their diligence and hard work, in meeting our stringent deadlines and accepting some of our suggestions (while properly rejecting others), made putting this book together a positive experience.

We also want to acknowledge the support provided by Parkland Institute and the University of Alberta Press. Particular thanks go to Dennis Haughey, Gordon Laxer, Bill Moore-Kilgannon, Glenn Rollans, and the members of Parkland's Research Committee, including the anonymous reviewers, for their critical questioning and valuable suggestions as the book evolved.

We would also like to thank several individuals — Bob Barnetson, Anne-Marie Decore, Susan Belcher El-Nahhas, Calvin Fraser, Noel Jantzie, Bev Lyseng, Eric Newell, Annette Richardson, Victor Soucek, David Watt, Diane Wesley, and Deanna Williamson — for their contributions which remain inserted, if only unconsciously, within the margins of this text. We also owe enormous thanks to David Odynak and Derek Briton for their technical support.

Finally, we want to acknowledge the many sacrifices made by our families over the past many months and the time we stole from them as we worked to complete this book. We will all be rewarded if this book makes this province a better place.

This book involved a genuinely collaborative effort on the part of the editors. No primacy to either party should be read into the order of editorship or authorship. Any errors or omissions contained herein are the sole responsibility of the editors.

— T.W.H. and J.L.K.

Contributors

H. Larry Booi is a social studies teacher at Strathcona Composite High School in Edmonton, currently on sabbatical leave and taking graduate studies in educational policy studies at the University of Alberta. He is a vice-president of the Alberta Teachers' Association and co-author of *Ideologies* (1997, 3rd ed.).

Lee Easton teaches in English at Mount Royal College and at the Centre for Communications Studies. He is currently completing a PhD in English studies and multimedia at OISE. His most recent publication includes "Phone Sex, Cybersex and Other Hi-Tech Sex Adventures: Just Like the Real Thing?" in Post II.

Judith Evans holds a PhD in psychology from the University of California and an MBA from the University of Alberta. She is president of Pragmatic Applied Research Ltd and a member of the Canadian Evaluation Society's National Council. She is also on the Capilano School Council.

David Flower has a PhD in historical geography from the University of Alberta. He taught high school social studies in Medicine Hat before joining the Alberta Teachers' Association where he is currently coordinator of communications.

Trevor Harrison holds a PhD in sociology. He specializes in political sociology and is author of *Of Passionate Intensity: Right-Wing Populism and the Reform Party of Canada*. He co-edited (with Gordon Laxer) *The Trojan Horse: Alberta and the Future of Canada*. He played a part in the founding of Parkland Institute and was Research Associate during its first year.

Jerrold Kachur has a PhD in the sociology of education and is an assistant professor in educational policy studies at the University of Alberta. He specializes in the sociology of comparative and international education. He is the Canadian research coordinator for a six-country study of teacher unions in the Pacific Rim, funded through the Latin American Center, UCLA. He has taught seventeen years in K-12 and post-secondary systems.

Kas Mazurek has a PhD in the history of education and is a professor of education at the University of Lethbridge. His research interests overlap the fields of comparative education, multiculturalism and minority group relations, the social contexts of educational ideas, policies and practices, and the logic of inquiry. He has co-edited (with N. Kach, R. Patterson, and I. DeFaveri) *Essays on Canadian Education* (Detselig, 1986) and (with N. Kach) *Exploring our Educational Past* (Detselig, 1992). His most recent book, co-authored with M. Winzer, is *Special Education in Multicultural*

Contexts (Prentice-Hall, 1998). He has just completed co-editing (with C. Majorek and M. Winzer) *Schooling and Society in Today's World: Comparative Studies* (Allyn and Bacon, forthcoming).

Dean Neu holds a PhD in accounting and organizational theory and is professor of accounting in the faculty of management at the University of Calgary. He is a member of the Alberta Institute of Chartered Accountants and recently received their Distinguished Service Award for his research and community service activities. He co-authored (with David Cooper) the chapter entitled "The Politics of Debt and Deficit in Alberta" in *The Trojan Horse* (1995), which debunked some of the myths surrounding Alberta's debt and deficit.

Frank Peters has a PhD in educational administration and is a professor in educational policy studies at the University of Alberta. He works mainly in the areas of educational governance, politics, and law. A former teacher and school administrator, Frank has recently been intensely involved in writing and speaking on the major restructurings taking place in Canadian education.

Tom Pocklington received his PhD in political science from Indiana University and is currently a professor of political science at the University of Alberta. His publications include *Democracy, Rights and Well-Being in Canada* (1999) and *The Government and Politics of the Alberta Metis Settlements* (1991). In 1997-98, Tom was president of the Canadian Political Science Association.

Dave Pysyk is a doctoral student in educational policy studies at the University of Alberta. He has previously served as a teacher, vice principal, principal, and deputy superintendent with various boards in Alberta.

Alison Taylor has an EdD in the sociology of education from the Ontario Institute for Studies in Education and is a professor in educational policy studies at the University of Alberta. Her research examines educational restructuring and reforms in Alberta.

Norm Yanitski holds a PhD in educational policy studies from the University of Alberta. He was a former school principal and is currently the director of Instructional Services and Continuing Education for the Elk Island Public Schools.

Beth Young has a PhD in educational administration and is an associate professor of educational policy studies at the University of Alberta. She is co-editor of *Women and Leadership in Canadian Education* and has otherwise written numerous articles on educational administration and policy.

Introduction

Public Education, Globalization, and Democracy: Whither Alberta?

Jerrold L. Kachur and Trevor W. Harrison

[T]hroughout the West . . . we are slipping away from [the] simple principle of high-quality public education. And, in doing so, we are further undermining democracy.
— John Ralston Saul[1]

Much has been written about the Klein "revolution" that began with the re-election of the Progressive Conservatives in Alberta in 1993. The idea that a revolution occurred has always been more myth than substance, a description fostered by government public relations experts and opponents alike for equally political purposes. Nonetheless, it is true that some substantial changes have occurred, no more so than in the field of education.

Education restructuring is not unique to Alberta, of course. Change has been occurring for some time and in all provinces, often with heated results: witness the Ontario teachers' strikes of 1997 and 1998. But Alberta was the first province to frontally attack the notion of equality of opportunity, replacing it with New Right policies redefining "opportunity" according to a new logic — competition, effectiveness, and standards — and to emphasize choice, vocationalism, and marketization. Long before Mike Harris, Ralph Klein's government was the first in North America to adopt the political strategy of Roger Douglas in New Zealand: create a crisis, then strike fast and hard before opposition can be mobilized against the new policies.

After 1993, Alberta became a beachhead for the introduction of many New Right ideas into Canada, imported most especially from New Zealand,

Britain, and the United States.[2] Thereafter, Alberta's policy reforms gained positive notoriety among various journalists, academics, and politicians already sympathetic to similar ideas. Later, some jurisdictions, particularly Ontario, also copied these policies. While other books have previously examined the totality of these changes, none has looked specifically at the changes made to Alberta education. This book fills that gap. Specifically, this book asks: what was done to education? How was it done? And — as Alberta embarks upon an era of post-deficit politics — what is likely to be done in the future?

Readers will discover that education restructuring in Alberta has been and continues to be ideologically driven. They will further learn that, under the guise of increasing public input, the government has in fact centralized authority and decreased equality of student opportunity while opening market niches for private entrepreneurs. Finally, readers also will discover something of how they have been manipulated by the Alberta government to "buy" these policies.

This book, however, is not narrowly about education. Nor is it — as much as we disapprove of many of the government's actions — a tirade against the Klein Tories. As Kas Mazurek notes in chapter one, "the current state of schooling in Alberta is not merely the consequence of a political agenda by the administration of Premier Klein." Rather, we criticize a set of ideas — often termed "neo-liberal" — which have narrowly construed the meaning, purpose, and value of education and have affected all public services in Alberta. The long-term consequences of these ideas pose irreparable harm to people, communities, and democracy itself. If the Klein government, and other governments, are to be faulted, it is for accepting neo-liberal ideas too easily while failing to understand or examine their far-reaching effects.

Ultimately, the editors call for a strategic realignment of educational interests around a politics of postmodern socialism.[3] At the core of such an approach remains a critique of capitalism, class, and power. Indeed, such a critique is essential to understanding current events, including — as this book goes to press — the ongoing crisis in global markets and the growing likelihood of a world recession. At the same time, given the history of the twentieth century, no such analysis can ignore the limitations — and dangers — of entrusting too much power in a centralized state. There can be no worthwhile socialist politics that is not also democratic, bottom-up, and responsive to local needs and initiatives.

A postmodern socialist politics integrates, in a genuine way, the perceptions and experiences of groups and individuals too long marginalized by dint of ethnicity, race, and gender; yet it also eschews the false tolerance of relativity and the new intolerance of particularistic voice. A postmodern socialist politics respects civil and individual rights, but it does not give way to the alienation and destructiveness of either "possessive" or "false" individualism.[4] Likewise, postmodern socialist politics includes intellectual rigour and a shared sense of community, but it does not fall prey to rigid notions of hierarchy and authoritarianism.

Public education in the post-war era, with which many of us are familiar, was based upon a particular political economy — capitalist in nature — and particular politically and socially liberal premises. With the rise of globalization, public education, as a kind of dutiful handmaiden to the old system, has itself been necessarily transformed. But it is important to understand that the seeds of these changes lay within the previous educational system. Certain elements of public education have made it as much a perpetrator as a victim of its own demise.

A failure to recognize the broad political and economic contexts in which education is embedded frequently confuses people and renders debates about education narrow and unrewarding. Too much emphasis — and blame — is placed on teachers and schools without consideration of the social conditions and political agendas that affect the classroom. As a result, education has become a way to avoid dealing directly with issues such as growing social inequality, changing family structure, the perceived rise in juvenile crime, and heightened consumerism. As a proxy for an economic battle, education is treated as both "the problem" and "the solution" for productivity decline and international competitiveness, thus diverting attention from more fundamental issues related to the inability of the business community to maintain economic growth, employ educated labour, and sustain the real wages of workers.[5] But why scapegoat education and not something else?

Anyone who has visited a newsstand or bookstore in recent years will immediately recognize the contentiousness of this question and the limited nature of many critiques of education. There, one will find a number of books and articles on public education, many strewn with such terms as catastrophe, failure, and bankruptcy. Nor are universities sheltered from this conflict. Some of the criticisms are different, encapsulated in terms like special interests, political correctness, rising tuition fees, and irrelevancy. But the gist is the same: something has gone terribly wrong with education.

These appeals hit home with the public. Parents already feel overworked and straitened by taxes. Now they are told that if drugs and violence don't claim their child, illiteracy and modem-impairment will. Even if their own experiences deny the threat voiced in some of these books, apprehension still remains. Maybe public education really is going to hell in a handbasket. Of course, public education also has its defenders. But for the parent, this simply adds to the confusion. Who's right? Who's presenting the "straight goods"?

This book provides a means by which parents, teachers, and concerned citizens can sort through the discrepant claims about public education and re-think the relationship between education and society. Ultimately, we argue that public education is inseparable from broader moral, economic, and political issues, in particular the construction of a democratic community and a just society.

This book does not claim to be "academic," although its scholarship is first-rate. In line with the recent seminal analyses provided by Lisac's

The Klein Revolution, Laxer and Harrison's *The Trojan Horse*, and Taft's *Shredding the Public Interest*, this book is intended not only to increase public understanding of education and the deep social, political, and economic changes occurring in Alberta, but to goad readers into action and to shape the future direction of public education.[6] The contributors to this book — many of them scholars familiar with existing research in their specialization — were instructed to keep to the facts when dealing with evidence, but otherwise to write with a point of view and in a reader-friendly way, keeping citations of academic research to a minimum.

In order to fully understand the situation in Alberta, it is first necessary to review what has gone on in education and to escape the illusion that Alberta is unique. While possessing some unique characteristics, events in Alberta are nonetheless part and parcel of a host of world-wide economic, political, technological, and other changes generally called globalization.

Globalization and the Welfare State

Globalization is the buzzword of the 1990s. Everybody says it, imagining that they are all talking the same language. But what is it? In a general sense, globalization involves a combination of broad, cultural, economic, political, and technological forces that are changing the ground rules for human interaction on a worldwide scale. But such a broad definition tells us both too much and too little.

One major problem in defining globalization is that the term is frequently confusing. On the one hand, ideological and structural changes (e.g., cultural interaction and the emergence of a "global village") are occurring simultaneously; on the other hand, there are the consequences of globalization (e.g., the rise of religious fundamentalism and ethnic nationalism), which are separate from its core elements. Efforts to define globalization as the emerging "global village" or as increased internationalism oversimplify a term that needs clarification.

Our stance is not so forgiving. Quite simply, globalization involves the worldwide extension of a specifically capitalist form of production, including a global division of labour and the promotion of rampant consumerism and competitive individualism. In practical terms, globalization means the heightened mobility of capital, fostered by modern technologies, and the reorganization of production under the direction of large multi-national enterprises whose power and wealth frequently rival — even surpass — many states. It means that while some people and countries are becoming richer, many are becoming poorer. Globalization further means a reduction, shifting, or transformation of state powers. Some of these powers have been taken over by multi-national corporations or other non-governmental organizations. Other powers have shifted upward to new, transnational bodies, such as the World Bank and International Monetary Fund (IMF), or downward to various levels of government.[7]

Education is necessarily implicated in this neo-liberal approach to globalization.[8] The "new consensus" assumes that competitive advantage in the global economy goes to the country with the best-educated workforce. As economic policy, education has taken on greater political significance in terms of the quality of national education and training systems and the universal spread of schooling, computers, and high-speed communications. Economic and educational initiatives focus on investments in new technology, the quality of human resources, and attracting foreign capital. At the same time, however, governments have found it more difficult to acquire the necessary revenues to pay for these initiatives. Usually concurrent with reform, then, are declining living standards, stagnant or slow growth, and increased unemployment. Alberta has been a leading promoter of this model.[9] As Trevor Harrison notes in chapter three, the demands of the new knowledge-based economy require large investments in education, science, and technology. However, a resource-based economy, such as Alberta's, faces unique challenges in adopting this model as a matter of faith. Likewise, as Lee Easton notes in chapter two, much of educational reform is tied up with the creation of a new kind of worker — the "perpetual learner" — able both to produce and consume the latest technologies.

But globalization has also changed education in another way.[10] The institutions of modern, mass public education were expanded and redefined, along with other public services, after the Second World War. The expansion of these services — encapsulated in the phrase "welfare state" — was part of a historic compromise between capital, labour, other social classes and cultural groups, and the state. This compromise was meant (among other things) to reduce class conflict (a staple prior to the war) and to provide a fiscal hedge against capitalism's inevitable booms and busts. For capital, the compromise ensured the cooperation of workers and their unions; also, it provided low-end consumers with the money necessary to purchase mass-produced goods. For workers, the arrangement ensured increased wages and benefits based on an expanding economy. For the state, the gains came in the form of increased popular support from previously marginalized groups, as well as from workers, for whom the welfare state provided increased rights of social citizenship. While these rights varied from state to state, in general they included a commitment to full employment, guaranteed forms of income maintenance (unemployment insurance, pensions, social welfare), public health care, and expanded opportunities for publicly funded education (including post-secondary education). These same rights also promoted strategies for the inclusion of cultural minorities within a democratic civic culture. In Canada, for example, the politics of education and inclusion focused primarily on policies related to language, multiculturalism, and feminism.

But by the late 1970s, the welfare state compromise began to unravel. The unravelling occurred on two fronts: economic and socio-political. On the economic front, business began complaining of declining profit margins, resulting from increased competition and public demands. On the socio-political front, the complaints of business were reinforced by corporate groups such as the Trilateral Commission, an organization made up of leading corporate executives, intellectuals, and high government officials from the United States, Europe, and Japan, who actively questioned the "excesses of democracy" and appealed to the growing and popular resentment of an economically threatened middle class.[11]

Business addressed the problem of declining profits in two ways. First, it began seeking out new investment opportunities abroad in order to increase capital accumulation. Thus began a process of corporations moving production to areas of cheap labour, untapped resources, and limited government regulation and taxation. Second, business used foreign expansion as a lever for demanding changes at home from both labour and the state. These demands included, among other things, lower corporate taxes, deregulation, and undermining union contracts. Business began to pressure the state to act as a broker in arranging regional and global foreign investment agreements (North American Free Trade Agreement [NAFTA], Asia Pacific Economic Cooperation [APEC], and the Multilateral Agreement on Investments [MAI]), which serve the double purposes of facilitating business and placing brakes on welfare state programs and expenditures. Gradually, these foreign investment agreements undermined the capacity of states to act on behalf of their citizens. Legislative power shifted to the executive, while executive power shifted to the departments of finance, trade, and industry. The economic and political underpinnings of the welfare state compromise quickly began to crumble. In its place, a new development model was implemented throughout many Western countries based on structural adjustment policies recommended by the World Bank, IMF, and the Organization for Economic Cooperation and Development (OECD).

In the first decades of the unravelling, corporate taxes declined and middle-class taxes and unemployment rose, while government commitments to social programs remained static. It wasn't a pretty sight, but nonetheless the welfare state limped on. By the early 1990s, however, a lot of people — particularly members of the disgruntled upper-middle class who felt overtaxed — wanted the "social" part of the welfare state put down. Led by populist politicians aping forms of anti-political politics, debt hysteria encouraged attacks not only upon the welfare state but upon the *idea* of government in general.[12]

But the welfare state did not run aground on financial reefs alone. By the 1980s, the socio-political environment had changed and the welfare state faced considerable resentment from increasingly conservative middle-class males and private-sector workers, who felt their traditional advantages had been eroded by "special interests": various marginalized groups (e.g., women and visible minorities) and entrenched public-sector professionals and their clients (e.g., welfare recipients). Likewise, other conservatives, such as religious fundamentalists, disliked the increasing secularism, pluralism, and moral relativism encouraged by modernity, of which the welfare state and the education system were a part.

These economic, political, and cultural critiques provided the popular bases for a political coalition known as the New Right. Ideologically, this coalition married neo-liberalism (or economic liberalism) to residual forms of political and social conservatism.[13] The New Right's first political victories were in Britain, under Margaret Thatcher in 1979, and in the United States, under Ronald Reagan in 1980.[14] Then starting in 1984, the New Right experienced a second wave of victories, beginning in New Zealand, before entering Canada through Alberta. Here, as elsewhere, a focus upon education was a necessary part of these victories.

New Right Ideology and Educational Reform in Canada

Under the Canadian constitution, provinces have responsibility for education. This control is complicated somewhat by the federal government's fiscal authority: witness Paul Martin's announced "millennium scholarship fund" (see below) and the anger expressed by some provinces over this federal "intrusion." Nonetheless, the Chrétien Liberals have taken a neo-liberal turn since 1995 and downloaded power to the provinces in all areas, including education.[15]

In Canada, no less than in Alberta, education has long been the site for broader ideological debates (Kas Mazurek, chapter one). Beginning in the early 1970s, Canada experienced a series of economic, social, and political crises that continue, in one form or another, to beset the country and that have a major impact on education. Almost immediately, education became a scapegoat for many of these problems.

The criticisms of education came from all fronts. Social democrats, for example, berated progressive education for failing to deliver on social equality, arguing that liberal schooling in a capitalist society actually produces social inequality by socializing students for their future roles as members of a compliant and proficient labour force. They further denounced Canada's education system for failing to do enough to deal with continuing racism and sexism.[16] Likewise, traditional conservatives faulted education for failing to instill "proper" social and moral values and otherwise undermining the stability of the "traditional" (that is, nuclear and patriarchal) family.[17] But by far the most influential critique of Canadian education was that launched by business people, various neo-liberal organizations (e.g., the C.D. Howe Institute, the Fraser Institute, the Economic Council of Canada), and members of the intellectual community.[18]

In several important ways, neo-liberal critiques of education merged with conservative concerns. Like many conservatives, neo-liberals argued for increased parental "choice"[19] and decried the seizure of education by a so-called "iron triangle" of teacher unions, educational bureaucrats, and university theoreticians, in coalition with other "special interests."

More so than the conservative critique, the basis of neo-liberal criticisms was that Canada's competitive position in the global marketplace had been compromised by poor educational performance and high costs.

Neo-liberals made several proposals for educational reform to address these economic concerns.[20] These proposals included increased links between school and work; enhanced "streaming" of students into educational programs; increased educational emphasis on science, mathematics, and technology as a means of addressing the Canadian economy's productivity decline; the reorganization of schools based on new managerial practices used in transnational corporations; greater use of performance measures to assess school quality; greater public choice in education to improve efficiency and accountability in school systems; and increased fiscal austerity ("doing more with less"). These latter two proposals, in particular, garnered enormous support from pro-business executives and their organizations who, by the early 1980s, saw in education and other public services opportunities for profit-making.[21]

In making these recommendations, neo-liberals adopted several human capital and supply-side assumptions: first, governments "cannot" create jobs — only business can do this; second, individual and national success in the new global economy is based on the supply of knowledge and skills; and, third, the "proper" role of government is to assure the development of this supply through economic incentives and disincentives. In this field of dreams, if people are educated, the jobs will come.

These assumptions, linking Canada's social, political, and economic problems to education and employment, are questionable. For one thing, while there is generally a correlation between education and productivity or improved social position (see Appendices D, F, and K), there is no *necessary* causal relationship between them.[22] The appearance of increased social mobility since the Second World War, for example, may be more accurately related to structural changes in the economy and the changing nature of credential and labour markets than to genuine changes in social-class position.[23] Furthermore, the provision of technical skills is only one of many school functions. Thus, a credential does not transparently represent skill or accumulated knowledge, but rather embodies a whole range of cultural, social, economic, and political functions. For example, public schools also function to babysit children, and post-secondary institutions act as holding-tanks for the unemployed.

These arguments aside, the neo-liberal explanation of Canada's problems in education found widespread support after 1980. While Canadians support public schooling, corporate executives, whose confidence in public education has dropped, tend to support privatization.[24] This change in business support provided the basis for the latest wave of intense education restructuring, which began in the 1990s.

The scope of government reforms of education across Canada in the 1990s, based largely on neo-liberal principles, include nine commonalties:[25] 1) the adoption and expansion of province-wide and national testing and student achievement exams; 2) the tentative statement of national standards (with the exception of Quebec) for science and other subjects; 3) the creation of partnerships between schools and corporations; 4) the establishment of parent advisory councils for administrators; 5) the formation of influential stakeholder commissions at provincial and national levels; 6) the centralization of control over funding and curriculum; 7) the reduction or elimination of the power of local, democratically elected school boards; 8) the regionalization of curriculum development and evaluation; and 9) the end of twenty-five years of sustained growth in spending on public education and the initiation of deep cuts in some provinces.[26] In short, education reform across Canada reflects certain neo-liberal similarities.[27] At the same time, different provincial governments promote varied emphases.

New Right provincial governments, in particular, have tended to politicize and involve the business community in efforts to restructure public education. In turn, the corporate sector has influenced the restructuring of Canadian schools in several ways. It has shaped the fiscal, monetary, and industrial policy of the Canadian state. It has provided a model for the internal reorganization of school bureaucracies along the lines of transnational enterprises. It has entered into partnerships with schools as the steering agent. And it has promoted the privatization, marketization, and commodification of educational services.

In pursuing these changes, the corporate sector has garnered public support from various social conservative elements by appealing to the "little person" against the incursions of the state and "special interests." Populist resentment against the welfare state, as embodied in the Reform Party, has been mobilized to free up state revenues for capital investments in the business sector and to undermine the universality of the social welfare state that previously garnered widespread support from all Canadians.

These changes have not gone uncontested. Indeed, a key aspect of the New Right assault on education has been its necessary conflict with various sectors of the educational community. In particular, given that schooling is a teacher-intensive process and that approximately four-fifths of the cost of education — as in other public service occupations — goes to labour, the cost-containment of education expenditures implicitly means lowering the real wages of teachers, increasing class sizes, and introducing organizational efficiencies.[28] To accomplish this task, governments have challenged the organizational power of teacher unions and their professional monopolies as service providers (see chapter ten) and have introduced non-standard work arrangements based on post-industrial models into educational settings (see chapter eleven).

Nowhere has the contest for the future of education been more pronounced than in Alberta. Indeed, in education, as in deficit reduction, health care, and welfare reform, Alberta has provided the model for the rest of the country and has forced the federal Liberal party and various provincial governments to reorganize their priorities along similar neo-liberal lines. So influential has been the Alberta model that it has pushed even social-democratic provincial governments in British Columbia and Saskatchewan to accommodate neo-liberal and neo-conservative interests. Is it a model worth following?

Education in the Klein Revolution

History is not always a good teacher. Nonetheless, it is a necessary starting point for understanding the present. In 1992, a politically desperate government, beset by its own record of fiscal incompetence and private sector subsidies, began rewriting the history of its own record. Key to this reconstruction was the selection of a new, charismatic leader and the cynical manufacture of a debt and deficit "crisis" around which to mobilize the electorate and — not unimportantly — distract the public from its record.[29] The government's facelift proved successful in 1993; and although showing wear and tear, it likewise pulled the government through again in 1997.

But there were many casualties. Some casualties were the direct result of government cuts: workers laid off, recipients of services left to fend for themselves. Other casualties were less tangible but involved the discrediting of government service and those who supported the public sector: a fracture in public discourse between "loyal" Albertans and "special interests"; a government-defined "enemies list"; the denial of any truth other than that approved by the one-party state.

Anyone familiar with the management "Bibles" that directed the Klein government's restructuring will recognize two common threads running through them, the first ideological, the second programmatic.[30] The ideological thread states that government services should be run by corporate principles, preferably through privatization of those services. The programmatic thread involves bringing public services into disrepute in order to garner public support for their privatization. These threads have become standard elements of Alberta's political fabric in recent years.

Health care provides a prime example. Health-care spending, it was alleged in 1993 and thereafter, was "out of control." Tough decisions had to be made. People had to take greater personal responsibility and count less on government support. Reinforcing these messages, the Klein government strangled health-care spending during this period, thereby opening up market niches for private exploitation.[31]

The same thing happened in education. Alberta education already was experiencing fundamental changes (see chapter one) when Ralph Klein took over as Alberta premier from Don Getty in December 1992. Following the 1993 election, however, the Klein government embarked on an even broader social and political revolution that involved, among other things, significant changes to education.

Not all of these changes were necessarily bad, nor unusual in the context of educational change occurring elsewhere. As Frank Peters notes in chapter six, for example, "changes to educational funding have . . . put in place a more equitable funding system than formerly existed." Likewise, as both Frank Peters and Judy Evans note (chapters six and twelve respectively), the government's efforts to decrease the number of school boards from 141 to 63 have surely proved a worthwhile endeavour. Similarly, the attempts to involve parents at the grassroots level through school councils hold some promise. Finally, we may note positively the expansion of curriculum options for students and the increased accommodation of work schedules to the needs of individual teachers (chapter eleven).

At the same time, we do not know exactly how these changes will play out. While restructuring created more equity among school boards, the reduction of spending levels — as Dean Neu and Frank Peters identify in chapters six and seven respectively — suggests we might only be seeing equality in a race to the bottom. Similarly, neither parents nor students are well served if decreasing the number of school boards results in the centralization of government power or the takeover of school councils by well-organized and parochial zealots. Finally, the "freedom to choose" — whether of workplace schedules or of curricular offerings — too often masks the real powers of owners and managers, as Jerrold Kachur points out in chapter nine.

At the heart of concerns about the Klein government's actions on education lies its neo-liberal understanding of human capital development and its often coercive and manipulative manner of implementing changes. Since 1993, the government has justified educational change using fiscal arguments, as it has with health care. But in garnering support for its changes to public education, the government also has appealed on other grounds. First, the government has justified changes to education on the basis of making Alberta more globally competitive — an appeal directed specifically to the government's supporters within the business community. Second, the government has justified changes to education on moral conservative grounds, allowing members such as Stockwell Day free rein to attack public education for a whole host of alleged social and cultural wrongs.

In appealing to these elements, this government has talked more openly than previous administrations of business-school partnerships (chapter four), openly courted the appeals of private-school lobbyists (chapter eight), and recently increased the proportion of funding available to private and charter schools (chapters nine and twelve). There is no question that public schooling in Alberta, as with the provision of many other services, is becoming a private affair.

Education in Alberta is being privatized in three ways. The first, most obvious way is the growth of private schools, supported by public funds. One measure of this growth is the increased number of private enrollments. The government's own figures show that private enrollments have gone from about 13,000 in 1986 to 20,000 in 1996. The second way is through the entry of business into classrooms, from kindergarten through grade twelve to all post-secondary levels. Educational institutions have increasingly become a site for profit-making, often by large corporations (see chapter four). The lines between public and private, non-profit and profit, have grown blurred.

The third way in which education is being privatized is more subtle and involves the increasing transfer of costs to individuals and families. Reduced funding and taxpayer support means that core elements of education in Alberta are now paid for through fees, raffles, auctions, bingos, and assorted other fund-raisers. Likewise, schools have been forced to depend on parent volunteers to act as librarians and teacher aids — at least in the early grades. Because resources vary from rich to poor districts, the government's promotion of "community development" is really a code for re-introducing a high degree of inequality based on local conditions, something supposedly eliminated when taxing authority was removed from the school boards. Furthermore, the more effective that volunteers, charities, and small businesses are at supporting educational services, the more easily government is able to justify getting out of the "education business." As we describe below, this process of privatization complements a larger process of debt-mongering and provincial government reform.

The privatization of education in Alberta is not an accident. Rather, it is the result of constant lobbying by private-school operators and influential members of the Progressive Conservative party (chapters eight and nine). Privatization appeals to two of the Klein government's major constituencies: business and moral conservatives. For business, the privatization of education creates market niches for possible exploitation. But privatization also provides moral conservatives an escape from the valueless purgatory of public schools, while enhancing the status qualifications of the wealthy and their offspring. As Trevor Harrison (chapter three) notes, both cases reflect the increasing tendency under globalization for certain groups to seek out "physical refuge in gated communities and an ideological safe-haven in an often narrow provincialism."

In short, since 1993 the Klein government has introduced a series of changes that have fundamentally undermined public education in Alberta. At the same time, Albertans (like most Canadians) remain outwardly highly supportive of public education. How, then, has the government been able to mobilize public support for the changes it has introduced? The answer lies in the government's manufacture of Alberta's continuing fiscal crisis.

Riding Alberta's Perpetual Debt Cycle

Shortly after the Harris government came to power in 1995, a firestorm was set off in Ontario. The province's Minister of Education, John Snobelen, was caught on camera commenting on the need to "create a crisis in education" in order to mobilize public support for the kind of changes planned by his government.[32] Many people were astonished by this revelation, if only for the boldness of the statement and the fact that it had actually been recorded. The tactic was not new, however. Much of the Harris' government's blueprint for educational reform had been taken from Alberta. Likewise, the idea of creating a crisis for political purposes also had Alberta's fingerprints all over it.

Alberta's deficit crisis[33] from 1993-97 was based on three arguments: first, that deficits and debts were out of control; second, that social expenditures (mainly education, health, and welfare) were the cause of the deficit crisis; and third, that the crisis could not be dealt with by increasing revenue through either taxes or a reliance on economic growth. Individuals were "overtaxed," corporations would simply "leave town," and Alberta's resource-based economy was too volatile. The crisis, it was alleged, could be dealt with *only* by massive cuts to social spending.

The first of these arguments has some basis in fact. Expenses were out-distancing revenues, although not by as much as the government claimed.[34] The second argument is demonstrably false: the cause of the deficits and debt was attributable to corporate — not social — welfare.[35] The third argument is more assertion than fact. Individual and corporate taxes in Alberta are well below Canadian averages.[36] Most of Alberta's major industries (oil, gas, tourism, services) must be located in the province — they can't just get up and walk away.

Nonetheless, the illusion of a deficit crisis held Albertans in thrall from 1993 until 1996. Thereafter, however, the Klein government's political use of the "crisis" brought decreasing returns. By 1996, many Albertans were increasingly concerned that the cuts to education and health, in particular, had gone too far, too fast. While still convinced that government deficits needed redress, they began to demand that more money be put into these social areas. Perhaps more importantly, however, the government's embarrassment of riches became apparent in 1996 as oil and gas revenues skyrocketed. In 1995/96, for example, Alberta's budget surplus was $1.1 billion. This rose to $2.5 billion in 1996/97 and $2.7 billion in 1997/98 (see chapter six and Appendix A).

It was in these changed circumstances that Ralph Klein — the arch-chameleon of Canadian politics — and the Alberta Tories remade themselves in the months leading up to the 1997 provincial election (see chapter five). They acquired a kinder, gentler, more conciliatory image, Yes, tough decisions had to be made to deal with past "accumulated deficits" (the debt), and some people had been hurt. But the worst was over, and the "house" was still standing. Now it was time to "reinvest" in Albertans.

This theme of reinvestment continued after the election. Reinvestment was the centrepiece of the September 1997 Growth Summit, a meeting of prominent delegates from various sectors of Alberta society (see chapter five). Held in the absence of a fall sitting of the legislature, the Summit was promoted as an opportunity for "average Albertans" to set the priorities for the government and the province. One may be skeptical of the Summit's intents. Nonetheless, there is no doubt that the key recommendation coming out of the conference was for increased spending in areas of social infrastructure, particularly education. Premier Klein himself said so in summing up the conference. The government, supposedly, had heard. It would reinvest in something called "people development" (see chapter three), a commitment reinforced shortly thereafter by delegates to the Tory convention.

Then something happened. On November 26, 1997, Treasurer Stockwell Day announced that Alberta's entire budget surplus for 1997/98 would go towards paying the province's net debt. This statement was followed on December 16 by Premier Klein's announcement of plans to tackle the province's gross debt, estimated at $15.5 billion. Like Medusa's head, the government had apparently cut off one "debt-snake," only to find that it had multiplied two-fold. There was only one way to beat the serpent: social expenditures must continue to be squeezed. Thus, the stage was set for the Alberta budget of February 1998.

A Tale of Two Budgets

Treasurer Stockwell Day's budget was meant to herald a new direction for the government. Some of its key points, however, seemed all too familiar. For example, the government acceded to the interests of oil and gas corporations in scrapping, a year ahead of time, a machinery and equipment tax that annually brought $98 million to the Alberta Treasury.[37] Curiously, the budget also contained a drop in Alberta's personal income tax (PIT) rate to forty-four percent (of the federal rate) in order to compete with Ontario, which had recently dropped its rate to forty-five percent.[38] Combined with a repeated promise never again to raise taxes, these measures have lessened the Alberta Treasury's capacity to react to economic shocks, such as the sudden drop in oil prices that occurred in the early months of 1998 (see chapter three). As this book goes to press, the government is once again facing a "deficit" and is talking about further cutbacks.

But the main failure of the budget, in the eyes of some critics at least, was that it made only token reinvestments in education and health — not enough to keep up with population growth and inflation (see chapter six). This, in spite of the fact the government had amassed a budget surplus of $2.7 billion in 1997/98. For defenders of public education, the Alberta government's commitment of only a few months earlier seemed to have slipped a notch.

At first glance, the Alberta government's approach to spending on education seemed particularly miserly and inadequate when compared to the federal government's 1998 budget. The centrepiece of Paul Martin's federal "education" budget was a $2.5 billion, multi-year Canada Millennium Scholarship Foundation. It also featured an enhanced Registered Educational Savings Plan (RESP), accessible to parents, and a more favourable schedule of loan repayments for post-secondary students.

This action sounds good. But we must remember that it was the Liberal government who cut an estimated $3 billion from federal transfers for post-secondary education and created the funding and tuition problems in the first place.[39]

Is the approach taken in Martin's budget really different from that taken by the Alberta government? We would argue that, behind rhetoric and partisanship, the differences are in fact superficial. Neo-liberal assumptions underwrite both budgets.[40] Both governments have accentuated concerns about public deficits and debt. Both budgets, in turn, placed enormous faith in human capital investment and the healing powers of the market as the major means for addressing Canada's ills. That the approaches taken by both governments are not so far apart is underlined by the fact that Martin's budget was praised by Ralph Klein and Stockwell Day. Indeed, Klein and Day stated that the federal government was merely following Alberta's lead.[41]

Nonetheless, Martin did take his argument in an interesting direction to reveal an underlying political problem for neo-liberals. He prefaced the 1998 federal budget with remarks about "education" as the means to preserving the middle class in an age of globalization. The problem, as understood by Canada's finance minister and many others, is the decline of the Canadian "middle class," a reference to the well-documented[42] decline of real income for working people (the actual tax-paying "public") in Canada since the mid-1970s, the so-called "disappearing middle" during the 1980s, and the accelerating disparity between rich and poor in the 1990s (Appendix K). The increasing class polarization in Canada is an economic reality and a growing political problem which requires a solution of sorts: "There is no better way to reduce the gap between rich and poor, no surer way to widen the mainstream . . . and no better way to provide a higher quality of life for Canadians than to facilitate the path to greater education."[43] Martin even promoted more education as job creation! The current assumption about a relationship between education and the economy presupposes more skills, more jobs, more income: a neat causal relationship. The federal government is not alone in holding this theory; certainly, neither the Alberta government nor many Albertans would disagree. The ticket to a middle-class life, they assume, is an education. It follows that the real problem with education is that there is not enough to go around!

Martin's educational strategy is wrong on at least three counts. First, in individualizing financial assistance, based on academic achievement, he stands squarely against the notion of universal public education. Second, a focus on star candidates at the post-secondary levels does not counter the damage done through cuts in other social areas that hurt educational outcomes at the lower levels and for average students. Third, the emphasis in Martin's budget on supplying educational skills, with little regard for the availability of good paying jobs where existing skills can be used, harbours some risky assumptions. The fact is, Canada already has one of the best-educated workforces in the world, yet its unemployment rate continues to hover near double digits. "More" education misses the point.

We do not disagree that education and the labour market are — and should be — related. Nevertheless, we do suggest that the relationship between education and "jobs" is not as clear cut as the Day and Martin budgets, with their neo-liberal assumptions, imply (see Appendix K).[44] What if, after increasing educational spending, Alberta's and Canada's economies do not prosper? Whither public education?

Much political debate today involves a phony conflict, the rhetorical equivalent of confusing a World Wrestling Federation contest with the real thing. Beyond partisan excess, one of the really striking aspects of current political debates is the degree to which critics — on both the left and the right — unconsciously imbibe liberal assumptions that ultimately undermine their own critiques. That "we are all liberals now" is no more true than in education.

The Life and Times of Liberal Education

Liberalism has many faces: political, social, and economic. There is much in political and social liberalism that remains serviceable today and must not be abandoned: political equality for the individual, the rights of freely chosen association, the promotion of self-determining freedoms and authenticity, the opportunities for self-development, the basic legal and civil rights of individuals. These values, for which many have fought and died, must be retained.

In education, even though liberalism hasn't completely delivered the goods, it promotes equality of opportunity and social achievement based on merit rather than family, race, gender, or social class. Liberal education further supports — although this is usually overstated — the provision of opportunities for working-class children to get a university education. Liberal education continually experiments with new teaching techniques and strategies to enhance the development of students, while eliminating many of the more repressive measures of power and coercion previously inflicted on generations of students by a conservative education. Yet something is missing from this cornucopia of liberalisms that have dominated the latter half of the twentieth century.

Of the many forms, it is economic liberalism that today predominates. Economic liberalism's overweening popular appeal is exhibited, on one level, by the current tendency to equate education with economic growth even while many people, including the well-educated, are experiencing declining incomes and uncertain job prospects. The strength of liberalism is reflected at a deeper level, however, by the fact that many who would otherwise declare themselves conservatives or socialists subscribe to similar beliefs. In general, most people are unable to reflect critically upon public education and its place within the political economy of capitalism — as if education could somehow be immunized from the contagious influences of politics and economics that inform its everyday activities.

Given this blind spot, proponents of public education are ill-prepared to understand, let alone criticize, its predicament in the wake of globalization.

At the same time, public education has also abandoned values. It is not that public education is immoral; moral conservatives over-reach in making this accusation. But, given its socially liberal roots, it is amoral. Social liberalism assumes that pro-social values arise spontaneously and that moral values in general are culturally relative and cannot be justified rationally — after all, everyone has a right to a perspective. Similarly, mistaking knowledge for psychic identification, sincerity, or just plain getting things done, liberal educators have called for a thousand values and "sensitivities" to blossom. But too often the only product has been weeds: a garden strewn with the worst excesses of consumerism — mediocrity, redundancy, and an appeal to the lowest common denominator — mixed with an all-too-prevalent dose of embedded insensitivities: violence, racism, and sexism. Unwilling to make judgements about the truth or rightness of social morality, liberal pluralists provide no intellectual grounding beyond a narrow notion of the individual. More importantly, they fail to comprehend, let alone teach others, about the collective power of material interests, specifically class interests, in shaping experience and belief. This proliferation of competing and contradictory values, reinforced by a cultural commitment to immediate payoff, plays into a general social climate of rising cynicism, malaise, and fatalism regarding economic determinants.[45]

For their part, radicalized social liberals, usually romantic and individualistic, tend to forego factual distinctions and moral judgements, promoting instead confused thinking as the highest order of postmodern playfulness. These "radicalized" theorists have become circumspect even about the mildest demand for discipline — even if it means maintaining a boundary between fact and fiction. Claims to truth, logic, and method — as well as the "foundation" for informed social critique — are thrown out the window as if, in the words of culture critic Raymond Morrow, "to prefer vegetarianism over cannibalism is ultimately a simple matter of taste."[46] But, what then is the aim of education? What kind of student do we want? What do we mean by a "standard of excellence"? What is left to arbitrate the merits of globalization? The market.

Like neo-liberals, conservatives have tended to blame education for a loss of certain social values and for the rise of various social ills which are seen as detrimental to the Canadian economy. But conservatives prescribe only modest proposals for containing and minimizing the effects of the market, which have arguably created much of the instability and insecurity underlying these trends. As Arthur Schlesinger, Jr., remarks: "The unfettered market conservatives worship undermines the values — stability, morality, family, community, work, discipline, delayed gratification — conservatives avow."[47] Thus, conservatives continue a trend they have followed since Edmund Burke (1729-1797) in accommodating themselves to capitalism. It is all very good to criticize selfish individualism, vapid consumerism, and an immoral culture — the Jerry Springer show comes to mind — but unless we understand the economic underpinnings of such modern phenomena, these things will keep coming at us. In tying themselves to a defense of capitalism, conservatives fail the test of social realism.

Traditional and moral conservatives also miss when they argue for a single self-evident and universal standard. Such calls too often mask an authoritarian fist, behind which lurks a desire to return to a hierarchical and unequal society. A conservative agenda which re-introduces a religious education, based on restrictive Judeo-Christian beliefs, simply will not work in Canada today. Indeed, it would fracture the country into a multiplicity of separate fundamentalisms and solitudes.

What *is* needed is a postmodern socialist recognition of certain basic values common to all cultures and religions — respect and courtesy, social and personal responsibility, self-discipline, honesty and courage — to be instilled by schools in a committed way. Of course, the specific content of these values must be determined through a democratic process of public debate and critical reflection. But education could play an important role in this process of democratic awakening.

Public education cannot be blamed for every blemish on the social fabric. Critics of all political stripes have gone too far in making these attacks. At the same time, teachers and administrators have gone too far since the 1970s in presenting education as the universal solution. Schools have made substantial progress in several areas. Children *are* becoming educated. Canadians, as a whole, *are* functionally literate. Our rates of post-secondary education rival any other country. Schools today *are not* as racist, sexist, or class-ridden as in the past, although each of these issues continues to exist in various degrees and a two-tiered system of education does seem to be emerging. Likewise, schools today *are not* as authoritarian as they were only a few short years ago.

But public education's defenders cannot rest. Moreover, they must not fall into the trap of defending public education on the terrain of neo-liberal expectations: a mere investment in future jobs. Neither can the defence be based on some narrow appeal to education's capacity to instill collective morality. Public education can only be defended on the basis of its capacity to develop human potential and promote democracy.

Democracy and the Struggle for Public Education

C.B. Macpherson argued years ago that Alberta was subject to dominance by a single party and a social structure adverse to a thriving democracy.[48] Although some elements of Macpherson's argument have since been successfully challenged,[49] it remains difficult to argue with his overall conclusion. Kevin Taft remarked that democracy in Alberta has been on vacation. This may be an understatement. The reality is that democracy has too infrequently visited the province.

As his life's work attested, Macpherson believed firmly in genuine, participatory democracy. Building on his legacy, we contend that universal public education — broadly conceived — is a necessary if insufficient foundation for maintaining an active and participatory citizenry. Public education is a fundamental element in the establishment, maintenance, and transformation of democratic citizenship, not only through *what* is taught, but through the process of *how* things are taught[50] and as the means for understanding and transforming the unequal conditions of social existence.

Current discussions of education pay too much attention to its role in preparing for work — a reflection, as we have noted, of the neo-liberal thrust of our times. This approach ignores, however, the inter-relatedness of the economy, society, and public and private realms. Ultimately, an information-based, high-tech economy is the product of a particular kind of society: one extremely open to change and democratic in the broadest sense. Yet education in the larger sense means more than technically retooling the workforce, or the emergence of professional classes, or even the encouragement of a manufacturing culture in the schools and colleges in order to preserve a productive base.[51] It also implies a deep understanding of why our world is changing, of how other people and cultures feel about and respond to these changes, and of what we have in common — as well as what divides cultures, classes, and nations. It should provide also a safe space for the development of personal autonomy and social criticism. We are more than a little uneasy about a wholesale adoption of one model of social development without a comprehensive and detailed dialogue committed to the development of social equality, individual freedom, and equitable access to resources. Democracy is about providing a legitimate place and opportunity for people to voice their concerns and be heard. It is also about changing the conditions in which we learn and labour with the goal of a better future for all. Too many voices have been sacrificed on the altar of restructuring. It is time to reclaim our voices and take that place, that space.

Notes

The authors wish to thank Deanna Williamson and Gordon Laxer for their suggestions on earlier drafts of this chapter.

1 *The Unconscious Civilization* (Concord, Ontario: Anansi, 1995), 65.

2 B. Elliott and D. MacLennan, "Education, modernity and neo-conservative school reform in Canada, Britain and the US" in *British Journal of Sociology of Education*, 15:2 (1994): 165-85. For the similarities among the Canadian, British, and American states that distinguish them from other welfare states see G. Esping-Andersen, *The Three Worlds of Welfare Capitalism* (Oxford: Polity, 1990).

3 The term is taken from R. Burbach, O. Nunez, and B. Kagarlitsky, *Globalization and its Discontents: The Rise of Postmodern Socialisms* (London: Pluto Press, 1997). The individual

contributors to this book may define their approaches in different ways. Arguably, we feel that their analyses are congruent with many of the assumptions of postmodern socialism.

4 The term "possessive individualism" was made famous by C.B. Macpherson, *The Political Theory of Possessive Individualism: Hobbes to Locke* (Oxford: Oxford University Press, 1962). The term "false individualism" is taken from John Ralston Saul, *The Unconscious Civilization*.

5 See the Science Council of Canada, *Reaching for Tomorrow: Science and Technology Policy in Canada 1991* (Ottawa: Minister of Supply and Services, 1992).

6 Mark Lisac, *The Klein Revolution* (Edmonton: NeWest Press, 1995); Gordon Laxer and Trevor Harrison, eds., *The Trojan Horse: Alberta and the Future of Canada* (Montréal, Black Rose Books, 1995); Kevin Taft, *Shredding the Public Interest* (Edmonton: University of Alberta Press and Parkland Institute, 1997).

7 See R. Barnet and J. Cavanagh, *Global Dreams: Imperial Corporations and the New World Order* (New York: Touchstone, 1994); G. Teeple, *Globalization and the Decline of Social Reform* (Toronto: Garamond Press, 1995).

8 P. Brown and H. Lauder, "Education, globalization, and economic development" in *Journal of Education Policy* 11 (1996): 1-24; R.S. Pannu, "Neoliberal project of globalization: prospects for democratization of education" in *Alberta Journal of Educational Research* 42:2 (1996): 87-101; S. Aronowitz and W. De Fazio, "The new knowledge work" in *The Jobless Future: Sci-Tech and the Dogma of Work* (Minneapolis: University of Minnesota Press, 1994), 13-56.

9 A.H. Halsey, H. Lauder, P. Brown and A.S. Wells, "The transformation of education and society: an introduction" in *Education: Culture Economy Society* (Oxford: Oxford Press, 1997), 8.

10 D. Drache and M.S. Gertler, eds., *The New Era of Global Competition: State Policy and Market Power* (Montreal and Kingston: McGill-Queen's University Press, 1991); M. Molot, "The Canadian state in the international economy" in *Political Economy and the Changing Global Order*, R. Stubbs and G. Underhill, eds. (Toronto: McClelland & Stewart, 1994), 511-23.

11 P. Marchak, *The Integrated Circus: The New Right and the Restructuring of Global Markets* (Montreal and Kingston: McGill-Queen's University Press, 1991); R. Cox, "Knowledge, politics, and neo-liberal political economy" in *Political Economy and the Changing Global Order*, R. Stubbs and G. Underhill, eds. (Toronto: McClelland & Stewart, 1994), 75-88; J. Calvert with L. Kuehn, *Pandora's Box: Corporate Power, Free Trade and Canadian Education* (Toronto: OSOS, 1993).

12 T. Harrison, *Of Passionate Intensity: Right-Wing Populism and the Reform Party of Canada* (Toronto: University of Toronto, 1995).

13 Neo-liberalism might also be termed "classical," "laissez faire," or libertarian. The various forms of conservatism include traditional, ethno-religious, or populist. Neo-liberalism and conservatism combine easily into bureaucratic and paternalistic forms of corporatism. For a detailed description see D.S. King, *The New Right: Politics, Markets and Citizenship* (London: Macmillan, 1987).

14 While the governments of these countries have since changed, we would argue that the Bush-Clinton administrations in the US and Major-Blair administrations in the UK have largely continued and consolidated the neo-liberal thrusts begun under Reagan and Thatcher, respectively.

15 The Liberals have increased their business orientation and emphasized decentralization and the downloading of social services. See Maude Barlow and B. Campbell, *Straight Through the Heart: How the Liberals Abandoned the Just Society* (Toronto: HarperCollins, 1995). For details related to post-secondary education see Canadian Association of University Teachers, *CAUT Bulletin* May 1997: 1-11.

16 See Sandro Contenta, *Rituals of Failure: What Schools Really Teach* (Toronto: Between the Lines, 1993). In the same vein as Contenta is Heather-Jane Robertson and Maude Barlow's *Class Warfare: The Assault on Canada's Schools* (Toronto: Key Porter.Books, 1994). Their criticism of the business agenda found some favour with teachers across Canada, but was panned by the business press, especially *The Globe and Mail*. Unlike Contenta, Robertson and Barlow are not critical of Canadian education as an institution of domination and inequality but defend its accomplishments in the post-war period. The fundamental problem, as they see it, lies not with the schools — which are increasingly forced to deal with an increasing diversity of problems and an inadequacy resources brought by government cuts — but with the organization of an economy that protects the vested interests of the business community and middle classes and cannot provide adequate employment and income for Canada's highly skilled and educated workforce. Robertson and Barlow also point to Alberta as a leader in wrong-headed education reform.

17 A traditional, and fairly balanced, conservative approach is taken by Andrew Nikiforuk in *School's Out: The Catastrophe in Public Education and What We Can Do About It* (Toronto: MacFarlane Walter & Ross, 1993). A journalist, author, parent, former teacher, and columnist on education, Nikiforuk's approach to education is reminiscent of arguments made famous in the 1950s by Hilda Neatby in *So Little for the Mind* (Toronto: Clark Irwin, 1953). Like Neatby, Nikiforuk rails against inadequate and ineffective teacher-training and calls for a return to intellectual rigour and authority. His position stands firmly against the business interest to turn schools into high-tech knowledge factories. Likewise, he also distances himself from the humanist, populist, or religious penchant for dumbing-down education in the name of child-centred learning, popular democracy, or religious authoritarianism, respectively. A more extreme conservative position is reflected in *Alberta Report*, which has carried on a long tirade against public education. For example, the cover of its July 5, 1993 issue read, "OUT OF CONTROL: The great socialist experiment in public education has resulted in rampant school violence, runaway costs, poor performance and furious parents. The alternative is privatization."

18 In response to the arguments of social democrats, conservatives, and neo-liberals, another (counter-) critique has emerged in recent years based on liberal humanist principles. See P. Emberley and W. Newell, *Bankrupt Education: The Decline of the Liberal Education in Canada* (Toronto: University of Toronto, 1994). While sharing some ground with traditional conservatism, liberal humanism also ushers in a kind of liberal lament for the passing of tolerant pluralism. Specifically, liberal humanists argue that the best qualities of liberal education have been undermined by five contradictory forces — business, ethnic advocacy groups, educators, radical intellectuals, and religious fundamentalists — resulting in intolerance and a polarization of debates.

19 By making this pitch to parental "choice," neo-liberals are able to garner support from a small but vocal group of what might be termed small-town populists. Joe Freedman, MD, a radiologist from Red Deer, Alberta, provides an example of the latter. He is a leading lobbyist in the province for charter schools. He runs the Society for Advancing Educational Research (SAER), which released *Failing Grades: Canadian Schools in a Global Economy* and a *Proposal for an Alternative Model School* (see chapter eight for more information).

20 For examples, see S.B. Lawton, *Busting Bureaucracy to Reclaim Our Schools*. Montreal: Institute for Research on Public Policy (IRPP), 1995. Some other titles published by IRPP in Montreal are E.G. West's *Ending the Squeeze on Universities* (1993); P. Coleman's *Learning About Schools: What Parents Need to Know and How They Can Find Out* (1994); and B. Wilkinson's *Educational Choice: Necessary But Not Sufficient* (1994). This list goes on with new material produced annually.

21 The Fraser Institute has a very specific five-year plan for promoting "the privatization of education." Fraser Institute, "Toward the New Millennium: A Five Year Plan for the Fraser Institute" (unpublished document).

22 See D. Blanchflower and R. Freeman, "Why youth employment will be hard to reduce" in *Policy Options* 19:3 (April 1998): 3-7; and H. Levin and C. Kelley, "Can education do it alone?" in *Economics of Education Review* 13:2 (1994): 97-108.

23 See appendices. For a recent comprehensive review of literature on schooling and the social order, see "Educational opportunity and social reproduction" in Terry Wotherspoon, *The Sociology of Education in Canada* (Toronto: Oxford University Press, 1998), 155-92; and T. Dunk, S. McBride, and R. Nelson, *The Training Trap: Ideology, Training and the Labour Market* (Winnipeg/Halifax: SSS/Fernwood, 1996).

24 D. Hart and D.W. Livingstone, "The 'crisis' of confidence in schools and the neoconservative agenda: Diverging opinions of corporate executives and the general public" in *Alberta Journal of Educational Research* 44:1 (1998): 1-19. See for example, *Edmonton Journal*, 8 September 1998, A1.

25 J. Lewington, *Globe and Mail*, 3 September 1997, A4. Other summaries can be found in various issues of *Globe and Mail*: 27 January 1995; 22 February 1995; 20 May 1995; 21 September 1996; 17 May 1997.

26 See F. Gendron, "Funding public school systems: A 25 year review" in *Education Quarterly Review* 4:2 (Summer 1997): 27-42. Although university financing as a percentage of Canada's GDP is currently at one of its low points, the overall trend appears to have been more stable — unless, of course, the recent downward trend in government grants to cover operating expenses continues. See D. Little, "Financing universities: Why are students paying more?" in *Education Quarterly Review* 4:2 (Summer 1997): 10-26.

27 R. Dale, "The state and the governance of education: an analysis of the restructuring of the state-education relationship" in *Education: Culture Economy Society*; R. Manzer, *Public Schools and Political Ideas: Canadian Educational Policy in Historical Perspective* (Toronto: University of Toronto, 1994).

28 A. Hargreaves, *Changing Teachers, Changing Times: Teachers' Work and Culture in the Postmodern Age* (New York: Teachers College Press, 1994); G. Whitty, "Marketization, the state, and the re-formation of the teaching profession" in *Education: Culture Economy Society*; S. Robertson and H. Smaller, eds., *Teacher Activism in the 1990s* (Toronto: James Lorimar, 1996).

29 See Laxer and Harrison, eds., *The Trojan Horse*; Taft, *Shredding the Public Interest*.

30 See, for example, M. Hammer and J. Champy, *Reengineering the Corporation: A Manifesto for Business Revolution* (New York: HarperBusiness, 1991); D. Osborne and T. Gaebler, *Reinventing Government. How the Entrepreneurial Spirit is Transforming the Public Sector* (New York: Plume, 1992).

31 See G. Flanagan, "Cutting health care: the hidden cost" in *Alberta Views* 1:2 (Spring 1998): 20-26.

32 *Toronto Star*, 13 September 1995, A3.

33 When government expenses (e.g., health services) exceed government revenues (e.g., taxes), it is called a "deficit." Budget deficits are carried over on each following year and accumulate as "government debt." However — aside from fudging the numbers — the deficit and the accumulated debt can be accounted for in many ways, because the calculation of a government's assets is open to a variety of interpretations; thus, defining the deficit and debt becomes part of many governments' public-relations' strategies.

34 See D. Cooper and D. Neu, "The politics of debt and deficit in Alberta" in *The Trojan Horse*.

35 Taft, *Shredding the Public Interest*.

36 M. McMillan and A. Warrack, "One-track (thinking) towards deficit reduction" in *The Trojan Horse*.

37 *Edmonton Journal*, 18 February 1998, A7.

38 See *Edmonton Journal*, 12 February 1998, A1. The symbolic measure, designed to protect Alberta's "bragging rights" to having the lowest taxes, ultimately failed when the Ontario government subsequently lowered its rate to 40.5 percent (*Globe and Mail*, 6 May 1998, A8). But Alberta's overall personal taxes still remain lower than any other provincial jurisdiction when other factors are considered. For example, Ontario's provincial sales tax (PST) of eight percent costs the average taxpayer between $1,250 and $2,953 per year (*Edmonton Journal*, 6 January 1998, A6). Additionally, Alberta is the only province with no capital or payroll tax (Alberta Economic Development and Tourism, *The Alberta Advantage in Action*. April, 1997, 16-17).

39 *Globe and Mail*, 25 February 1998, A1, A6-A8.

40 For a review of neo-liberal federal policy assumptions for education and knowledge see S. McBride, "Investing in labour market policy" in A. Johnson and A. Stritch, eds., *Canadian Public Policy: Globalization and Political Parties*, 1997, 53-72; A. Stritch, "An innovative economy: science and technology policy" in *Canadian Public Policy: Globalization and Political Parties*, 73-98.

41 *Edmonton Journal*, 25 February 1998, A5.

42 See Appendix K.

43 *Globe and Mail*, 25 February 1998, A1, A6-A8.

44 See also D. Blanchflower and R. Freeman, "Why youth employment will be hard to reduce" in *Policy Options* 19:3 (April 1998): 3-7.

45 For a more thorough discussion of this argument, see Charles Taylor, *The Malaise of Modernity* (Concord, Ontario: Anansi, 1991).

46 R. Morrow with D. Brown, *Critical Theory and Method* (Thousand Oaks: Sage, 1994), 52.

47 A. Schlesingler, Jr., "Has democracy a future?" *Foreign Affairs* 76:5 (1997): 2-12, quotation on 8.

48 C.B. Macpherson, *Democracy in Alberta: Social Credit and the Party System* (Toronto, University of Toronto Press, 1953).

49 See E. Bell, *Social Classes and Social Credit in Alberta* (Montreal: McGill-Queen's University Press, 1993). Also Alvin Finkel, *The Social Credit Phenomenon in Alberta* (Toronto: University of Toronto Press); D. Laycock, *Populism and Democratic Thought in the Canadian Prairies, 1910 to 1945* (Toronto: University of Toronto Press); J. Richards and L. Pratt, *Prairie Capitalism: Power and Influence in the New West* (Toronto: McClelland and Stewart, 1979).

50 K. Osborne, *Teaching for Democratic Citizenship* (Montreal: Our Schools/Our Selves, 1991), 6-7.

51 See P. Kennedy, *Preparing for the Twenty-First Century* (New York: Random House, 1993), 340-41.

Globalization and Educational Change

1

Passing Fancies: Educational Changes in Alberta

Kas Mazurek

The changes outlined in this plan will alter substantially the character of the educational system.
— Alberta Education[1]

Regardless of whether there is or is not a clear overall plan, there is no doubt that important changes are taking place.
— Alberta Teachers' Association[2]

Public schooling is not today, and has never been, a static enterprise. The evolution of Alberta's education system is marked by profound changes to the goals of education, curricular content, pedagogical strategies, evaluation tools, expectations, and responsibilities placed on teachers. Are these changes comprehensible or are they chaotic and patternless?

All too often, the latter interpretation is advanced. Most people criticize education in Alberta as a "faddish" enterprise, one explained metaphorically as a pendulum that oscillates wildly between extremes of ideology and practice without apparent rhyme or reason. Not true. Changes in educational orientations and practices have, over time, indeed been dramatic. But, as this chapter will show, these changes are not haphazard; they are the effects of clearly identifiable forces. In this sense, schooling in Alberta follows an orderly, discernible, pattern of change over time.

That order, however, cannot be recognized by looking at education from the inside, so to speak. Schools are almost wholly reactive institutions. Existing under direct political control, subject to the pressures of public opinion, constantly under media scrutiny, and sensitive to social, cultural, demographic, economic, and political fluctuations, the enterprise of public schooling is always in the process of being redefined and reconstituted by powerful external forces and interest groups. The specific changes taking place in public schooling at any given time are the result of social forces and the agents who mould them. This chapter surveys the most important changes to education and identifies the social forces and individuals that have made schooling in Alberta what it is today.

Historical Foundations of Schooling in Alberta[3]

Alberta was not yet a province in the closing decades of the nineteenth century; it gained provincial status in 1905. Before that, it was part of a region in Canada called the North-West Territories. During its early history and its first three decades as a province, the social forces that defined the character of schooling in Alberta were stark and transparent. There was little doubt in the minds of the dominant social groups — the economic, political, racial, and cultural elites — that schools existed as convenient and powerful instruments for the attainment of specific social objectives. There was also little thought given to hiding these ambitions. What is transparently good may be left transparently obvious. And so, public schools were assigned ideological mandates and were expected to pursue them with messianic zeal. The early objectives to build a nation and nurture capitalism are well documented. These objectives included the mission of "civilizing" various minorities into the dominant White Anglo-Saxon Protestant (WASP) culture.

This mission is starkly illustrated in the case of Canada's aboriginal population and epitomized in the cultural genocide experiment known as the residential school movement. There, notions of racial and cultural superiority intersected, resulting in a concerted effort to replace the cultural consciousness of one race with that of another. This federally sponsored educational experiment was manifest most clearly in the schools — residential and other — established for Native Americans in the prairie provinces.

However, the aboriginal population was not alone in being singled out for cultural extinction; there was also the worrisome "ethnic" element with which to contend. Although many new immigrants to the territory came from Ontario, the United States, and Great Britain, a substantial number came from continental Europe. Greatly troubled by the stubborn persistence of cultural cohesion within many "non-preferred" immigrant groups in Alberta — particularly the Slavic and other peoples who settled in rural bloc settlements — the dominant culture charged schools with the task of assimilating the diverse ethnic populations. As David Goggin, the territorial superintendent of schools, bluntly put it, the "only truly successful way" to achieve assimilation was "to gather the children of different races, creeds, and customs into the common school, and 'Canadianize' them . . . . Though they may enter as Galicians, Doukhobors, or Icelanders, they will come out as Canadians."[4]

Because language and religion are key elements of most cultures, both provided flashpoints for the politics of education. Language was thus an integral element of WASP imperialism. Until English became common to all, ethnic assimilation could not be assured. Accordingly, in the unrelenting drive to make Alberta an exclusively English-speaking province, schools were called into service. Alberta's multilingual populations were not to see their linguistic pluralism reflected in public schools.

Added to this focus on Anglo-conformity was a religious dimension. Clearly, Roman Catholicism was a thorn in the side of those who dreamed of a Protestant Canada. Constitutional provisions for separate schools existed but were a source of dismay for educational leaders from the Ottawa river to the Rocky Mountains. Egerton Ryerson, the central figure in the development of public schools in Ontario, expressed openly that schools were to be important institutions for "religious" assimilation. His ideas were echoed throughout the west, especially by public school promoters in Alberta, who adopted the Ontario model. They hoped that in time Catholics and Catholicism could be swallowed up by the numerically dominant Protestant population.[5]

Further interwoven into all this was nationalism. The political and educational elites feared the "balkanization" of Alberta (and the other prairie provinces) into ethnic, linguistic, and religious enclaves, because it threatened the integrity of the new dominion, challenged central Canadian and British power, and lowered resistance to American interests. Elite fear of balkanization assumed hysterical proportions with the advent of World War One. Democracy and the Canadian state were in peril from within. Whereas the "Canadianization" of Alberta's diverse population was a noble social ideal in pre-1914 Alberta, in the years immediately following it was deemed necessary for survival. Nation-building was a duty schools were expected with some urgency to fulfill.

However, the national democratic aspiration of the Dominion was not the only ideology that needed to be nurtured. Capitalism was the foundation that made the opening of the west possible — the source of Alberta's wealth, and the hope for its future. Be it for clearing forests into productive farmlands, mining coal for industry and transportation, or labouring in small businesses and factories, suitable workers were in great demand and short supply. The duty of the schools was therefore clear. For the great majority (the farmers and workers), an elementary school education, consisting of a smattering of literacy and numeracy skills, was desirable; but the inculcation of a good work ethic in the form of industry, punctuality, and deference to authority was *a necessity*. For a select few (the managerial and professional middle classes) who would complete high school and might even go on to university, the inculcation of higher-level thinking and problem-solving skills, the ethics of "professionalism," and high aspirations was also a necessity.

The above, by no means exhaustive, outline illustrates some of the main contours of the social context within which schools operated and which defined the character of schooling in that era. Dominant groups — defined by race, ethnicity, culture, language, religion, national orientation, political ideology, and economic status — advanced their agendas through the public schools. However, two cautions warrant citation.

First, it is worth stressing that the plural — i.e., dominant groups — is used throughout. Clearly it is a mistake to homogenize the architects of the cultural, political, and other orientations of public schooling noted above into one undifferentiated entity. Groups are never singularly monolithic; differences, divisions, and disputes will always be found. Still, too much must not be made of such differences. Public schooling was designed in early Alberta to reproduce the particular roles of its own highly stratified and structured society. Schooling, as scholarship has documented, was emphatically not value-free during the early era. It is equally clear which individuals, groups, and agendas were instrumental in shaping the value orientations of schools.

Second, it would be a mistake to read conspiratorial undertones into any of this. As stated earlier, historical documentation makes clear that the agendas advanced through public schooling were very "public" and forthright during this era and represented a confluence of powerful interests. There were no "hidden agendas." This openness is because schooling was characterized by what is in retrospect a naïve, whiggish, historical ethnocentrism. Inherent in the above social, political, cultural, economic, linguistic, and religious prejudices is a notion of social, political, cultural, economic, linguistic, and moral progress. The dominant groups who used Alberta's schools to advance their agendas may best be thought of as a coalition of leading thinkers who possessed an intellectual and moral certitude that the world can become a better place and that their ideas were indeed the "right" ones. Why hide one's agenda if that agenda is the blueprint for progress itself?

The Emergence of Progressive Education

Why indeed? It is almost as if the question of progress was literally asked by the educational establishment during the turmoil of the Great Depression. Political reorganization, marked by emerging farmer-labour alliances in the 1920s and in combination with the economic crisis of the 1930s, created a watershed period across Canada. In 1935, the United Farmers of Alberta (first elected in 1921) was thrown out of office and Social Credit elected. The "agenda" for "progress" for public schooling has perhaps never been more clear in Alberta than it was in this era of progressive education (see chapter three). Starting with a vengeance in 1936, the significance of the Aberhart government's educational reforms cannot be over-emphasized.

Like every other province and nation during the Great Depression, Alberta was struggling to find a remedy for the economic and social gloom into which the industrialized world had plunged. Desperate measures were needed; the "old" way of doing things was simply not working. In this furnace of fear and uncertainty were forged many radical social experiments. Fascism, communism, and liberal capitalism were fighting a no-holds-barred battle for control of the nations of Europe; Roosevelt's New Deal was fundamentally reshaping the economic, political, and social character of the United States; the Cooperative Commonwealth Federation took root in Saskatchewan to germinate ideas that would later transform Canadian social policy; and an incredulous Canada looked on as Albertans elected a Social Credit government whose social and economic policies were, to put it mildly, unorthodox. Social, political, and economic experimentation was rampant, and one such experiment was progressive education.

It mattered little that progressive education was borrowed wholesale from a contentious American source — John Dewey and his colleagues at Columbia University — or that progressive education was itself a derivative of the much older "New Education" movement in Europe. What did matter is that Alberta's educational establishment — led by Hubert Newland[6] — grew inspired with the promises offered by an educational philosophy that was revolutionary, transformative, and that literally presented the regeneration of humanity and society? Aided by the zealous salesmanship of Newland and his colleagues, progressive education took root in Alberta.

Philosophically, progressive education was broadly compatible with other ideologies spawning on the prairies. It respected the uniqueness and innate intelligence of the individual, while at the same time emphasizing cooperation and group solidarity. It sought to foster self-initiative, a broad range of intellectual and practical skills, and a practical "can do" approach to problem solving, while rigorously applying the scientific method to all inquiry and enshrining participatory democracy as fundamental to educational practice and political discourse. In these regards, it simultaneously tapped into the cooperative orientations Albertans had developed under the United Farmers of Alberta administration, glorified the rugged and practical individualism of a predominantly rural Alberta, rejected the academic "bookishness" of a school curriculum irrelevant for farming and working Albertans in favor of applied problem solving, and offered the promise of a transformation of society through the liberation of individual talent and initiative in the cause of a common good and general social progress.

In its attempt to fulfill these promises, progressive education wrought a transformation of public schooling in Alberta which was truly monumental in its proportions. Virtually everything changed when the education system was developed — for the most part — during this period: large administrative units were created; the powers of local boards were redefined; a new Teaching Profession Act defined the nature of the profession; mandatory membership led to the formation of the Alberta Teachers' Association (ATA) (although its primary influence was more on contract bargaining than policy); cooperative and interdisciplinary learning was mandated through the enterprise program; massive curricular revisions (particularly the integration of existing distinct subjects and the creation of new options with a practical focus) were undertaken; explicit new teaching objectives (such as the inculcation of a scientific attitude, creative self-expression, and tolerance) were introduced; a restructuring of the organization of school levels was effected; evaluation criteria and procedures for students and teachers were redefined. That the preceding is only a partial listing is testimony to how profound the changes were under progressive education to the practice, content, and organization of schooling.[7]

The years 1935-40 witnessed the creation of a school system that, on the surface, was unrecognizable from the perspective of what existed before. Different as the new system was, however, it was still a creation of its social environment and it still served social, political, economic, and ideological objectives. Although cultural assimilation was no longer emphasized, it remained the implicit aim of schooling. Now school children would be assimilated into the culture of pragmatic, scientific rationalism. Religious bias was no longer everywhere interwoven into curriculum and pedagogy. It didn't need to be: there was now a new, universal religion called the scientific method. The inculcation of worker virtues compatible with a capitalist economic order was no longer openly espoused. Again, it didn't need to be: self-motivated students bound by the ethos of cooperative work habits fit perfectly into the bureaucratic machinery of industry.

In short, new content but the same old functions; schools remained institutions consciously employed to perpetuate identifiable values and to serve rather clear, specific, predetermined ends. And the ultimate objective for progressive education was, quite literally, the transformation of society itself. Both for John Dewey and his disciples in Alberta, "social reconstruction" was the ultimate objective; schools were merely the chosen instruments for achieving that objective. The experiment lasted until mid-century. It then imploded, undermined by weakness from within and pressures from without.

"Progress" Meets Tradition

In a real sense, progressive education never had a reasonable chance of succeeding. Even if the concept was sound, it never marshalled the resources necessary to realize itself in Alberta. It was an innovation imposed from the top down. While progressive education was the darling of the educational establishment, it never fully garnered grassroots support from practicing teachers. It was literally forced upon an unsuspecting teaching community; compliance with the orientation and practices of progressive education was imposed, not invited or negotiated. Not surprisingly, a great number of teachers did not buy into what they perceived to be merely a new educational "fad." Their support and participation, hence, were token.

However, even had there been full teacher support for this new approach, it is far from certain that the teaching force had the competence to implement it. Progressive education, being both novel and complex, was not fully understood by the teachers who were asked to implement it. It is clear that large numbers of teachers simply did not understand the theory behind progressive education and were only superficially able to apply progressive pedagogical strategies. Teachers were commonly only graduates of grade ten, eleven, or twelve, and their training usually consisted of less than a year in Normal School. The complexity of the new teaching orientation, especially without the assistance of extensive in-servicing, was simply beyond the ability of a relatively poorly educated and trained teaching force. Furthermore, some Catholic educators understood the pervasively secular nature of progressive education and rebelled against its inclusion in Catholic separate schools.

These internal problems were that much more critical when one considers the backlash against progressive education that developed outside the cocoon of the educational establishment. Emerging social pressures would result in the virtual negation of all that was created in the era of progressive education.

One powerful influence was an emerging moral condemnation. Progressive education's emphasis upon open-ended inquiry into virtually all matters meant that proponents rendered suspect absolute answers to moral, social, cultural, and political questions. Some religious, political, and cultural groups responded predictably: traditional social and ethical values were being undermined and the process must be stopped.

Another major blow to progressive education came from the university establishment. Following the lead of critics in the United States (where progressive education was criticized even earlier and more severely), a litany of complaints emerged about marginal literacy and numeracy skills of new entrants into post-secondary education. The causes of this were argued to be fourfold. First, it was claimed that the school curriculum had become so watered down that most meaningful intellectual substance had been removed. Academic rigour suffered because progressive educators were too concerned with making learning student-centered and student-directed. Second, the restructured curriculum prevented students from grasping the disciplinary bases of the sciences and humanities. This was deemed to be the fault of the enterprise method, which integrated disciplines and, to use today's terminology, taught subjects "across the curriculum." Third, allegedly subjective evaluation criteria had resulted in varied standards and unreliable grading. As a result, students were simply not prepared for advanced study. Finally, these problems were compounded by the proliferation of options that students were allowed to take. In the drive to make schools relevant and practical institutions, a great variety of non-academic options emerged. Students could graduate with a wide variety of courses on their transcripts which had little if anything to do with the traditional subjects associated with a core curriculum. Calls for the primacy of "core" school subjects emerged.

Such rallies against the "evils" of progressive education were not limited to disgruntled traditionalists and academics (who could be accused of merely wishing to preserve an intellectual and moral status quo). Teachers and parents also provided pragmatic complaints about the alleged legacy of progressive education's ideas and methods.[8]

Certainly the Soviet Union's launch of Sputnik near the height of the Cold War made inevitable an unflattering scrutiny of the current state of education across North America. Leaders mobilized fear and postured politically to introduce reform. They argued — not always accurately — that the western democracies had lost their technological edge; that schools must produce a new generation of scientists to regain that edge; that there must be a change in orientations and methods if the schools were to meet that challenge. This line of logic was every bit as compelling in Alberta as it was in the United States.

While Alberta did not have to worry about closing a technological gap with the Soviet Union, it did have its own concerns. The "post-industrial" age was already upon us as the 1950s unfolded. The schools' mandate could no longer be vaguely proactive (some utopian ideal of "social reconstruction"); it had to be concretely reactive (to keep up with the seemingly insatiable demands of industry and bureaucracy in the new technocratic society). Both labour and professional requirements demanded increasing levels of technical and intellectual skills as the economy changed fundamentally.

The combined effect of the above concerns and demands for reform formed a comprehensive and complete assault on progressive education. The classic summation of the time concerning all that was wrong with progressive education in Canada was Hilda Neatby's (1953) eloquent and popular *So Little for the Mind* (see introduction).[9] Therein she argued, before a responsive audience, that progressive education had abandoned all standards of rigour, had debased the most worthwhile subjects by treating them superficially and by including them alongside trivial studies, and had contributed to the decline of the best social, ethical, and political values to emerge out of the western intellectual tradition. The cure was obvious: a return to a core of essential knowledge and disciplines and a reaffirmation of traditional values.

That is precisely the direction schooling in Alberta took. In 1959, a Royal Commission on Education both reaffirmed the steps already taken and the contours of the path to follow. The Cameron Report[10] paints a picture of schooling which enshrines core subjects, a highly specific curriculum to clearly define the content of that curriculum, standardized testing to measure achievement levels, direct teaching methods, the instilling of a work ethic, and citizenship training.

Such was the new educational status quo. Alberta now had a school system that was clearly "traditional" in its conservative underpinning, content, and pedagogy — arguably the antithesis of the "progressive" system that had defined schooling in the previous generation. However, profound social forces were beginning to reshape Alberta and Canada in the 1960s.

Prosperity

As society changed, its momentum proved too powerful for schools to resist. Education in Alberta was once again to undergo a dramatic reconstitution. One major social change was economic. The prosperity Canada had enjoyed immediately after the war did not abate; instead it accelerated at an astonishing pace. One result of this was a chronic shortage of personnel at all levels, especially in technical fields and the professions. Opportunities were almost limitless for skilled people, and the demand for advanced education was enormous. The budgets and student populations of schools and post-secondary institutions exploded. Not only were students staying in school longer, but there were also more of them. Increasing immigration and the continuing tidal wave of baby-boomers strained the capacity of schools to find enough classroom spaces and teachers.

This boom had two results. First, schooling options increased dramatically. The need to keep more and more students in school longer and longer to supply the personnel needs of a rapidly expanding, increasingly diversified and technological economy meant that school offerings had to expand. Second, teachers themselves were a desperately sought-after labour commodity — there was a chronic teacher shortage. The combined effect was that teachers demanded and received increasing professional autonomy and schools responded to the new economic demands placed on them by increasing student choices.

However, these developments were more than a reflex response of schools and teachers to the demands of a market economy. Cultural forces also were at work which would prevent schools from becoming more than mere producers of human fodder for the mills of industry. The 1960s heralded an era of incredible social innovation and experimentation — in the arts and media, in social relationships, in political thought; indeed in all aspects of social life. A sense of empowerment gripped youth, in particular, and the feeling that a new age was dawning was in the air. Whether it took the form of overt rebellion against tradition and authority in the form of the sexual revolution or drug use, redefining identity through humanistic psychology and cooperative living experiments, or demanding a more direct form of participatory democracy through demonstrations or the student rights movement, it was clear that the 1960s generation would not be content to fit into the social and intellectual mould of the previous generation.

Schools were as affected by the changing social milieu as other institutions. The uniform curriculum, content, pedagogy, and governance which characterized the traditional educational system eulogized in the Cameron Report were no longer acceptable for a "do your own thing" generation. Educational experimentation was enthusiastically embraced; the results were dramatic. A student-centered orientation replaced the teacher-centered perspective; open-ended discovery and inquiry approaches replaced learning strategies focused on content and skill specificity; curricular options were greatly expanded at the expense of time allocated to the core curriculum; curriculum and pedagogy were adapted to student interests; standardized evaluation tools and procedures were abandoned; team-teaching, cooperative learning, inter-disciplinary study, and open-area classrooms were encouraged.

The final "seal of approval" by the educational bureaucracy on this new state of educational affairs (not that it needed one, as it was an established reality by that time) was given in 1972 by the Worth Report.[11] Therein is documented the full extent to which the new educational ethos and practices had permeated public schooling, the teaching profession, and faculties of education in Alberta. Incredibly, in the mere thirteen years separating the Cameron and Worth reports, the philosophy and practice of schooling in Alberta had shifted virtually 180 degrees. But this shift rather precisely matched major shifts experienced by society itself. Education could not have resisted such powerful social forces. However, further changes were on the horizon.

From Retrenchment to "Revolution"

The ink had barely dried on the Worth Report before a profound restructuring of schooling in Alberta slowly began again in response to new and powerful social changes. The full effect of this latest restructuring has only today, at the close of the century and millennium, been fully realized and incorporated into the school system.

Once again, change in the economic sector was a major impetus (see introduction and chapter three). In the early 1970s, the heady economic expansion that had been gathering steam since World War Two finally seemed to fizzle out. The causes for this change are disputed and varied — increased energy costs after the formation of OPEC, the flight of multinationals to areas offering a cheap supply of labour, international currency crises, escalating interest rates, and so on — but the results are clear. Changed economic realities ushered in changes to fiscal policies; social spending, it was argued, had to be reined in. As governments grappled with the question of how to do this, provincial debts accumulated and the crises deepened.

In the search for culprits, schools became an obvious and easy target. As is so often the case, the process began in the United States, then made its way into Canada. Emerging economic problems were, understandably, accompanied by social concerns. The problems of crime, violence, youth alienation, racial tensions, disparities in wealth, growing ghettos, and so on were not new to the United States. However, as unemployment rates climbed, wages stagnated, inflation rose, and taxes increased, working- and middle-class Americans began to sense the erosion of a way of life.

Part of the fear coalesced into an emerging perception that the United States was falling behind other nations in key areas such as science, technology, and manufacturing.

America's leadership in the post-industrial world was and is intimately tied to the theory of "human capital." The premise is that the economic realities of the modern world are such that human resources — in the form of problem-solving skills and technical and scientific knowledge for managers and professionals, and high literacy and numeracy skills for the labour force — are vitally necessary if a nation is to enjoy prosperity through economic growth. It is not merely financial capital and the physical assets of production that are vital; a highly educated labour force is needed to achieve a "competitive edge." Schools and post-secondary institutions therefore play a crucial role in the economic vitality of a nation by educating citizens to these high levels. The role of the state is to underwrite this prosperity by establishing and maintaining high-quality public schools.

But something seemed to have gone wrong. Since World War Two, the US had enjoyed a sustained economic boom. That boom, as human capital theorists argued, was made possible in large part by the country's pool of expertise — its well educated population. Year after year, the United States increased its advantage in technology, manufacturing, finance, marketing, and so on. Year after year, investments in education reached historic highs, as did completion rates for schooling. However, as the 1970s unfolded, signs emerged that the economic dominance of the US was threatened. Could it be that the educational system was no longer delivering in its duty to provide the highly educated labour force that human capital theory demands?

Disturbing suggestions of a marked decline in the quality of education in the US surfaced. Polls documented a decline in public confidence in public schools, Scholastic Aptitude Test scores showed a prolonged downward trend, universities complained about ill-prepared high-school graduates entering their programs, school administrators provided evidence of problems with students and teachers, and political leaders put quality of schooling in America on the public agenda. A concerted attack on public schooling took shape. The most damaging blows of all came from an all-out assault by the media. Major national newsmagazines, newspapers, and television networks aired a succession of hypercritical stories on public schooling; the effects were absolutely devastating. Perhaps the final blow came in 1983 when the prestigious National Commission on Excellence in Education sounded its now famous warning that "the educational foundations of our society are presently being eroded by a rising tide of mediocrity that threatens our very future as a Nation and a people."[12]

Alberta was quick to reflect what was happening south of the border. True, the province did not have nearly the same social concerns and problems. But there were commonalties — especially the way American research dominated the academic literature. Above all, Alberta was encountering an economic slowdown, the provincial government's public debt was beginning to accumulate, and a conservative, openly business-oriented administration was concerned about the size and cost of its public service agencies. Economic liberals and social conservatives could promote their agendas by using events in the US to their advantage. A climate of opinion strongly negative toward public schooling had emerged in the US, and the media kept Albertans aware of the heated debate.

Since the 1970s, declining performance ratings for education mirrored a universal decline of public confidence in all major institutions in Canada, the US, and the UK. Although public support for education since the 1970s has remained relatively high when compared to other institutions, there has been a definite decline in satisfaction with educational performance. While this assessment is more attributable to the rising expectations of the public and the demands of the business community than the poor job being done by Canadian schools,[13] governments nevertheless quickly turned their attention to public schooling. This very large and expensive bureaucracy emerged as an early and prime target for governments in the battle to reduce public-sector spending.[14]

In fact, a battle in Alberta began in the early 1970s as the government began to steadily reduce the share of its annual budget allocated to education (see chapter three). However, more fundamental and publicly visible changes to schooling had to wait until 1977 and the release of the Harder Report.[15] The Harder Report, published by Alberta Education, is a most significant document. In a real sense, it is the blueprint for changes to education that have taken two decades to fully realize. Unfortunately, as so often happens, the Report attracted the detailed scrutiny of only the academic community and activists within the Alberta Teachers' Association. Not until half a decade later did a broader spectrum of the public and front-line teachers begin to recognize the impact of the unfolding plan heralded therein.

The Harder Report begins with a curious, and undocumented, assertion. It claims to be

> . . . a response to requests for changes in our education programs from many segments of our society. In the main, these requests stem from the general dissatisfaction of the public with what they feel are short falls in the education system and the high costs of what they term mediocrity.

Serious charges, but what evidence is presented for such a "general dissatisfaction"? In the Alberta of the early 1970s, few seemed so seriously unhappy with the school system.

Nevertheless, a failure to provide factual justification did not stop the report from proposing a sweeping reform of the entire school system. An emphasis upon knowledge and skills relevant for employment; more instruction time in the core curriculum; a curriculum highly specified in content and skill levels by grade; a reduction of electives; criterion-referenced standardized tests; accountability through monitoring; citizenship training: these were all the elements of the so-called "back to basics" movement.

At first slowly and gradually, Alberta Education began to implement this blueprint for the reform of schooling. In 1981, standardized achievement tests in English, mathematics, science, and social studies were introduced at the grade three, six, nine, and twelve levels on a rotating basis. One year later, leaving examinations in these four subjects were made available for grade twelve students on an optional basis; the following year the examinations became compulsory and counted for fifty percent of the final grade. Two years later, the curriculum underwent a major change: time allocated to core subjects was increased; many options were eliminated; a new compulsory course in career, personal finance, and life management skills was announced. The pace soon quickened. The 1984/85 school year witnessed a veritable barrage of initiatives: Secondary Program Review; Consultative Committee on Tolerance and Understanding; Study of Private Schools; School Libraries Review; Teaching Profession Act Review; School Act Review; Evaluation of Student Achievement; Evaluation of School Programs; Evaluation of School Systems; Evaluation of Schools; Evaluation of Teachers; Standardized Exams; Core Curriculum; Spending Restraints; Replacement of the Board of Teacher Education and Certification with the Council on Alberta Teaching Standards.

Many events and pressures along the way helped justify these initiatives and reforms. As the debt crisis deepened, the calls for a streamlined and more "accountable" educational system increased. The business community continued to lament a deplorable lack of skills and work ethic in school graduates. The provincial and national media added fuel to the fire by producing a decade-long sequel of horror stories about declining standards and inflated grades, barely literate and numerate high-school graduates, incompetent teachers, indifferent educational administrators and bureaucrats, inadequate teacher-training programs, and so on. Grassroots parents' organizations emerged to pressure directly for school reforms. And the infamous "Keegstra affair" certainly didn't help.

In December 1982, James Keegstra was fired from his teaching position in a small Alberta town for teaching his students that there is an international Jewish conspiracy and that the Holocaust is an historical myth. He was subsequently charged and convicted under Canada's "hate crime" laws.[16] As *Alberta Report*[17] relates, the authors of a book on Mr. Keegstra received a letter from the then-minister of education in which he wrote:

> I do not consider "the Keegstra affair" to have been an "Important historical event" . . . . It is significant not in itself, but rather for the

window of opportunity it opened, which lent focus and power to a number of initiatives that had commenced in the years 1979-1982.

As recent events show, the fruition of those "initiatives" took place soon after the election of a Progressive Conservative government under Premier Ralph Klein. The years 1993-96 were a watershed. Five documents[18] tell the story of how the finishing touches were applied to Alberta's educational system over that three-year period.

Measuring Up comprehensively sets out an agenda for all government departments. It addresses what the goals for each department should be, indicates how each of the goals will be implemented, and outlines how each department will be measured and evaluated to ensure that stated goals are being met and policies carried out. *Meeting the Challenge* specifies how Alberta Education will comply. *Roles and Responsibilities in Education* details the specific responsibilities of all the constituents in the schooling enterprise: students, parents, school councils, school boards, superintendents, principals, teachers, staff, communities, and Alberta Education. *Teacher Education Policy Reform* specifically addresses the knowledge, skills, and attitudes teachers are expected to possess and ties these into certification requirements. *Accountability in Education* focuses on reporting and monitoring at the school and board levels.

The results attained over the 1993-96 period were dramatic. The government's "three-year business plan schedule for restructuring education" proposed a number of important changes. For 1994/95, these proposals included legislation to restructure education; provincial requisition and distribution of education property taxes; and reduction of school-board spending on administration and capital. For 1995/96, these proposed changes included getting charter schools piloted; teacher certification requirements updated; the number of school boards reduced; Alberta Education reorganized, downsized and cost recovery of department services increased; provincial assessment program expanded; school jurisdiction business plans required; and a new provincial funding framework created. For 1996/97, the proposed changes included having Career and Technology Studies implemented; local attendance boundaries removed; competencies for beginning and experienced teachers established; site-based management implemented; uniform provincial mill rates set; a overall budget reduction target (of over a quarter of a billion dollars) met.

In these recent events, we can clearly discern a movement which started at first almost imperceptibly at the opening of the 1970s, took concrete shape in the 1977 Harder Report, made major headway with the initiatives of 1984-85, and was virtually fully realized and implemented by the end of 1996. Today, there remains on the agenda only an ongoing fine-tuning, the outlines of which can be found in documents such as *An Integrated Framework to Enhance the Quality of Education in Alberta.*

A momentary plateau has been reached. But is it safe to say that Albertans and their government can now rest for a bit, as a period of consolidation in matters educational take hold? A cautious "yes" may be volunteered. Why? At a recent meeting of the Council of Ministers of Education, the following major current trends in education were identified[19]: more cooperation at regional and national levels; more accountability to the public; making information technology an integral part of education; providing less funding for education in general while ensuring that available funding is allocated to classrooms; fewer school districts and boards; a focus on curricular outcomes and standards to make schooling more relevant; improved levels of student achievement; more cost-effective ways to deliver programs; implementation of comprehensive, multi-year assessment programs tied to curriculum standards and outcomes; attention to school/work transition programs; and evaluation of current development and training programs.

It should be noted that Alberta is a "leader" in many of the above trends (see introduction). For the next little while, the government of Alberta and those of its citizens who are basically content with the current state of their province's educational affairs can watch, with deserved smugness, as other provinces take up the battle to get where Alberta is today. And a potentially divisive and ugly battle it may be — if the Ontario teachers' strikes in 1997 and 1998 are any indication.

■ ■ ■

In the meantime, five general conclusions may be drawn from this chapter. First, dramatic changes have occurred in schooling over the course of Alberta's short history. It is perhaps accurate to conceive of these changes as involving a series of "eras." It is inaccurate to portray such change as chaotic or random. This is because, second, changes in educational ideas and practices can clearly be associated with profound external (and sometimes internal) social changes. The changes that schooling took in form and substance were often fundamental and dramatic, but they were never random. They were a reflection of changes taking place in society at large.[20]

Third, those who consider the major changes that education underwent in 1993-96 something "imposed out of the blue" merely on the whims of a particular government under a particular leadership are sadly mistaken. It is well worth emphasizing that the current state of schooling in Alberta is not simply the consequence of a political agenda initiated by the administration of Premier Klein. As we have seen, the process which culminated in the dramatic restructuring of schooling in the 1993-96 period can be traced back at least two decades to the early 1970s. The "eras" of schooling we examined were not passing fancies; each took a long time to be realized and each had a durability lasting decades.

Fourth, there is no reason to believe that the process of change has come to an end. In light of the overview this chapter has provided, it is a pretty safe bet that the next generation of teachers will live to see continuing dramatic changes in their chosen profession. Unfortunately, this chapter also documents that changes in the past almost invariably happened without input from teachers except in their resistance to reform at the classroom level. To repeat: schools are almost wholly reactive institutions. It is astounding but true that teachers historically have been and continue to be almost completely, as the phrase goes, out of the decision-making loop.

This is a great source of frustration for the profession (see chapter ten). As the Alberta Teachers' Association laments in the landmark document *Trying to Teach*, "A common concern was that teachers' voices were not being heard — in fact, they were not even requested."[21] Nonetheless, this lack of consultation is indicative of the ATA's inability to present itself to the government and the public at large as having an important role in public policy formation, rather than merely a trade union bargaining for higher wages.

Fifth and finally, there is a lesson in this situation for faculties of education and teachers in training. Students in Bachelor of Education programs across Canada are poorly prepared in the skills of social-economic-political analysis. The focus of teacher education programs today is almost exclusively technical. Knowledge of subject-matter content, pedagogical strategies, evaluation techniques, lesson planning, classroom management approaches, and so on, combined with apprenticeship experiences in the form of teaching practica, characterize the education our future teachers receive. The strength of this education is that they enter the teaching profession with the technical skills to implement the curriculum as prescribed by Alberta Education. The weakness is that they have not developed the analytical skills or received the background knowledge that will enable them to understand the social context within which their profession is practiced and which has such a profound influence.

The ATA understands this and has issued both a call to arms and a warning:

> Public pressure for major educational reform is building throughout Canada and other countries. Undoubtedly, more change is going to occur. The question is whether teachers as a profession are prepared to take the initiative and to attempt to set the direction for those changes. If we decide not to exercise that initiative, there is little doubt that others will continue to impose their "solutions" on our classrooms.[22]

Little doubt indeed. Surely a logical place to begin is to raise and examine thoroughly these important issues very early in the career of professional teachers — in their professional training programs. Yet, while understanding the situation is difficult enough, teachers and their apprentices face huge challenges — as do many others in Alberta and elsewhere. As the next chapters show, the social forces that characterize globalization, and the political movements intent on remaking education, are formidable.

Notes

1 Alberta Education, *Meeting the Challenge: Three-Year Business Plan 1994/95 — 1996/97*, February 1994.

2 Alberta Teachers' Association, *Trying to Teach*, January 1993.

3 For more details on the historical foundations of schooling in the West, see D. Jones, N. Sheehan, R. Stamp, eds., *Shaping Canadian Schools of the Canadian West* (Calgary: Detselig, 1979); N. Sheehan, J. Wilson, and D. Jones, eds., *Schools in the West* (Calgary: Detselig, 1986); N. Kach, K. Mazurek, R.S. Patterson, and I. DeFaveri, *Essays on Canadian Education* (Calgary: Detselig, 1986); J. Barman, Y. Hébert, and D. McCaskill, eds., *Indian Education in Canada* (2 volumes) (Vancouver: UBC Press, 1986, 1987); E.B. Titley, ed., *Canadian Education* (Calgary: Detselig, 1990); N. Kach and K. Mazurek, eds., *Exploring Our Educational Past* (Calgary: Detselig, 1992); M. Battiste and J. Barman, eds., *First Nations Education in Canada* (Vancouver: UBC Press, 1995).

4 As cited in N. McDonald, "Canadian Nationalism and North-West Schools, 1884-1905" in A. Chaiton and N. McDonald, eds., *Canadian Schools and Canadian Identity* (Toronto: Gage, 1977), 71.

5 In Manitoba, this dream became a reality: the legislature eliminated separate schools in 1890.

6 Newland was president of Alberta Teachers' Alliance during the 1920s and supervisor of Alberta schools in the 1930s. He obtained his PhD in 1932 from the University of Chicago, a hotbed of progressivism.

7 See N. Kach, "Progressive Education in Alberta" in *Essays on Canadian Education*.

8 For another overview of the recent history of schooling and society in Alberta, see E.B. Titley and K. Mazurek, "Back to the Basics? Forward to the Fundamentals?" in E.B. Titley, ed., *Canadian Education: Historical Themes and Contemporary Issues* (Calgary: Detselig, 1990).

9 *So Little for the Mind* (Toronto: Clark Irwin, 1953).

10 *Report of the Royal Commission on Education in Alberta 1959* (Edmonton: Queen's Printer, 1959).

11 Government of Alberta, *Report of the Commission on Educational Planning*. A Future of Choices A Choice of Futures, 1972.

12 National Commission on Excellence in Education, *A Nation at Risk: The Imperative for Educational Reform* (Washington, D.C.: US Government Printing Office, 1983).

13 D. Hart and D.W. Livingstone, "The 'crisis' of confidence in schools and the neoconservative agenda: Diverging opinions of corporate executives and the general public" in *The Alberta Journal of Educational Research* 44:1 (1998): 1-19. Also see D. Livingstone and D. Hart, "Popular Beliefs about Canadian Schools" in R. Ghosh and D. Ray, eds., *Social Change and Education in Canada* (Toronto: Harcourt and Brace, 1995), 16-39.

14 Up to the late 1980s, public support for education across Canada remained strong. This strength, however, was identified by the Mulroney government as "the problem" with education and needed to be overcome in order for educational restructuring to occur. See

for example the government criticisms that underpin recommendations for reform: Steering Group on Prosperity, *Inventing Our Future: An Action Plan for Canada's Prosperity.* October 1992; Government of Canada, *Learning Well . . . Living Well*, Minister of Supply and Services, 1991. For Alberta see *Toward 2000 Together Moderator's Report On Conference Proceedings: Premier's Conference on Alberta's Economic Future: May 28-29, 1992 Calgary Alberta,* 1992.

15 Alberta Education, *Alberta Education and Diploma Requirements: A Discussion Paper Prepared for the Curriculum Policies Board.* Revised Fall 1977.

16 The case, which attracted both national and international attention, had far reaching consequerrces for the teaching profession. See K. Mazurek, "Indictment of a profession: the continuing failure of professional accountability" in *Teacher Education* April 1988: 56-69.

17 *Alberta Report*, November 25, 1985, 34.

18 Government of Alberta, *Measuring Up*, December 1994; Alberta Education, *Meeting the Challenge*, February 1994; Alberta Education, *Roles and Responsibilities in Education,* December 1994; Alberta Education, *Teacher Education Policy Reform*, May 1995; Alberta Education, *Accountability in Education*, January 1995.

19 "Key Trends in Canada." *CEC Today* September 1996: 7.

20 And, I would argue, other parts of the social sector such as health care, social services, and so on.

21 Alberta Teachers' Association, *Trying to Teach*, 24.

22 *Trying to Teach*, 26.

2

Constructing the Perpetual Learner: Education, Technology, and the New Economy

Lee Easton

[T]he computer has arrived in nearly every Canadian school board on the heels of what I call three lies and a threat. And they all merit some admittedly heretical questioning.
— Andrew Nikiforuk[1]

Writing recently in the *Globe and Mail*, education critic Andrew Nikiforuk attacks "the digerati" — a group including such technophiles as Bill Gates and Nicholas Negroponte — for perpetuating the myth that computers are now essential to schooling.[2] According to Nikiforuk, the current computer craze is simply another manifestation of trendy educators and technophiles looking for problems to suit their (computer) solutions. He further contends that the digerati "fear monger" by threatening that all those who resist the digital tidal wave that they risk becoming, or remaining, jobless. Nikiforuk, however, debunks these myths, arguing that the computer remains "just a glittery delivery truck" which is so far "pitifully empty of rousing ideas, moral parables or for that matter critiques of machine-driven schools."[3]

This chapter argues that the installation of new technologies is closely related to a corporate interest in producing workers who possess the aptitudes and attitudes appropriate to a just-in-time workforce. New technologies in education provide one avenue through which learning is redefined not only to promote work in the "new economy" but also to create habitual consumers of digital culture, much the way advertising did for industrial culture in the early twentieth century. These moves cannot be seen in isolation, however. The larger historical context of a shift from print to digital culture suggests that the dividing line between public and private is again being refashioned, this time primarily to suit the current neo-liberal climate and its right-wing supporters. This chapter argues that education is one of the primary sites where this "re-visioning" is underway, and that the public interest requires the creation of alternative visions for using technology that will replace corporate agendas with one which promotes greater social justice for all.

Retooling Education for the Digital Workforce

I broadly agree with Andrew Nikiforuk's critique of technology cited above: this work supplements his argument, however, by adding three critical points he misses. First, because he relies on what can be termed, kindly, a crude technological determinism where technology, not people, appear to be in charge, Nikiforuk fails to consider the powerful economic and social forces that also underlie the installation of computer technologies into schools. He downplays, for example, the position that computer installation in schools is driven not just by the rhetoric of a select group of technophiles but also by the education system's crucial role in producing literate workers. In this light, computer installation in schools emanates equally from industry's wholesale adoption of flexible production techniques such as just-in-time delivery, niche marketing, and specialized short runs as the preferred way to produce goods in the 1990s. Better known as post-Fordism, these forms of flexible specialization rely extensively on new information and communication technologies. Consequently, industry now demands skilled workers who can work in highly automated environments. In other words, just as Ford assembly-line workers eventually required minimal print literacy, so too post-Fordist "knowledge workers" now require minimal "computer literacy." While Nikiforuk correctly links the demand for computer literacy with the digerati's underlying threat of unemployment, he overlooks how this threat is directly connected to industry's desire to play a more direct role in matters of curriculum and pedagogy. After all, "flexible" workplaces need "flexible" workers who share attitudes and values to support the "flexible" organizations that these companies aspire to create. Where better to accomplish this shaping than through schooling? It is unsurprising, therefore, that business often supports school curricula that incorporate so-called "transferable skills" aligned with this type of workplace. These transferable skills usually include a capacity for teamwork, self-motivation, critical-thinking skills, and computer literacy. It is thus difficult to view computer installation in education to be solely about providing "skills." Rather, computer installation in schools is better viewed as part of a broader social project dedicated to producing a person with the attitudes and beliefs congruent with the new economy's flexible production techniques. Nikiforuk, however, seems reluctant to draw this clear link between technology, education, and business, an intersection that we must increasingly view as an emergent "industrial-education complex."

Second, and more significantly, Nikiforuk underestimates the extent to which the pressure to deploy new technologies in education results from the continuing right-wing project to re-write social relations around concepts of public and private such that education increasingly becomes a "private" rather than a "public" good. In this retooled vision of education, skills and knowledge inherently belong to an individual, so the matter of which skills and how they are obtained moves from a matter of public policy to one of private choice. Moreover, once education is re-written as a set of skills and "knowledges," the market's invisible hand, not government policy, will ostensibly better ensure that the mix of skills and training meets society's needs. New technologies play a critical role in this strategy since increased competition among institutions (which new technologies facilitate) not only provides learners/consumers with a myriad of convenient, competitively priced "learning experiences" but also encourages the production of courseware which can then be copyrighted and sold for profit. Of course, in this new economy, an institution must willy-nilly designate scarce resources to the building of virtual infrastructure or risk being "left behind."[4] Add in government funding such as Alberta's Learning Enhancement Envelope that makes such participation attractive, if not essential, and the nexus of education, emergent technologies, and business that I am describing becomes much clearer. In fact, this interconnection of cyber-technologies, education, and business agendas is intimately connected to concerns over teacher hiring, building physical infrastructure, and of course, the role of private education (see chapters eleven, seven, and nine respectively).

Third, Nikiforuk focuses his analysis on the elementary and secondary sectors of the education system. However, to understand the situation I am outlining, attention must be given to the post-secondary system, where the forces of post-Fordism have been busy renovating education for some time (see chapter four). Here in the post-secondary sector, especially in the community colleges, the startlingly new and unfamiliar nexus of education, markets, and information technologies is already firmly in place.[5] And here, in the post-secondary sector, we are already seeing the emergence of the new person that the education system at all levels will be responsible for producing: the perpetual learner. This "person's" sudden emergence in government documents and policy initiatives underlines my insistence that fundamental shifts in education are underway, shifts that this apparently "new" person embodies. I argue that a close examination of how these texts talk and think about this "perpetual learner" provides us with important details about who this "learner" is intended to be. Furthermore, since these documents guide institutional policies and actions, they also provide an excellent window through which to understand the complex intersection of industry, education, and new technologies which are rapidly (re)writing our beliefs around the proper role of public policy in education and the economy.

From Labouring Worker to Labouring Learner

Admittedly, the idea of "perpetual learning" is not new; concepts of lifelong learning and open education have circulated in society for years. In fact, life-long learning is usually construed as "continuing" education, extension courses, or even individual hobbies — recreation or simple self-improvement. However, this new sense of "perpetual learning" — with all its religious connotations of perpetual atonement for sins past — intensifies these concepts and re-arranges them, weaving them into what increasingly appears to be a web of corporate-driven, just-in-time skill "modules" leading to certification or accreditation. Not surprisingly, many of these courses are intended for delivery through distance-education methods, which rely heavily upon cyber-technologies. As close readings of texts that describe the perpetual learner also suggest, this individual apparently views education as a process largely designed to process raw "information" into value-added "knowledge." Such utilitarian views of education seem far removed from more traditional concerns around creating citizens who can critically participate in society or lead a "good life." Indeed, I would argue that the perpetual learner is a person who is trained to be a "perpetual consumer" of the Information Age's privileged product — information — and whose creation also works to further the re-writing of the dividing line between public and private. Part of this re-writing involves not just a shift in educational emphasis from "teaching" to "learning," as its proponents assert, but actually writes the teacher out of the education equation entirely. Arguably, as cyber-technologies increasingly disembody teachers, they become no-body at all.[6]

So who is this perpetual learner? In some ways, we simply don't know, since s/he remains largely a proposal of the digerati, a fabrication of a particular class's version of a workplace utopia.[7] The utopian texts authored by corporate managers and consultants "announce a new enchanted workplace where hierarchy is dead and 'partners' engage in meaningful work amidst a collaborative environment of mutual commitment and trust."[8] Like all such texts, however, this form of writing is not just an attempt to depict current social realities. Rather, it constitutes part of a larger project to enact or call into existence a vision of a new, transformed world.[9] This utopian quality — Nikiforuk suggests "coercive" is a better word — certainly accounts for the "Field of Dreams" feeling that permeates the debate around the new technologies in education.

Despite indications from various stakeholders suggesting substantial resistance to using cyber-technologies to deliver post-secondary curriculum, government and education officials remain largely dedicated to building the necessary virtual infrastructure to deliver post-secondary curriculum on the assumption that, "If you build it, they will come." As recently as November 1997, Alberta's deputy minister of Advanced Education and Career Development asserted that the anticipated enrollment pressures in post-secondary education would be met through deploying new technologies more intensively, not through increased faculty hiring or through building new physical infrastructure. The deputy minister's remarks are, of course, in keeping with the two such utopian texts circulating in Alberta's higher education circles: Michael Dolence and Donald Norris's *Transforming Higher Education*,[10] and the Ministry of Advanced Education's *A Vision for Change*. In these documents, the outlines of the perpetual learner begin to take shape.

According to the scenarios sketched by current advocates of educational technology, the perpetual learner is an individual who accepts that the economic forces of global competition require workforce flexibility. This perpetual learner also accepts that these skills and knowledge, like any software package, have a shelf-life but that, fortunately, information and communication technologies conveniently enable her to access the requisite upgrading to ensure her prosperity in this "new world order." The perpetual learner uncritically accepts that work comes and goes, moving onto the next project, acquiring, at personal expense, any missing accreditation or certification. Likewise, education also must reinvent itself to accommodate this "new" reality.

It is important to emphasize, however, that writers of these utopian texts often use the changing nature of work, resulting from post-Fordist production techniques, not merely to explain educational change but to legitimate the changes they advocate.[11] In short, rather than questioning the relationship between perpetual learning and cyber-technologies, these writers take the latter's growing prevalence as a way to authorize, not question, the futures they uncritically advocate.

The Employability Agenda

The growing intersection between post-secondary education and business must be briefly addressed. Most evidence suggests that the connection between industry and higher education is firmly established. These links regard not just joint research projects undertaken in our universities (see chapter four), but also the increasingly visible links between curriculum and employment, most notably in the congruency between college learning outcomes and the 1992 Conference Board of Canada's influential "Employability Skills Profile."[12] In Alberta, we see this link emerging in the concept of applied degrees. Similarly, the Ontario Colleges of Applied Arts and Technology have shifted their focus from meeting educational needs of students, defined through training programs established by faculty and administrators, to meeting the training needs enunciated by industry.[13] This change is mirrored in industry's new focus of managing workers' skill sets instead of workers' occupations, a move not surprisingly linked to the ideology of flexibility.[14] Certainly, perpetual learning means little if not maintaining constantly changing skills sets, which are deemed in constant need of upgrading as production changes make current ones redundant.

Three points must be made. First, constant skill upgrading parallels the constant upgrading of software that propels the information industry. This discourse of obsolescence, with its fetish for "the new," contains within it the problematic seeds of ageism and sexism which have yet to be fully examined.[15] Second, and more importantly, focusing on "skill sets" rather than "occupations," or in education on outcomes rather than quality, encourages the process of "unbundling" learning into identifiable "learning experiences." "Unbundling" education into discrete learning experiences enables one to envision education more as a series of just-in-time learning modules, conveniently delivered — of course — by cyber-technology than as a holistic undertaking which is a complicated social process. Third, we need not be cynics to note that unbundling education into byte-sized outcomes enables learners and managers to sort out unnecessary duplication and exact the most efficiency for their educational buck.

These developments are not a surprise. The alliance between the corporate lobby and pragmatic education policy-makers has created the conditions under which we now feel education "should not only produce 'enterprising' individuals for the enterprise culture they are trying to effect, but also produce *types of individuals* who have the attitudes and competencies appropriate to an emergent post-Fordist economy."[16] The perpetual learner is precisely this person since, practically speaking, s/he emerges from applying Total Quality Management ideas to education. Like any other "process/product," a perpetual learner becomes trapped within a ceaseless cycle of learning designed to eliminate defects, a quest that is at best quixotic since by its very definition a perpetual learner is necessarily incomplete. The more insidious aspect of new technologies in these writings is that users are always seen as insufficient, as necessarily incomplete: there's always more to know. Conveniently, this central lack is driven home via the vast quantities of information that one ceaselessly surfs, searches, and synthesizes. Little wonder radical cyber-theorists talk about adopting "voluntary illiteracy"![17]

From Print to Digital Economies: Perpetual Learners/Habitual Consumers

In his excellent book *Selling Culture*, Richard Ohmann[18] analyzes the emergence of mass culture between 1897 and 1911 along with its connections to technology and mass production. He argues that the central problem facing American culture between 1890 and 1911 was a crisis of oversupply instigated by the Second Industrial Revolution. The challenge then, as it seems to be now around the mass of information that cyber-technologies make readily available, was to sell the burgeoning output of mechanized production to a recalcitrant public. The innovation of advertising enabled producers to communicate directly to their potential market, bypassing the jobbers and small merchants who until then comprised the distribution channels. The emergence of advertising suggests that producers entered into a new social relation with the public, a relationship in which, with ever-growing resources, advertisers and producers bent their efforts to the creation of wants in their target market. In short, the solution to oversupply lay in the ability of the producers to effect a new type of person to consume the burgeoning industrial production, an individual who could be a "habitual consumer." According to Ohmann, this rewriting of social relations instigated by producers effectively changed what it meant to be a person in society.

Today's situation looks surprisingly similar, as merchants continue to find that on-line business for all its hype is singularly unrewarding and that, for all their hype, the Web and Internet remain largely irrelevant to many people. (Even the most optimistic figures suggest that over sixty percent of Canadians remain off-line.) In an early assessment of the problems posed by information technologies, observers have noted that even as the supply of information grows exponentially, information consumption increases much more slowly while knowledge application remains constant. The result is a substantial gap between the supply, demand, and application.[19] The solution to this gap ostensibly remains what was in the previous century: establish a new set of social relations that effectively change what it means to be a person in society. From this view, constructing perpetual learners means also constructing perpetual consumers for the voluminous amounts of information relentlessly produced by computer technologies. Just as introducing the practice of accumulative reading into the school curriculum created a host of habitual readers whose existence we now assume, so too does computer installation in the curriculum create habitual consumers of electronic culture. Computers in education therefore are more than Nikiforuk's apparently empty "glittery delivery trucks"; in fact they are vehicles for installing tendencies in people to act and think in given ways. In this case, the decisions around what these tendencies will be and in whose interests they will work are increasingly dictated by corporate interests.

The Erasing of Teachers and Students

Instructively, constructing the perpetual learner requires the erasing of what Donald Norris tellingly calls the "teaching franchise." Just as producers turned away from the jobbers and small merchants, who were the chief distributors prior to the era of mass consumption, so too education policy-makers increasingly turn away from teachers to deal directly with learners. This turn from the teacher is not necessarily wrong. The problem lies in that as learners take the stage, both teachers and students disappear. The difficult teacher-student relationship in all its human complexities is supplanted by a more commercial relationship driven by economic need and market "realities." Interestingly, teachers become redefined as simply "providers," a term that flattens the difference between human and machine, between teacher and trainer, between education and training. The strategy here is the classic one of the late twentieth century: when people won't go willingly, re-engineer the process and "re-describe" the job.

I want to be absolutely clear on this point: new technologies *do* offer potentially exciting avenues of new learning. In fact, as an educator who works with these technologies, I want to stress the potential here is immense. For those who believe that students need to discover their own ways of gathering, sifting, and producing their own knowledge, rather than accepting ideas which are passively transmitted, the Internet, the Web, and other related technologies offer exciting opportunities for such education. Moreover, the curricular emphasis on teamwork, communication skills, and computer literacy is not inherently undesirable; on the contrary, these remain eminently desirable propensities to be encouraged. However, we cannot ignore how these skills are currently made to work to support a set of attitudes and beliefs that are often incongruent with notions of community and of the public good. The question becomes whether we can endorse such a project, no matter how desirable the skills on offer, especially when the underlying project is to "reformat" people as if they were software.

A Bigger Picture:
Reworking the Boundaries of Public and Private

To elaborate more on how this reformatting operates, let me turn to the larger picture in which I situate the perpetual learner. Digerati are fond of suggesting that we are in epochal shift from a print-based culture built around the book to a digitally based culture based on digitized information.[20] While such theoretical speculations offer many problems, they also suggest interesting possibilities. Again, history is a useful guide. In *The Private Tremulous Body*, Francis Barker[21] traces how aspects of our current beliefs about the qualities that an individual should possess emerged in seventeenth-century England in conjunction with the growing number of available print texts and the ensuing debate around censorship. The large quantity of print texts led to a concept of the individual where, it was argued, a person was sufficiently self-disciplined, serious, and self-controlled to make state regulation of printers unnecessary. In essence, these seventeenth-century debates re-wrote the division between public and private such that an individual undertook to censor herself privately rather than assigning the task to the State. Moreover, this division was closely tied to emerging divisions between mind and body, as well as to notions of propriety and decorum centred on the body.

Like print texts in the seventeenth century, debates over digital technologies are contributing to re-drawing the line between public and private especially in the notion of "home work." But we might better focus on the manner in which new technologies are used to "download" questions around employment and economy from the public-policy domain to that of the private. Just as seventeenth-century writers constituted individuals as capable of censoring themselves, so the perpetual learner privately monitors her own skill profile without state interference. This new worker/learner assumes from the outset that no business will sustain them in the long run. In Dolence and Norris's writings, for example, a woman learns that her job is about to be terminated as part of a corporate reorganization. Rather than question the re-organization, the reasons for it, and the (in)justice in her imminent unemployment, Kathleen pluckily gets on the Net and arranges for "upgrading" so that she can compete for a new job. As all good workers of the future will assume, Kathleen knows she must take responsibility for her career and not leave such responsibilities to business or government. As a self-disciplined, self-assessing worker, Kathleen must take on the responsibility for keeping her skills current; if she doesn't, the fault is hers, just as presumably the benefits of re-skilling also are hers. Ignoring the latter tenuous assumption — one regularly made by right wing theorists — how might we locate these perpetual learners in more critical terms? These ideal learners are, notably, middle class and presumably white: they exist in a world that has been appropriately called elsewhere "enchanted."[22] They are largely unencumbered by the pressures facing the students I see: money woes; childcare challenges; excessive work loads at school, work, and home; and, of course, systemic sexism and racism.

The efficiency and effectiveness of devolving responsibilities around employment readiness onto the individual cannot be underestimated: self-motivated, self-assessing, self-disciplined workers keep companies lean while effectively removing training/re-skilling questions from issues of social concern to issues of individual concern. A key aspect of the perpetual learner is the incorporation of the skills formerly provided by the government or companies into a set of attitudes and behaviors that are expected of an individual. In effect, the questions of job skills, employability, and professional development are no longer social or even, really, corporate considerations. They are ultimately privatized. We need no further evidence that such a move is afoot than to observe Ontario's recent attempts to "re-form" education. Starting in September 1997, from Grade seven to twelve, each student will be required to set annual plans outlining goals and decisions around education.[23] We need only remark that such disciplinary techniques are drawn directly from that now well-established practice of the corporate sector — the business plan.

■ ■ ■

I want to end this whirlwind with two brief thoughts about the future social spaces of education and the role of teachers there. The construction of the perpetual learner tends to draw our attention away from the equally troubling emergence of the "virtual professor." Critics often emphasize that cyber-technologies seriously challenge the university library, the heart of a modern university and the campus that surrounds it.[24] Reconstructing the campus as the "education commons" poses distinct challenges for those institutions where the campus is the focal point of their educational endeavor. As an information commons gradually supplants the library and learners increasingly access the Net for learning, the campus as a social and socializing space becomes displaced. This is only one aspect, however, of the challenge. Cyber-technologies also threaten to loosen the ties of the individual faculty member to the institution. I recently attended a video-conference[25] featuring distant education specialist Greg Kearsely, who spoke enthusiastically of how cyber-technologies allow market forces to enter into education at the level of the instructor. As Kearsely states, "All I need is a good server and the appropriate connections to become a virtual professor." For some educators, this intensification of market forces in education is to be devoutly welcomed, not feared, since in their view the market will enable the best practitioners to prevail. I have many concerns here, but I want to stress that like the perpetual learner, virtual professing takes education increasingly out of the social and public realm into those of the individual and the private. For private-sector education, such a move provides the long-sought "level playing field" where information or knowledge visibly contained (and stunningly, interactively, presented) in web-based modules means more than the social aspects of education.[26] The invisible social aspects are reconfigured, diminishing some and emphasizing others. Since the manner in which such re-balancing occurs ultimately depends on the values that are at play, the question of social space and post-secondary education requires urgent attention.

Remember that education is the future game. While I agree with Andrew Nikiforuk's conclusion that computers might legitimately remain a part of any curriculum mix, we must question whether containment of computer technology — that is, to continue to do the same thing but with different tools — is the best strategy here. While this path offers us safety, we might more wisely seize cyber-technologies to imagine them differently. For example, rather than envision these novel tools as a means to produce "perpetual learners" who are, by definition, designed to become cogs in the digital infrastructure currently under construction, we might imagine the potential of these emergent technologies as a way to construct "unruly subjects."[27] This unruly person must possess the perpetual learner's generic skills but ideally also have a propensity — even a calling — to utilize these skills towards the ends of greater social justice rather than private gain. Such a project, however, entails engagement with the new technologies, seeing in them more than their Machiavellian application by the new virtual class. It means devising different visions of who — or what — we will become through these novel tools, debating what we want for ourselves and for others. To our advantage, such questions invoke values, not discussions of hard drives, processor speeds, and bandwidth size. To accomplish this task, we need our own utopian texts which offer uses for new technologies that struggle to maintain the value of the public, that seek to enable persons to make their own choices around technology without coercion, either implicit or explicit. We need to remember that technology is not a product but a process: something people do, not something done to people.

Notes

1 *Globe and Mail*, 3 October 1997, D3.

2 Nikiforuk derives this term from popular usage captured best in the title of John Brockman's anthology, *The Digerati: Encounters with the Cyber Elite*, which comprises writings from a cross-section of individuals working with and around digital culture.

3 Nikiforuk, *Globe and Mail*.

4 See, for example, the local press coverage of the Southern Alberta Institute of Technology's decision to devote $25 million to developing a "virtual campus." Other institutions are expected now to compete with SAIT's decision to go virtual.

5 J. Kenway with C. Bigum and L. Fitzclarence, "Marketing education in the Postmodern Age" in *Journal of Education Policy* 8:2 (1993): 108.

6 E. McWilliams makes this same point in several of her recent writings on technology, education, and the body. See, for instance, "Introduction: pedagogies, technologies, bodies." in *Pedagogy, Technology and the Body*, E. McWilliams and P. G. Taylor, eds. (New York: Peter Lang Publishing, 1996), 1-12.

7 P. Gee and C. Lankshear, "The new work order: critical language awareness and 'fast capitalism' texts" in *Discourse: Studies in the Cultural Politics of Education* 16:1 (1995): 8.

8 Gee and Lankshear, 7.

9 Gee and Lankshear, 8.

10 *Transforming Higher Education: A Vision for Learning in the 21st Century* (Ann Arbor, Michigan: Society for College and University Planning, 1995).

11 M. Hickox and R. Moore, "Education and Post-Fordism: a new correspondence" in *Education for Economic Survival: From Fordism to Post-Fordism?*, P. Brown and H. Lauder, eds. (New York: Routledge, 1992), 98.

12 Corporate Council on Education et al., *Employability Skills Profile: The Critical Skills Required of the Canadian Workforce* (Ottawa: Conference Board of Canada, 1992).

13 D. Smith and G. Smith, "Re-Organizing the jobs skills training relation: From 'human capital' to 'human resources'" in *Education for Work, Education as Work: Canada's Changing Community Colleges*, J. Miller, ed. (Toronto: Garamond Press, 1990), 178.

14 Smith and Smith, 187.

15 K. Woodard, "From virtual cyborgs to biological time bombs: technocriticism and the material body." in *Culture on the Brink: Ideologies of Technology,* G. Bender and T. Drucker, eds. (Seattle: Bay Press, 1994), 58.

16 S. Ball, cited in J. Kenway et al., "Marketing education," 115.

17 H. Bey, *T.A.Z: The Total Autonomous Zone, Ontological Anarchy, Poetic Terrorism* (Brooklyn: Autonomedia, 1991), 129.

18 R. Ohmann, *Selling Culture: Magazines, Markets and Class at the Turn of the Century* (New York: Verso, 1996), 85; italics added.

19 D. McQuail and S. Windahl, *Communication Models for the study of Mass Communication,* second edition (New York: Longman, 1993), 202-203.

20 This thinking is based on the ideas of media theorist Marshall McLuhan who argued that electronic technologies are driving human civilization into totally new social relations. McLuhan's work has been extended into the area of digital technology, most notably by Derek De Kerkhove.

21 F. Barker, *The Tremulous Private Body: Essays on Subjection* (New York: Methuen, 1984), 45-49.

22 Gee and Lankshear, 8.

23 Ontario Ministry of Education and Training, *Backgrounder.* May 1997.

24 M. Peters, "Cybernetics, cyberspace and the politics of university reform" in *Australian Journal of Education* 40:2 (1996): 173.

25 G. Kearsely, *The Web and Education.* Video conference at Mount Royal College and University of Alberta, 23 October 1997.

26 I understand that such a move is double-edged given that simply attending one institution instead of another confers various social advantages that the information commons might alleviate. Still, if the social relations which structure the physical world are largely re-inscribed in cyberspace, the advantage may be worth little.

27 T. Miller, *The Well-Tempered Self: Citizenship, Culture and the Postmodern Subject* (Baltimore: The Johns Hopkins University Press, 1993).

3

The "Alberta Advantage": For Whom?

Trevor W. Harrison

The message is clear . . . . We've been told that people development is a priority.
— Premier Ralph Klein, summing up the 1997 Growth Summit[1]

While the Klein government could justifiably claim widespread support during the period 1993-96 for tackling the public debt, public-opinion polls repeatedly showed significant concern regarding two particular areas of government cutbacks: health and education.[2] This concern turned to bewilderment and increasing anger in the latter two years of the mandate as cuts continued despite rising government surpluses from hefty oil and gas revenues. Indeed, by 1997, many Albertans were beginning to view the debt-and-deficit beast conjured up by the government as little more than a mouse on steroids.

Thus, even Albertans long critical of the Klein government viewed with some optimism the latter's re-election to a second mandate in the spring of 1997. Many believed that an era of "post-deficit" politics was at hand, heralded by "reinvestments" in key areas of social infrastructure, including education. The premier's concluding comments at the Growth Summit, in the fall of 1997, that increased money would be spent on education only fueled this belief (see chapter five).

But others remained skeptical. For too many years, low taxes and budget cuts — captured in the slogan "the Alberta advantage" — had dominated political speechcraft in Alberta. The Alberta government's curious budget of February 1998 (see chapter six) — a mix of tax cuts and meagre spending increases, at a time when revenue projections were shaky[3] — followed by the recommendation of the Alberta Tax Review Commission in the fall of 1998 of a provincial flat tax[4] only raise anew concerns over the current government's view of the role of public services and education in the Alberta economy.[5]

This chapter deconstructs the notion of "the Alberta advantage" with an eye to pointing out the politics underlying educational investment in Alberta. The chapter argues that the Klein government is continuing, albeit with a vengeance, a time-worn tradition of developing Alberta's export economy, in the short-term, at the expense of the province's social infrastructure. The chapter further argues that while this approach to development benefits some businesses, high-end income earners, and "star" students, it will ultimately leave the province, as a whole, unprepared educationally to meet the economic, political, and social challenges of the twenty-first century. The chapter begins with a brief examination of certain contradictions within Alberta related to income, education, and work, and Alberta's expenditures on education.

Scenes from a Resource Hinterland

Scene One: The average income of Albertans in 1996 was $23,511 — third highest in Canada, after Ontario ($23,910) and British Columbia ($23,857), and above the Canadian average of $22,681.[6] Yet, amidst this plenty, there are increasing signs of economic disparity and hardship. Food banks have become a regular feature of the urban landscape. A recent federal government report notes that, "In Calgary, the share of poor families living in very poor neighbourhoods increased from 6.4 per cent to 20.3 between 1980 and 1990. In Edmonton, the share shot up from 4.1 per cent to 28.3 per cent."[7]

Scene Two: On average, people in Alberta are as well or better educated than people in the rest of Canada.[8] Fourteen percent of Albertans hold university degrees, right on the Canadian average; twenty-eight percent hold a post-secondary certificate or diploma (compared with twenty-seven percent nationally); and eleven percent have taken some amount of post-secondary education, compared with nine percent elsewhere. At the same time, the percentage of *unemployed* persons in Alberta with a post-secondary certificate or a university degree is second only to Nova Scotia,[9] while the unemployment rate in Alberta for persons with low educational attainment (e.g., less than high school) is much lower than the Canadian average.[10]

Scene Three: Despite having the lowest taxes in Canada, Alberta was able (between 1987 and 1997) to lower its per capita deficit more than any other province, to achieve the lowest debt-to-GDP ratio in Canada, and to post a budget surplus in 1997 of over $2 billion.[11] But Alberta also spends far less than most provinces, including some of the very poorest, on maintaining its social infrastructure. In 1996/97, Alberta spent less money per capita on education than five other provinces, including New Brunswick (see chapter six and Appendix B).

In short, Alberta is a wealthy province marked by growing economic inequalities and poverty amidst plenty. Alberta is also a province where having a "good" education by no means ensures employment, but where having a "poor" education need not altogether be a hindrance to getting some sort of a job. Somewhat bizarrely, Alberta is a province featuring high incomes and low taxes, but also underfunded — some would say deteriorating — public services.[12] These contradictions can only be explained in the context of the province's reliance upon primary resource extraction (e.g., oil, gas, forests, grains) and the peculiarities of political power which this reliance produces. One means of understanding these contradictions is to take seriously the meaning of "the Alberta advantage."

Education and "the Alberta Advantage"

If there is a single phrase that sums up the Klein years in Alberta, it is the "Alberta advantage." The precise phrase was first trotted out by then Finance Minister Jim Dinning in his 1995 budget paper to justify budget cuts and low taxes, but can be traced back to previous keepers of the public purse.[13]

It would be easy to pass off "the Alberta advantage" as just a catchy slogan. Certainly, the phrase is in part this, but it is more. Rather, "the Alberta advantage" provides an index for understanding the ideas that inform economic development in the province.

At the same time, it should also be noted that the term, like all political slogans, is open to various uses. *Calgary Herald* editorial writer, Bob Bragg, for example, identified two meanings of "the Alberta advantage" in the fall of 1997, shortly after the Growth Summit. Bragg, who was covering Ralph Klein's trip to Japan at the time, noted that the premier's rendition of it for local audiences usually emphasizes low taxes, a deregulated and welcoming business environment, and a balanced budget. By contrast, his short speech to the Japanese Federation of Economic Organizations emphasized Alberta's "strong culture of science and technology," a clean environment, and a workforce that "is the most productive in the nation, one of the most highly educated in North America and one of the youngest in the industrialized world."[14]

These contradictory interpretations of "the Alberta advantage" are important; indeed, they point to genuine conflicts within Alberta's political and social structure. For now, however, unearthing the term's meaning requires taking a look at Alberta's history.

Not unintentionally, the term "Alberta advantage" is modelled on David Ricardo's very old concept of "comparative advantage." Ricardo, an influential nineteenth-century British economist, coined the term in arguing for the benefits of free trade (another very old article of faith in Alberta). Specifically, the theory of comparative advantage states that a country can maximize national income by specializing in producing those goods or resources in which it has a comparative cost advantage with its competitors.[15] Working in the classical liberal economic tradition, Ricardo (and others) assumed that countries (or, presumably, regions) that adopted this logic would, in time, acquire the capital necessary to develop economically. Later economic theorists, however, were more skeptical.

Especially skeptical was a twentieth-century Canadian economist, Harold Innis. Based on what he observed empirically in the Canadian case, Innis developed what is termed "staples theory."[16] The theory's primary argument is that staples-driven economies are prone to certain problems unrecognized by Richardo's theory. The major factors of production — capital, technology, and skilled labour — are readily imported rather than produced locally, while profits from the resource sales are either exported or poured back into resource development. The result is underdevelopment, on the one hand, and over-specialization, on the other. When world prices for the staple are high, the economy booms; but when the prices are low, the economy goes bust.

On the surface, Alberta's economy today does not altogether fit Innis' classic description of dependent development. Myths of range-riding cowboys aside, for example, Alberta today is the most urbanized (or sub-urbanized) province in Canada. It is also, as I have noted, very wealthy and politically influential.

Nonetheless, Alberta today remains extremely open, dependent on resource-extraction, and tied to external trade and investment. This dependency leaves the province unusually subject to economic turbulence generated elsewhere. Indeed, Alberta's economy remains the most volatile in Canada, itself buffeted in the summer and fall of 1998 by collapsing markets in Asia and elsewhere. Lacking a developed internal economy, Alberta government revenues and unemployment rates sometimes fluctuate wildly. This volatility is characteristic of a staples-driven economy. And it has important consequences for educational spending in the province.

Royalties obtained from resource extraction during the boom years have allowed Alberta to maintain the province's education and retraining systems at a high (but declining) level, offsetting both low — and dropping — taxes and/or increased government subsidies to the business sector[17] and low personal taxes. One negative consequence of low taxes, however, in combination with an over-reliance on resource royalties (and, increasingly, gambling revenues),[18] is chronic instability for program spending during lean periods. Given that social welfare, health, and education incur the largest expenditures of any departments, anywhere, they are the most targetted for cuts when the inevitable downturn occurs.[19]

From the perspective of strict economic rationality, staples-based economies impose another consequence upon education. Given the volatile nature of the economy, its lack of diversification, and concentration on labour intensive work, there is little need to have an *overall* highly skilled workforce. Except on the margins of labour-force reproduction, those few high-skilled workers and professionals who are required are often imported, along with the necessary capital and technology.[20]

It should be noted that, in the Alberta case, *both Ricardo and Innis were right*: Alberta's comparative advantage in certain resources has made the province extremely wealthy *in the aggregate*; and Alberta also remains economically dependent as a result. Where Ricardo and Innis are wrong is in overlooking the fact that, while the economy creates a context for development, whether or not a region like Alberta fully develops is ultimately a product of political decisions and actions taken within — not external to — the province.

Political Power, Education, and Economic Development in Alberta

Much of Alberta's history reveals a people trying to overcome economic dependency. Before 1947, Alberta was a poor province. Social Credit, the governing party from 1935, was supportive of small government, balanced budgets, and markets, but not of Big Capital and not at the expense of people. Perhaps because Aberhart himself was a former school principal, early Social Credit was awash in schoolteachers; indeed, the first Socred caucus had as many teachers as farmers.[21] Throughout the 1950s and 1960s, Alberta outspent the other Canadian provinces on education and other social services.[22] And Albertans, perhaps viewing education as a hedge against hard times, were likewise highly supportive of educational spending. But these were the political inclinations of a people living in a chronically poor region at the tail-end of the global economy. The discovery of oil at Leduc, outside of Edmonton, in 1947 changed Albertans' hopes and dreams.

The years following Leduc saw the Alberta government, led by Ernest Manning, take what is termed a "rentier" approach to the province's oil resources. Since 1929, the provincial government had owned the mineral rights under more than eighty-five percent of Alberta's land. Rather than taking the risk of developing Alberta's oil industry on its own, Manning's government allowed foreign (mainly American) oil companies to locate and extract the oil in return for three types of revenues: deposits on exploration, bids on drilling rights, and production royalties.[23]

The discovery of oil set in motion changes to the province's economy and class structure. In the wake of oil came American capital, American expertise, and American ideology. The effects were most noticeable in Calgary, which became the headquarters for the invading multi-nationals. But the changes occurred everywhere. In time, Edmonton became the province's service centre, the north was opened-up, and Alberta's rural communities became industrialized. By the late 1960s, a home-grown group of capitalists had also arisen in the province. Their leader was Peter Lougheed.

In 1971, Lougheed's Tory party defeated the Socreds, ending thirty-six years of rule. Lougheed represented a new breed of Western politician: young, urbane, cocky, and — at least in terms of provincial rights — a nationalist. Under Lougheed's tenure, government spending gradually shifted away from social infrastructure — including, it should be noted, education — and concentrated instead on "building up a huge surplus, which was used to spur industrialization and diversification."[24] Kevin Taft has noted, for example, that subsidies on industrial development (broadly defined) were twenty-four times larger in 1994/95 than when the Tories came to power in 1971.[25]

Despite Lougheed's efforts at diversification, however, Alberta remained largely tied to oil and gas when he retired. Alberta did not diversify so much horizontally as vertically, with forward linkages (e.g., to petrochemicals) and backward linkages (e.g., to oilfield services) growing out of the oil and gas sector. By contrast, Don Getty's years as premier saw relatively more diversification of Alberta's economy.

In 1985, for example, the energy sector made up almost thirty-six percent of Alberta's gross domestic product (GDP), followed by business and commercial services at just over fifteen percent. In 1995, however, business and commercial services comprised twenty-one percent of Alberta's GDP, while energy was only eighteen percent. Moreover, several other sectors — manufacturing, transportation and utilities, finance, and retail and wholesale trade — are now very important, each representing over ten percent of GDP.[26] Nonetheless, Alberta remains largely a resource-based economy, with oil and gas its main exports, followed by agriculture and forestry. Even many of its secondary industries are in fact "offshoots" of the extraction industries. Why, for all of the rhetoric, has Alberta failed to achieve economic diversification?

The answer is simple. While economic development in a staples-producing region requires a strong, interventionist state in order to promote development, this concentration of power makes it an easy target for seizure by those sectors already benefitting from the existing economy. As Kevin Taft has demonstrated, a huge portion of Alberta's government expenditures involve subsidies primarily to the province's dominant sectors: oil and gas, big agriculture, and forestry.[27]

The Lougheed-Getty years reinforced the power of those sectors of the economy whose wealth resulted from Alberta's comparative advantage in what they produced. With this power, they thereafter continued to direct resources into areas that reinforced specialization in certain goods, at the expense of developing Alberta as a whole. Alberta's economic elites, concentrated in the oil and gas sector, grew fat living off the avails of heavily subsidized staples extraction.

It is important to note that this elite was not then, and is not now, opposed to big government *per se*. Members of this elite, in Alberta and elsewhere, oppose the social welfare state because of its distributionist ethic. But they do support big government in the form of the corporate welfare state.

By the early 1990s, however, government expenditures were running well ahead of government revenues. A series of financial boondoggles — bad loans to questionable business enterprises — and the Meech Lake fiasco added to growing public discontent with the Tories. In the fall of 1992, Getty resigned. His party was on the political ropes. The Empire of the Bow River, however, quickly found a more-than-adequate replacement for Getty in the person of Ralph Klein.

Under the guise of balancing the budget and making Alberta more competitive (see chapters five and six), the Klein government took a sharp right turn, slashing government spending, cutting public service jobs, deregulating the economy, and privatizing government services. In the rhetoric of the time, the least government was the best government and, presumably, no government was best of all.

In this context, the government also "reinvented" education after 1993. Funding for public education was cut severely (see chapters six and seven), although less than funding for health and social services. Funding for post-secondary education was also reduced. Both educational systems were "reorganized" (see chapters five and seven) along corporatist lines.[28]

Following the Growth Summit in 1997, however, the Tories also embraced something they termed "people development." Ralph Klein subsequently defined the term as meaning "education."[29] Does this mean that "the Alberta advantage" is no longer based on low taxes but rather on the skills of its people?

No. The reinvention of education in Alberta is designed to link education and training more than ever to the needs of Alberta's major resource industries (i.e., oil, gas, forestry; see chapter five). Post-secondary education in Alberta serves industry in at least two ways. First, it provides a ready supply of skilled labour for the province's industries (hence the continued emphasis on the technical trades). Second, universities conduct research and development of use to industries, which they would otherwise have to perform in-house and at their own expense (see chapter four).

It is easy to understand why Alberta's corporate sector has embraced recent changes to education in the province. But why have so many Tories — many of them cut from the same rural cloth as their Social Credit predecessors — tied education so tightly to the needs of Alberta's increasingly "lean" industrial sector? And why have they tended to reject the needs of public and post-secondary educational institutions and their administrations, employees, and students?

Patronage would be an easy answer to these questions. Certainly, the Tories receive a considerable amount of money from corporations. Ideology may also be at work, insofar as at least a few Tory MLAs seem hostile to the notion of anything that is "public." Yet, it remains true that most Tories support public education, if only because they view it as a source of social cohesion. Personal psychologies may provide part of the answer, particularly in regards to higher education. One gets the sense, for example, that some Tory MLAs are self-conscious of their own academic credentials, while others are simply skeptical of "book learning" and pride themselves on having learned in the "school of hard knocks." Finally, there is the issue of politics. People who have attended meetings with Alberta's current ministers note that certain areas of higher education — the social sciences and the arts — are an especially tough sell in caucus, in part because people from these disciplines are viewed by the government as among its most vocal opponents and critics.[30]

There may, however, be another, deeper reason for the Tories' skepticism towards higher education. That is, it may be that they are simply hard pressed to understand how such things as the arts and social science "fit" into the Alberta economy. They have no mental "schema" in which to place these fields. Unskilled and semi-skilled labour, engineers, technicians, electricians, carpenters, plumbers, and beauticians, yes. But where do political scientists, playwrights, ecologists, and all those nurses, social workers, and teachers fit in? Why fund public education in disciplines and specialties that do not immediately lead to employment in Alberta's unique labour market? This logic may sound offensive, even bizarre, to some, but it is perfectly understandable from the point of view of a political and economic leadership whose view of the world has been shaped by the demands of a resource-based economy. Turning decision-making over to private business seems a rational solution for resolving fiscal shortfalls, cultural conflicts, and school-based problems (see chapter four).

At the same time, as we have seen, staples-based economies are subject to severe economic turbulence, while fostering significant social inequalities. To ignore these problems is particularly risky as Alberta prepares for the twenty-first century and the competitive forces unleashed by globalization.

Education and the Global Economy

Few governments in Canada have embraced — at least rhetorically — globalization as strongly as has Alberta's. Government documents are strewn with allusions to "global competitiveness."[31] As an extremely open, export-driven economy, such an emphasis is only natural. Moreover, this emphasis has been pronounced for some time: both the Lougheed and Getty governments took steps to enhance foreign trade, including opening a series of Alberta "trade offices" abroad. However, much of the Klein government's current approach to education and economic development is extremely short-sighted and, as such, will likely leave Alberta ill-prepared to meet the challenges of globalization.

Like aged generals readying to fight the last war, current government policies remain over-reliant upon time-worn mantras. Slogans about free enterprise and hard work will not cut it in the new global economy based on coordinated sectoral organization and high-technology transfers; neither will policies based on low taxes, low wages, and resource exports. Indeed, such policies carry — in the long run, at least — high risks for Albertans. What is an "advantage" today may be a hindrance tomorrow.

Several factors make current government policies risky. First, the province faces a growing number of resource-rich competitors. Second, Alberta's continued fiscal dependence on fossil-fuels and forests (and allied service industries) is at odds with current global pressures to curtail greenhouse emissions. Third, the number of jobs in the primary and even secondary sectors has been dropping for decades. Increasingly, those jobs that are created — and their precise number is another issue — will be in the tertiary sector, in professional, technical, and low-end services. Alberta will not escape these trends.

Moreover, the 1998/99 Alberta budget escalates these risks. In continuing to lower personal and corporate taxes — the latter, merely another form of business subsidy — the government leaves the funding of vital social programs at the mercy of uncertain revenue streams (oil, gas, liquor, and gambling). Alberta is increasingly becoming locked into the status of a resource hinterland to the world economy.

Nor should we rely too heavily on the emerging business-education partnerships to rectify this problem (see chapters four and twelve). As in the past, these partnerships cater to the needs of existing industries. They do not diversify or expand Alberta's economic base. More importantly, they do not fully develop Alberta's most important resource: its people.

Too often in recent years, workers — and Albertans in general — have been treated as a means to an end: economic growth. In fact, the reverse is true: economic growth is a natural consequence of investments in people. The countries, regions, and even cities that will prosper in the globalized world of the twenty-first century are those which encourage knowledge-based post-industrialism and which possess a universalized learning culture.[32] Additionally, their respective governments will spend more — not less — on social infrastructure (health, education, welfare). This is because the more open an economy, the greater the necessity for social expenditures to offset the economic and political turmoil accompanying the opening of borders to trade.[33]

To their credit, some members of Alberta's political and business elite, including former Premier Peter Lougheed[34] and Syncrude's Eric Newell, have begun warning of the dangers of deteriorating health and educational systems, and of the growing gap between haves and have-nots. Nonetheless, one senses that many members of Alberta's elite remain antagonistic to the broad social and political transformations that must accompany their support of economic globalization. At times, this elite appears to believe it can find physical refuge in gated communities and an ideological safe-haven in an often narrow provincialism. Attempts to privatize public services, including most especially education (see chapter nine), reflect efforts by some elite members to protect their entrenched class and regional interests.

■ ■ ■

Polls repeatedly show that Albertans value education and are particularly supportive of public education. In order to prepare for the twenty-first century, however, Albertans must accept the notion that public education must be supported by stable funding. Accepting this notion means that changes must be made to Alberta's tax structure. Resource royalties, booze levies, and VLT revenues alone will not ensure the funding necessary for long range educational planning.

Albertans must also free themselves of the belief that education is only a means to an end, a tool in the service of the economy (specifically, of corporations set on extracting resources for external markets). Education must instead be viewed as an important — though not isolated — element in developing equally, equitably, and as a whole society. Accepting this view means that Albertans must begin asking some fundamental questions, such as: for whom is Alberta's economy truly working?

Finally, education must be geared to the development of competent citizens, aware of their own and society's broader social and political interests. The real "Alberta advantage" lies in achieving this goal.

Notes

I wish to thank Jerrold Kachur for numerous valuable suggestions made on previous drafts of this chapter.

1 *Edmonton Journal*, 1 October 1997, A11.

2 See K. Hughes, G. Lowe, and A. McKinnon, "Public attitudes toward budget cuts in Alberta: Biting the bullet or feeling the pain?", *Canadian Public Policy* 22(3) (1996): 268-284. Note the lack of discussion, however, about social welfare. Even today, in the midst of talk about "reinvestments," social welfare issues remain off-limits to debate. Yet social welfare issues play an important role in the problems facing Alberta's educational system.

3 The budget ratified previous commitments to increase government funding to school boards by $380 million over three years and to adult education by $7.5 million over the same period (see *Edmonton Journal*, 12 February 1998, A1), but these did not keep up with either inflation or increasing population demand (see chapter six). Shortly thereafter, the price of oil began to slide, dipping below $15 (US) per barrel on March 6. The government's own budget projection was $19.12 (US) for 1998 and $17.50 (US) for 1999.

4 *Edmonton Journal*, 29 October, 1998, A1.

5 I say "curious" because virtually no one in Alberta — except a few business groups — has called for tax cuts. The government has repeatedly failed, over the past two years, to sell the idea of tax cuts to Albertans who, instead, have demanded increased spending, particularly in the areas of health and education.

6 F. Wein, "Regional inequality: Explanations and policy issues" in *Social Inequality in Canada: Patterns, Problems, and Policies*, J. Curtis, E. Grabb, and N. Guppy, eds., third edition (Scarborough: Prentice Hall Allyn and Bacon Canada Inc., 1999), 272.

7 Report quoted in the *Edmonton Journal*, 27 October, 1998, B9.

8 Taken from Statistics Canada, December, 1996, B-16 and B-18. See also Alberta Economic Development, "Education," *Facts on Alberta* (Edmonton: Alberta Economic Development, June 1997), 3.

9 Alberta Economic Development, "Labour Force," *Facts on Alberta* (Edmonton: Alberta Economic Development, June 1997), 7.

10 See Statistics Canada, December, 1996, B-16 and B-18. For example, while fifteen percent of the unemployed in Canada had less than a grade-eight education, the percentage of unemployed in Alberta with such few credentials was so negligible as to not be counted.

11 Canada West Foundation, *Back from the Brink* (Calgary: Canada West Foundation, 1998).

12 A study published by the Western Centre for Economic Research (WCER) in 1994 stated, "In Alberta the social return to a university degree is competitive with alternatives but lower than the average for Canada." *Valuing Education in Alberta. What Are the Returns to Our Investment?* (Edmonton: WCER, University of Alberta, 1994), v.

13 See S. Drugge, "The Alberta tax advantage: Myth and reality" in *The Trojan Horse: Alberta and the Future of Canada,* Gordon Laxer and Trevor Harrison, eds. (Montreal: Black Rose Books, 1995).

14 R. Bragg, "Alberta Advantage proving to be the opposite for workers" in *Edmonton Journal,* 17 October 1997, A20.

15 For an excellent exposition of this theory, see chapter two of R. Lairson and D. Skidmore, *International Political Economy: The Struggle for Power and Wealth* (Toronto: Harcourt Brace College Publishers, 1997)

16 See D. Drache, ed., *Staples, Markets, and Cultural Change: Selected Essays of Harold Innis* (Montreal: McGill-Queen's University Press, 1995); also, Gordon Laxer, ed., *Perspectives on Canadian Economic Development* (Toronto: Oxford University Press, 1991).

17 See Kevin Taft, *Shredding the Public Interest: Ralph Klein and 25 Years of One-Party Government* (Edmonton: University of Alberta Press/Parkland Institute, 1997).

18 Incredibly, Alberta's 1997/98 budget forecasts revenues of $660 million, for the first time surpassing oil royalties as a source of revenue. If oil revenues are unstable, gambling revenues are even more so. What will the Alberta government do if oil revenues continue to drop and/or anti-VLT referendums are ever passed in Edmonton and Calgary?

19 *Back from the Brink,* 12.

20 J. Richards and L. Pratt, *Prairie Capitalism: Power and Influence in the New West* (Toronto: McClelland & Stewart Ltd., 1979), 310.

21 A. Finkel, *The Social Credit Phenomenon in Alberta* (Toronto: University of Toronto Press, 1989), 32.

22 Finkel, *The Social Credit Phenomenon,* 122 and 144.

23 This paragraph owes much to J. Barr, *The Dynasty: The Rise and Fall of Social Credit in Alberta* (Toronto: McClelland and Stewart Ltd., 1974), 139-143.

24 E. Shaffer, "The political economy of oil in Alberta" in *Essays on the Political Economy of Alberta,* D. Leadbeater, ed. (Toronto: New Hogtown Press, 1984), quote on 183.

25 Taft, *Shredding,* 47. By contrast, the Alberta Science and Research Authority (ASRA) has warned of Alberta's declining investment in research and development (R & D). In 1980, per capita R & D in Alberta was the highest in Canada, but was second lowest by 1994, at nearly seventy-five percent of the Canadian average. One may question how much of this investment was in genuine research. But the ASRA also makes the point that business investment in R & D in Alberta has fallen behind business investments in R & D elsewhere (ASRA, *Sustaining the Alberta Advantage,* September 1997).

26 Alberta Economic Development and Tourism, *The Alberta Advantage in Action* (Edmonton: Alberta Economic Development and Tourism, April 1997), 2.

27 Taft, *Shredding.*

28 Trevor Harrison, "Making the trains run on time: Corporatism in Alberta," in *The Trojan Horse.*

29 Said Premier Klein, "This thing called people development, when translated, means education" (see the *Edmonton Journal,* 13 October 1997, A9). The term "people

development" enjoyed a brief shelf-life, the premier repeating it on several occasions over the next few months (see M. Lisac's column, *Edmonton Journal*, 14 February 1998, A12).

30 Author's personal correspondence. It seems unlikely that this book will alter this perception.

31 See, for example, Advanced Education and Career Development, *Alberta Careers Beyond 2000* (Edmonton: Advanced Education and Career Development, 1996). The "occupational profiles" document published as part of this series lists the projected impact (positive, negative, or neutral) of globalization on particularly occupations.

32 See, for example, R. Reich, *The Work of Nations* (New York: Alfred A. Knopf, 1991); P. Kennedy, *Preparing for the Twenty-First Century* (New York: Random House, 1993).

33 See D. Rodrik, "Sense and nonsense in the globalization debate," in *Foreign Policy* Summer 1997: 19-37.

34 In a speech to Edmonton business and academic leaders in the fall of 1998, Lougheed stated, "I do not believe that government should be passive," and "I believe that as a matter of fiscal policy and responsibility — yes a balanced budget, but basic education should be first and foremost" (*Edmonton Journal*, 9 October, 98, A5).

4

The Marketing of the University

Tom Pocklington

*[T]he Faculty of Engineering and Computer Science at
Concordia University [faces] serious problems, which the
University will have to address, but they are not unique to
Concordia. They have their origins not in the intrinsic
wickedness of any of the persons involved nor in
particular defects of the University's administrative
structures. Rather, they are the almost inescapable
pathology of the surrounding research culture, of systems
of scholarly assessment, research funding and industry-
university-government cooperation which have developed
in Canada over the past 25 years, and ultimately of
developments in scholarship which, if not universal, are
certainly widespread.*

From *Integrity in Scholarship: A Report to Concordia University*[1]

On August 24, 1992, Valery Fabrikant, a Research Professor in the Faculty
of Engineering and Computer Science at Concordia University in
Montreal, shot and killed four of his male colleagues and seriously
wounded a female secretary. No one has, or could, make a case that these
were justifiable homicides. It is most unlikely that Fabrikant had anything
in particular against the four colleagues he murdered, and the secretary
probably just happened to be at the wrong place at the wrong time.[2] It
would be preposterous to maintain that anyone but Fabrikant was
responsible for the murders he committed. Nevertheless, among the
factors motivating Fabrikant's crimes was his exploitation by senior
colleagues, which even included taking credit for his ideas for the purpose
of acquiring scholarly recognition, research grants, consulting fees, and
research contracts (including contracts with private companies owned

by the senior professors). In conversations with scientists from British Columbia to Nova Scotia, I was assured that the less virulent forms of this pathology, as distinguished from Fabrikant's personal demons, are quite widespread in Canadian universities. The problems become more and more severe as researchers depend increasingly for funding on private corporations. (See chapters three and five regarding links to science, technology, and the Alberta economy.)

Since the more general aspects of Canadian and Alberta universities have been covered elsewhere,[3] this chapter focuses on a relatively new concern. It argues that Canadian universities have reached a new high-water mark (or depth of subservience) in their relationship with business during the past two decades. This new, much closer, relationship between business and university is already harming universities and threatens to do even more harm in the future. I look primarily, as a case in point, at the changing relationship between business and the University of Alberta.

Of course, universities were never ivory towers, completely untainted by vocationalism.[4] Even the medieval universities had faculties of law, and the small private universities of the early days of the United States and Canada devoted themselves primarily to the training of clergy. Business in particular has, for some time, had a profound influence on universities. Government-appointed businessmen have long dominated the governing boards of universities. Likewise — but certainly not exclusively — universities have long contained outspoken evangelists for liberal capitalism, especially in departments of economics and schools of business. Moreover, our economy has been essentially liberal-capitalist for more than 150 years. It is not surprising that the bulk of university graduates (not just graduates in marketing and electrical engineering but also those in anthropology and drama) end up working in the private sector. Several close connections between universities and business have been long-standing matters of fact.[5]

What *is* new in the past quarter-century is that universities (especially large, research-oriented universities with big medical schools) and business have entered into new forms of "partnership."[6] The university brings to the partnership "intellectual property" (ideas that can be sold or transformed into goods and services that can be sold). Business brings to the partnership the money to buy the university researchers' ideas and/ or the capital and entrepreneurial skills required to create "spin-off" companies to commercialize these ideas. This change is most pronounced in the United States and is increasingly evident in Canada.[7]

Because the new partnership between universities and business is so important, let us make sure we grasp it by looking at it in a slightly different way. Prior to the 1970s, almost all of the research done in universities was "pure" or "basic" research. This research was motivated by a desire to discover truths about the universe, regardless of their practical utility. "Research and development" (R & D), the application of science to practical problems, was generally not the job of universities. R & D was the responsibility, first, of the business corporations themselves, and second, of the national and provincial research councils set up by governments specifically as agencies of R & D. Beginning in the 1970s, however, universities became more and more involved in R & D. Why did this happen?

The Growth of Research and Development

Three factors contributing to the growth of R & D during the past twenty-five years are reasonably clear: cutbacks in government funding beginning in the late 1960s; changes, around the same time, in American patent law that made the sale of ideas by universities highly profitable; and simultaneous political triumphs by the New Right.

The first of these factors requires a brief historical sketch of universities from the mid-1950s to the early 1970s. Between the end of World War Two and the end of the 1960s, universities grew at an unparalleled rate, first to accommodate the returning servicemen (and then their children), then to absorb the "baby boomers." For example, in this period in Ontario, a cluster of five more-or-less autonomous universities was transformed into a "system" of fifteen universities governed by a common funding formula. Likewise, in Alberta, the lone university, the rapidly growing University of Alberta in Edmonton, was joined by a university in Calgary, which quickly became a "multiversity"[8] in its own right, as well as the smaller University of Lethbridge and the distance-education Athabasca University. In this period, the expansion of the traditional faculties (and, of course, endless capital construction) was accompanied by the addition of new professional schools and institutes. At the same time, there was a growth of graduate studies in all fields. Doctoral degrees were awarded by Canadian universities that, a few years earlier, were leaving the education of their aspiring professors to the elite English and American universities. From the late 1950s to the late 1960s university professors were definitely in a sellers' market, and they did not hesitate to take advantage of their position, individually and collectively. Salaries rose sharply. Teaching loads were reduced. Quantity and occasionally even quality of "research" became the measure of professorial prestige, as did the ability to increase one's salary and reduce one's teaching. Because of their excellent bargaining position, professors could get the time, the money, and the graduate assistance to concentrate on research.

However, by the end of the 1960s (slightly later in Alberta), expansion in university education came to an end. Governments were simply no longer willing, as they once had been, to spend huge amounts of money on universities, particularly on their research activities. This attitude meant a changing reward system, and if professors were to continue to live in the manner to which they had become accustomed — namely, one in which research is the name of the game — they would have to find more dollars for scholars.[9] Government priorities set the agenda, and fiscal restraint had an impact on university life at every level.[10] The universities accommodated materialistic assumptions and had to justify their utility in hiring, programming, student activities, and faculty involvement.

For many years prior to the cutbacks (and still today), the largest source of funds for research has come from the so-called national granting councils. These are the Medical Research Council (MRC), the National Science and Engineering Research Council (NSERC), and the Social Sciences and Humanities Research Council (SSHRC). The second largest source of funds has been departments and agencies of provincial governments. When these two main sources of funding were cut back, researchers complained and lobbied, but they also sought an alternative source of funds. There was only one major alternative source: business. So the campaign for research funding by the private sector began. With its directly profitable applications, however, R & D was of far more interest to business than was basic research. Thus, the decline of government research funding in the early 1970s is an important part of the explanation of the shift of university research from basic to R & D in the early 1970s.

A second factor in the shift was the result of a change in American law. In 1968, the University of Wisconsin succeeded in acquiring an "Institutional Patent Agreement" from the Department of Health, Education and Welfare. In effect, this agreement gave the university, rather than the government, title to inventions made with federal funds at universities. With this development, universities could profit from the sale of "intellectual property," even if that property was created wholly or largely through the use of federal funding. In 1980, this practice was generalized through passage of the Bayh-Dole Act. Now all universities could retain title to their inventions derived from federally funded research. Canadian practice generally followed the American model, although there is much more diversity here than in the US because the laws in this area are less codified.[11] In any case, US patents are important to Canadian R & D. Congenial legislation was a second factor essential to the shift from basic research to R & D in both countries.

The final factor contributing to the shift away from basic research towards R & D in the universities is the ever-accelerating commercialization of the culture in which universities are embedded. Thatcherism, Reaganism, and Mulroneyism were little more than warnings of what was to come by way of triumphs for the New Right.[12] Distrust of government, obsessive "downsizing" of workforces, transformation of full-time jobs into part-time, and vastly reduced expenditures on health, education, and social benefits are just the most obvious signs of the commercialization of our society at large. Its largest mirror in the university was the increasing number of administrators and professors who were involved in selling ideas for profit.

The Scope of the New Partnership

How far has the new "partnership" between universities and business gone? It is impossible to provide a comprehensive, quantitative answer to this question. Using the University of Alberta as an example, however, it is possible to cast some light on the question.[13] I'll confine myself to three specific indicators of the new partnership: the huge emphasis on medicine and the virtual neglect of the liberal arts by sponsors of research; the corresponding requirement that Arts professors take on much heavier teaching responsibilities than Medicine professors; and the growth of the university bureaucracy devoted to fostering the commercialization of "intellectual property."

First, at every university that emphasizes "partnership," medicine (and to a slightly lesser extent the other "health sciences") is the rock-star/supermodel/world class player. For example, in 1996-97, forty-three percent of the funds for sponsored research went to the University of Alberta's Faculty of Medicine. (Science was a poor second with twenty-three percent and Arts, the University's biggest faculty, a dismal last at two percent.) In contrast, Medicine received only thirty-six percent of the total amount granted to the University by the federal funding councils, while Science and Engineering received fifty-five percent and Arts nine percent. This is one indication that Medicine receives a much larger portion of its research funding from business than do other faculties. (The other big benefactors of business funding are engineering and forestry.)[14] Faculties most likely to exhibit short-term profitability and commercial utility find money for research.

This point is reinforced by a second indicator, a comparison of student/teacher ratios in the faculties of Arts, Science, and Medicine. In the 1996/97 academic year, the faculties of Arts and Medicine at the University of Alberta each had about 350 full-time academic staff members; Science had about 270. There were close to 5100 undergraduate students in Arts, about 4800 in the Faculty of Science, and 425 in the MD programme of the Faculty of Medicine.[15] Even if we count in the supervision of advanced students, which vastly increases the relative teaching responsibilities of professors of Medicine, the student teacher ratios in the three faculties look something like this: Arts — 17:1; Science — 20:1; Medicine 3.5:1. It is hard to avoid the conclusion that Medicine is a giant research institute with a small associated teaching enterprise. What does this have to do with marketing? Well, professors of medicine need time to test drugs, do licensed research, and create spin-off companies. When time "makes cents," the University makes sure they have time.

Third, the extent of the partnership between business and the universities is indicated by the sizeable bureaucracies set up by big universities to foster the relationship. Today, there are people systematically marketing university research, and the partnership of inventive professors and capitalists interested in high technology is not left to chance. Every large university now has a vice-president in charge of research. In contrast to just a few years ago, the VP (Research) wields clout comparable to that of the VP (Academic). (Until recently, the VP [Academic] was unrivaled as the president's second-in-command, or, at universities in which the president chose to concentrate on fund-raising and courting politicians and chambers of commerce, the effective chief administrator.) Martha Piper — formerly the University of Alberta's VP (Research) and now President of the University of British Columbia — promoted the virtues of university-business collaboration in an array of glossy brochures. She also held numerous press conferences, which were reported uncritically. At one point, considerable effort went into getting part of the faculty to wear buttons proclaiming that "Research Makes Sense." As far as I know, no one asked publicly what kind of research "makes sense," or when it makes sense, or for whom it makes sense, or even, most basically, what it means for research to "make sense."

Perhaps even more important than the office of the VP (Research) itself is the adjunct of that office known at the University of Alberta as the Industry Liaison Office (ILO) and at other large universities by the same or a similar name.[16] According to James W. Murray, the Director of the University of Alberta's ILO, its purpose is:

- To catalyze Collaborative Research Projects and Develop Industrial Partnerships
- To identify and Protect Intellectual Property
- To Out-License University Developed Technologies, Software, and Know-How
- To Promote Local Economic Development Through the Creation of University Spin-Off Companies
- To promote international collaboration and trade in creating global knowledge based business.[17]

To these ends, the University of Alberta's ILO employs no fewer than thirty people, which makes it the largest operation of its kind in Canada. By one measure, then, the University of Alberta leads the country in marketing the university. Moreover, it has recently created Research Technology Management Inc. (RTMI), a for-profit corporation one hundred percent owned by the University. RTMI has a distinguished board of directors and is intended to create up to six spin-off companies per year by such means as providing seed money, hiring senior management, and producing and implementing an initial business plan. Part of the business of the University of Alberta is business.

Problems with the Growth of Partnership

The marketing of the university grows feverishly, and what's wrong with that? What's wrong with the university getting a fair financial return for its commercially viable ideas, especially if the university devotes the return on investment to still more research and the research is valuable in creating jobs and improving people's quality of life? In small doses, this focus would not be a problem, especially if it were to be confined to the professional faculties whose central concerns are closely connected to R & D, such as in agriculture, engineering, forestry, and some parts of medicine. But it is difficult to justify universities or researchers subsidizing private companies. There are major problems here, of which I want to discuss the two most important.

The first problem is that time devoted to R & D is time eliminated from basic research. This is unfortunate for three reasons. First, universities (if not always in practice at least in theory) have long been conceived as places where scholars are bound to seek the truth (or, at least, a closer approximation to it). They are not supposed to be servants of the economic elite. Second, as universities reward applied research unduly, career patterns are redirected away from pure basic research. Scholars whose natural bent is seeking answers to questions with no obvious or immediate applications are induced to waste their time on applied research. And third, R & D as *applied* research depends on *basic* research. If academics devote too much time, effort, and resources to applied research, the basic research available for application shrinks. In other words, excessive attention to applied research to the detriment of basic research is self-defeating.

The second problem resulting from the marketing of the university is that it leads to an overemphasis on research generally *at the expense of teaching* throughout the university, not just in the areas where the sale of "intellectual property" is most likely to fetch a good price. This overemphasis on research is commonly supported by three wildly implausible postulates, each of which can be easily confuted. The first is that teaching and research are thoroughly mutually supportive, so that time spent on research invariably enriches the researcher's teaching. The truth, however, is that most serious undergraduate teaching concentrates on simplifying and enlivening ideas that the teacher has thought about much more broadly and deeply in his or her research. The second implausible postulate (an extension of the first) is that excellent teaching and excellent research are inseparable.[18] Good teaching requires practice. The best researchers, however, especially in the life sciences, don't teach much, so their teaching is bound to suffer. Moreover, the most demanding teaching is at the introductory levels, but high-profile researchers are increasingly opting out of the teaching of beginning students, so even if we suppose that they *could* be the best teachers, they are not so in fact.

The third implausible postulate used to support an overvaluing of research and an undervaluing of teaching has to do with class size. According to this belief, teaching/learning that takes place in huge classes without demanding written assignments is as good as, if not better than, that which takes place in small classes in which there is an opportunity for students to ask questions, engage in dialogue, and submit written assignments that receive careful scrutiny and extensive comments by the teacher. Such thinking, however, is more a self-serving justification than an honest evaluation of today's teaching environment. The postulate's chief function is to support the overemphasis on research by permitting scholars to teach a few large classes with machine-graded evaluations, thereby freeing them from the classroom to spend more time in the laboratory, the field, or the library.

The importance of these two problems was strongly underlined by the scientists I interviewed. On the matter of deflecting scientists from basic research to R & D, the point was made most strikingly, to my surprise, by some engineers. According to them, schools of engineering used to make room for two quite different types of researchers. On the one hand, there were engineering professors whose work was tightly focussed on the technological problems of a particular industry, such as automotives. On the other hand, there were academic engineers whose work was highly theoretical, more like that of physicists, mathematicians, or computer scientists. There are still engineers of the second kind, who tend to identify themselves as "lone wolves" rather than "team players." But engineers of both types told me that the "lone wolves" are an endangered species because they pay a price in career advancement for their failure to attend to the realities of the marketplace.

As to the overemphasis on research at the expense of teaching, even in areas in which commercialization is not a major factor, interviewees told me that mathematicians are particularly vulnerable. On occasion they have been castigated by their scientific colleagues for lack of "productivity." Moreover, it has been made clear to them that the appropriate way to increase their publications is to teach fewer but larger classes.

■ ■ ■

What, if anything, can people interested in the university ideal do to reverse the trend towards the ever-increasing marketing of higher education? The most important step toward answering this question is to avoid the extremes of romantic optimism and cynical resignation. By romantic optimism I mean the belief that the university can be thoroughly transformed from within — and especially from within the Faculty of Arts — by sermonizing about a better world. The increasing commercialization of the university stems in no small part from the increasing commercialization of the surrounding culture. In an era when National Hockey League teams sell the *names* of their arenas (for example, the Corel Centre in Ottawa and G.M. Place in Vancouver), nothing is to be gained by heroic posturing by professors of English and Political Science. On the other hand, there is even less to be said for cynical resignation. By cynical resignation I mean the view that we are subject to relentless "forces" — cultural imperatives, or capitalist markets, or "globalization." Such views, in my opinion, vastly underestimate the role of human agency. Opposition to the marketing of the university is most common in arts faculties, and arts students, their professors, and their allies should do what they can. I make two modest proposals, one that is essentially a rear-guard action, the other more offensive in nature.

The rear-guard action is to stop reproducing the obsession with research, and the devaluation of teaching, that is characteristic of the most commercialized parts of the university. Instead of opposing the trends evident in the health sciences, engineering, and forestry, arts faculties are emulating them. As I have discovered in interviews across the country, "successful" careers for professors in the social sciences and humanities are now based — as elsewhere in the university — almost exclusively on quantity of refereed articles[19] in narrowly specialized academic periodicals. As a result, there has been a decline in the number of courses taught, an increase in class sizes, and a growth in team research and multi-authored publications. One step that can be taken by humanities and social-science professors and students is to resist these trends, a bit of genuine progressive conservatism.

The offensive step is for universities to promote incisive criticism as a social good every bit as important as the creation of saleable technology. Of course, even corporate executives, like university presidents and deans of arts, regularly declaim about the importance of liberally educated students who can think broadly and write clearly. But they don't put their money where their mouths are. They endow chairs in business schools, hire engineers as consultants, and create companies in partnership with pharmacists. Moreover, there is no sign of corporations hunting desperately for the best of the arts graduates ahead of the least able products of the business schools. What about, as a very modest start, a university requirement that, for every hundred dollars used to purchase the university's "intellectual property," businesses contribute ten dollars to a fund for basic research, the liberal arts, and student financing in these areas?

Notes

1 H.W. Arthurs, R.A. Blais, and J. Thompson, *Integrity in Scholarship: A Report to Concordia University* (Montreal: Concordia University, 1994), 3-4.

2 Arthurs, Blais, and Thompson; also J. S. Cowan, *Lessons from the Fabrikant File: A Report to the Board of Governors of Concordia University* (Montreal: Concordia University, 1994).

3 G.A. Jones, ed., *Higher Education in Canada: Different Systems, Different Perspectives* (New York and London: Garland, 1997). See also *Maclean's Magazine, The Maclean's Guide to Canadian Universities 98*, 1998.

4 B. Clark, *The Higher Education System: Academic Organization in a Cross-national Perspective* (Berkeley: University of California, 1983).

5 See A.B. McKillop, *Matters of Mind: The University in Ontario 1791-1951* (Toronto: University of Toronto, 1994); W.H. Johns, *A History of the University of Alberta 1908-1969* (Edmonton: University of Alberta Press, 1981).

6 R. Pannu, D. Schugurensky, and D. Plumb, "From the Autonomous University to the Reactive University: Global Restructuring and the Re-forming of Higher Education" in *Sociology of Education in Canada,* L. Erwin and D. MacLennan, eds. (Toronto: Copp Clark Longman, 1994), 499-526. See also "The Knowledge Factory: A Survey of Universities" in *The Economist,* 4 October 1997.

7 The best Canadian source for the developments described in the text, even though it focuses on Ontario, is P.D. Axelrod, *Scholars and Dollars* (Toronto: University of Toronto Press, 1982). For contemporary business influences, see H. Buchbinder and J. Newson, *The University Means Business* (Toronto: Garamond, 1988); H. Buchbinder and J. Newson, "Corporate-University Linkages in Canada: Transforming a Public Institution" in *Higher Education* 20 (1990): 355-379.

8 "Multiversity" is the term coined by Clark Kerr, then President of the University of California, in his seminal work, *The Uses of the University* (Cambridge, Massachusetts: Harvard University Press, 1963), to refer to universities that do not have a "soul," in the sense of a single unifying purpose, such as glorifying God, training clergymen or producing informed citizens. The multiversity carries on a wide range of activities, from teaching the classics through training people in dentistry, producing good basketball teams to selling technology to industry without worrying about how these activities fit together.

9 G. Schrimpton, "The Crisis in Canadian Universities" in *The Political Economy of Canadian Schooling,* Terry Wotherspoon, ed. (Toronto: Methuen, 1987), 185-210.

10 *Postsecondary Education Issues in the 1980s* (Toronto: Council of Ministers of Education, Canada, 1982); *From Patrons to Partners: Corporate Support for Universities* (Montreal: The Corporate Higher Education Forum, 1987); *Report: Commission of Inquiry on Canadian University Education* (Ottawa: Association of Universities and Colleges of Canada, 1991).

11 D.E. Massing, ed., *AUTM Licensing Survey: Fiscal Year 1991 – Fiscal Year 1995* (Norwalk, Connecticut: The Association of University Technology Managers, 1996), 2-4.

12 In preference to "the New Right" there are those who make a distinction between neo-conservatives and neo-liberals, the supposed difference being that the latter are sympathetic rather than hostile to such groups as gays, single parents, and the unemployed. However, since "neo-liberals" think it is "fiscally irresponsible" to spend money to assist the disadvantaged, we seem to have here a distinction without a difference.

13 In regard to "partnership," the university of Alberta is not typical of all North American universities, or even all Canadian universities. "Partnership" does not assume anything like such large proportions at the University of Victoria or York University, although these universities certainly do engage in partnerships, let alone Brandon or Acadia. But it is typical of large, research-oriented universities with big medical schools on both sides of the border. For example, the fact that the University of Alberta lags far behind Stanford and considerably behind the University of Toronto in royalties received, but well ahead of Vanderbilt University and the University of Manitoba, does not mean that these institutions differ significantly in their commitment to market "intellectual property."

14 *Edmontonians,* March 1997, 5.

15 These figures somewhat overestimate the disparity between Medicine, on the one hand, and Arts and Science, on the other. Although they exclude the MA and PhD students taught and supervised by faculty members in Arts and Science, there is a larger *proportion* of students in Medicine pursuing advanced work beyond the MD than graduate students in Arts and Science.

16 Canadian universities with such an office include British Columbia, Simon Fraser, Northern British Columbia, Alberta, Calgary, Regina, Saskatchewan, Manitoba, Toronto, Queen's Western, Waterloo, Guelph, Lakehead, Carleton, McMaster, Ottawa, Montréal, Laval, Concordia, McGill, Québec à Montréal, Dalhousie, and Memorial.

17 J.W. Murray, *A Presentation to Members of the National Key Laboratories of China* (Edmonton: Industrial Relations Office, University of Alberta, 1997), 3; emphasis in the original.

18 In their recent compilation of assertions about universities, D. Bercuson, R. Bothwell, and J. Granatstein assert, without any show of evidence whatsoever, that "the best university teachers are invariably the best researchers." See *Petrified Campus* (Toronto: Random House, 1997), 88.

19 "Refereed articles" are articles assessed favourably by anonymous peer reviewers as a condition of publication.

The Politics of Educational Restructuring in Alberta

5

Orchestrating Delusions: Ideology and Consent in Alberta

Jerrold L. Kachur

*You told us education is crucial to your children's future
... We have heard you. We are putting our children and
young people first.*
— Ralph Klein, 1998 *State of the Province* television address[1]

Many people were hopeful that the Alberta Growth Summit in September 1997 signalled a new direction for the province. A selected few championed social investment at the Summit and challenged the business lobby's interest in tax cuts. The projected 1996/97 budget surplus of $2 billion (later finalized at $2.7 billion) and the Summit's decision to promote "people development" (see chapter three) led many critics to look forward to the restoration of social spending as part of the Alberta Advantage. But hope faded, and the Alberta government emphasized that people development depends on conditions: later, much later, after the debt is paid off.

The notion of people development, however, created an optimistic mood for community workers, teachers, and nurses heartened with signs of potential relief. As usual, government consultations and media events created a modicum of "trust" between ruler and ruled, and confidence was restored. Like survivors of a car wreck, Albertans optimistically believed that their ordeal was over and that the crash had been "just an accident." When explaining social events, Albertans seem to have difficulty in distinguishing acts of god or the forces of nature from human agency. Driving the highway known as the Klein revolution apparently is risky, filled with drama — and delusion.

A set of ideas, or ideology, while helpful as a shortcut to understanding, can function as a delusion, a symptom of mental illness, or, if preferred, a false belief, misconception, hallucination, or even misjudgement about the nature of reality. This chapter examines the way Albertans attempt to make sense of reality and delusion. It focuses on the ideological function of the consensus-building forums, particularly the 1997 Alberta Growth Summit process, and similar events in the 1990s. This chapter looks at the "stakeholder" consultation process as the vehicle whereby dominant social groups create a broad-based alliance and establish a system of "permanent consent" that justifies the existing social order and increases inequality, while claiming to do the opposite. The chapter further shows both the differences and substantial continuities in the orchestration of consent. More specifically, I show how the Progressive Conservative party under Ralph Klein led the province and articulated a belief system that is accepted as true by a majority of Alberta's population — in spite of facts that might show otherwise.

Understanding the relationships among consensus-building politics, economic restructuring, and educational reform requires looking at the Alberta government's assumptions as well as its organizational processes and strategic priorities during the 1990s. To accomplish this task, I describe Alberta's economic-development model and its connections to the everyday assumptions of many Albertans and the broad assumptions of New Right ideology. I outline the symbolic effect of the premier's persona and his pronouncements about Alberta's future. And I analyze in detail the government's consensus-building strategies: how the Klein government orchestrates the popular ideas of Albertans in the interest of economic liberalism and social conservatism.

Public Education and the New Economic Model

Since the early 1990s, Alberta has embarked on a New Right agenda, enjoining economic liberalism to social conservatism. Economic liberals, or neo-liberals, promote ideas about the free market, individualism, and a minimal state and play a dominant role in the alliance; social conservatives play a secondary role and tend to promote hierarchy, authoritarianism, and a public-order state.[2] The Alberta government has borrowed New Right ideas from Britain and the United States and has developed a new common sense about school reform.[3] This new thinking[4] shapes the way the government adjusts the province's staples-based economy and reorganizes contemporary education to meet the demands of globalization (see chapter three).

From 1993 to 1998, Klein's application of neo-liberal economic policies and practices to education was directed primarily at two goals, both intended to provide advantages for Alberta's traditional resource sector, to develop new technologies in the areas of scientific research, and to reorganize the training of skilled labour. Early in his leadership, Klein specified, "Well-educated and highly trained people are the key to achieving our goals. We need results-based education that prepares students to meet emerging technologies and to deal with change more rapid than at any other time in the past."[5] To do this, Klein intended to maintain infrastructure and quality, to simplify access to financial assistance for students, and to consolidate programming. These goals were to be accomplished in part through diversified and privatized forms of provision in education (see introduction).[6] He also wanted "to immediately launch a broadly-based call for public input into a practical, long-term plan for adult learning with particular emphasis on increased training and retraining opportunities in the labour market."[7]

The logic of the new economy and educational reform across the country requires governments to emphasize scientific research and technological applications. In Alberta, however, it also means appealing to the public about the importance of investment possibilities for big corporations and small businesses in new technologies (see chapter four). So with some urgency (but not too strongly, lest it appear undemocratic and self-interested), Alberta's economic, political, and scientific elites have also had to impress their logic on Albertans that a neo-liberal, post-industrial development model offers the *only* option.

If successful, Alberta's new technology-based revolution will transform information into knowledge, knowledge into intellectual capital, and "intellectual capital into an economic engine that will increase competitiveness and wealth."[8] Prosperity, thus, depends on both a culture of innovation and advances in technology in the resource sector and in related new clusters of advanced industry in computing, software, biotechnology, health sciences, pharmaceuticals, micro electronics, and telecommunications.[9] To achieve this goal, the economic, political, and scientific elites also call for more technology-oriented "education" and the protection of many high-risk ventures, as well as the facilitation of partnerships between scientific researchers and industrial research departments.[10] In other words — according to neo-liberal logic — the government must cut social services to free revenues to support technological innovation and *corporate welfare* while emphasizing the importance of education. Thus, the government links education and the economy such that subsidies for private profit go hand-in-hand with greater attention to quality management, labour training, international marketing, technological innovation, and development of resource-based industries.[11] Political success also depends on mass appeal and the necessity to say one thing and do another, especially if it means cutting one kind of education to support another.

In addition to technological innovation, the government's second goal is to reorganize educational inputs and to provide a highly skilled and flexible labour force. In the case of students, the corporate and political elites require a specific kind of skill development to increase the supply of scientists, engineers, technologists, and other skilled workers on a cost-recovery basis. Success here is measured by the provision of (relatively inexpensive) qualified workers and by the organization of tripartite partnerships among government, educational institutions, and industry to create a seamless school-to-work transition. Within this economic matrix flows another presupposition: the political subordination, or acquiescence, of labour unions and professional organizations — especially the Alberta Teachers' Association. In the latter case, the government and its backers required political strategies to counter the potential and real resistance of teachers and their allies (see chapter ten).[12]

The driving force behind the new economic model came from deep and brutal cuts to the social sectors (see chapters six and seven). Quite simply, the government promoted "doing more with less" as if it were a natural need. Thus, the provincial deficit and debt loomed large as an impending apocalypse; in keeping with some bizarre logic, education had to be cut in order to save it. With a crisis-management plan in hand, the spin-doctors complained — contrary to fact[13] — that the education system was falling apart. Alberta students, they said, were not exiting the system prepared for the new world order and the system was too costly, with teachers paid too much for doing a lousy job. Alberta's schools needed market-discipline. The business model would offer up a good spanking to those who wouldn't sit up straight and listen to the music. The Alberta government followed up its belief with action, slashed with great severity in the public sector,[14] and "reinvented" education. The "new student" was to be delivered to market through an appropriate mix of programs and new linkages to industry. Most importantly, the private sector would be freed for new business opportunities.

Thus, the Klein government embarked on an accelerated set of educational reforms in 1994 that met little resistance. The government, speaking a language of public concern for education and democracy, implemented the corporate agenda, appeased the school reform movement, created a new "common sense" about economics, technology, and education, and captured the imagination of "ordinary Albertans." What emerged in the process was a unique strategy based on the political economic realities of Alberta and a synthesis of ideas related to neo-liberalism, strategic planning, public consultation, and the imperatives of political survival. In the name of democracy, Alberta got something other than democracy: a top-down, neo-liberal approach to science and technology, labour markets, and public education that reinforced — rather than challenged — traditional patterns of resource-based development.

New Right Ideology and Education Reform

How then did the neo-liberal economic development model for education become "common sense"? New Right ideology — as a new common sense — seems to explain the way the world works and what ordinary individuals should do to get ahead in it. At the everyday and metaphorical level, this common sense in Alberta shares remarkable similarity to a religious morality play. The preordained drama is played out on the Field of the Lord, where the competitive marketplace is God and money is the way to keep score on the road to Heaven. As social explanation, New Right ideas may appear as the rational conclusion reached through a worldwide consensus of social scientists. In common-sense politics, people's everyday understanding of metaphors and the complementary experts' theories get blurred. Public-relations entrepreneurs are paid to use these blurred meanings so politicians can mobilize the public for change. In so doing, prescriptions for reform may appear as self-evident or omnipresent "to everyone" — even when they are not.

The popular understanding of many Albertans has been that their problems result from some kind of personal failing; that is, a failure of an individual's moral will or cognitive development — for example, the absence of a work ethic or lack of intelligence. This failing morality or psychology may be extended to personifications of institutions. For example, Corporate Canada, the ideal achiever in Alberta, provides jobs according to its means and pays workers according to their merit. There are always some people who seem to lack ambition, education, skills, ability, or experience to take advantage of economic opportunity — and thus they are deservedly unemployed or poor. Governments — "the Nanny State" — should not intervene in the "natural order" by creating jobs or promoting security. "Big Brother" should not distribute welfare cheques or maintain a minimum wage. Inversely, signs of poverty and unemployment may reveal individual deficits in moral will or cognitive development. Government policies that regulate the marketplace or shelter the poor from corporate judgements are considered wrong, not only because they constrain the rewards of "entrepreneurs," waste money, sap incentive, promote indignity, and cause economic decline; they are wrong because they impede the measurement of "real" human worth as viewed through the lens of the metaphorical morality play.

In a similar vein, government debt represents the collective failure to combat sin, while recent government policies of the Klein variety are meant to reassert the will of the Father over the degenerate sinner. Fiscal discipline — a cold shower — is used to motivate the appropriate behavior. A good spanking for the less fortunate is intended to restore the work ethic and to put the lost soul back on the road to salvation. Economic shock treatment restores the senses — that is, capital accumulation and the prerogative of the chosen few.

The above morality play also assigns a special function to schooling. Increasing rates of poverty are intimately (and usually inaccurately) linked to a lack of educational opportunities and a failure to develop marketable skills. It is "common sense" to understand schooling as the answer to unemployment, welfare, and poverty. To deal with this "poverty-cycle," conservatives relive the morality play, business neo-liberals promote growth and "skills," and the "caring" professions assume that more schooling is the ticket to success.[15] Likewise, while educators may express broader goals unrelated to the development of human capital — such as democratic citizenship, personal development, or cultural tolerance — for the most part they, too, see education as an "investment" in technical skills where more is always better. Under close inspection, most educational deficits are treated as ideological proxies for explaining either the economic or moral deficits of individuals. Thus, in "explaining" the poverty cycle, Albertans unreflectively — and inaccurately — promote a pervasive ideology that implies a natural relationship between morality, schooling, employment, and individual success (see Appendix K). In Alberta, "education" is primarily the alternative form of capital accumulation. Everywhere, when there is a failure to accumulate, Albertans see deficits in individual morality, intelligence, motivation, behavior, and skill; they don't see a structural dynamic of political economic and socio-cultural conflict. Why not?

The House that Ralph Built

Build your house on the solid rock of the Lord our King. While the Market is God, the central and symbolic Father-figure for the New Right drama is just a nice guy, played by Ralph. New Right ideology requires a symbolic figure like Premier Ralph Klein to embody contradictory social goals and to interpret the conflicting facts and values of life. In the House of Alberta, the Father states the facts, interprets the values, judges the past, and predicts the future. Government, also symbolized by Ralph, thus retains the prerogative to define the meaning of balanced budgets and Alberta's debts in all its details — leaving the "big" decisions to the little people.

Ralph Klein symbolizes the sovereign authority of the common folk and embodies the prophet from humble origins who knows the Way. A man of the people, he walks with elites. He is individual and province, rich and poor, a walking contradiction. And herein lies his appeal: based on taste (good and bad), there is something about him for each person to like. Political decisions are based on how good it feels to walk with him or to talk with him. Loyalty, rather than intellect, is given an audience. And like all good prophets, Ralph speaks in parables.

Klein's favourite parable is that of the house, once brought low by spendthrift sinners, now restored to moral and fiscal health. It is a parable easily understood by most Albertans. Ralph's television address in 1994 emphasized balancing household income with expenses and credit-card payments. In January 1998, he extended the analogy to include household renovations. Life makes difficult demands: balancing renovations, revenues, and expenses. "It was hard," he says, "and sometimes we felt angry and frustrated. But we stuck to the plan, and today we have a solid, affordable home with room to grow." Ralph continues: enjoy the new look — but only for a while. Two things remain to be completed: education and debt repayment.[16]

This parable seems to make a lot of sense to a parent under the ever-present pressures of mortgage payments. She shuffles the child off to classes, sits down for a coffee-break, pays bills for electricity, water, and school supplies, and then dips into an over-extended bank account just to make ends meet. Although the economics of a province are much more complex than balancing the household bank account, it provides a model for getting on with business. In reality, however, it mystifies the complexity of Alberta's situation.

Father Klein, and Albertans overall, take pride in sticking to the "plan" to pay down the mortgage, even if they didn't initially agree to the plan. This rendition of history returns to familiar themes for the Father of this Household. Klein's 1993 election campaign material declared "He Cares, He Listens" — a refrain that later gave way to scolding critics as special interests and whiners. Then Klein apologized: "Sorry. We didn't have a plan." He reassured Albertans and hinted that the toughest part was over. He would plan "better" next time. But by the 1997 election campaign, he would brag, "I said what I was going to do. And I'll do it again." The Growth Summit followed the election. Klein consulted "stakeholders," but not elected MLAs, and promoted briefly "people development."

People development, however, requires dealing with that damn mortgage and a newly christened objective: "accelerated debt reduction." Was the Father really uncertain about what to do? As he retreated to his study, all ears waited to hear his answers in the January 1998 television address. Albertans anticipated the event: "The budget is balanced. The economy is strong. Albertans are working hard. And they are proud of what they have done. What's next?"

At last, the Father revealed his thoughts: another plan — an "Agenda for Opportunity." He focused on his children. He committed himself to government services, "everything from schools to hospitals to roads." He recalled the past four years and described how Albertans had set out to ensure that the financial house was in order. The sacrifice had been for "our children and grandchildren," whose future had been burdened by "deficit and debt."

The pattern was familiar. However, there was no clear statement on how the Father's commitment would be accomplished, nor how much it might cost or who could pay for it. Moreover, there was that ever-present bugbear: fiscal responsibility, committed to no deficits (but also no tax increases), debt repayment, and new efficiencies.[17] "People development" was subordinated to the "Alberta Advantage." Can there be a more deluded state than that of a Father who cannot buy his hungry children groceries because he has the burden of a $2.7 billion surplus? When would Albertans ever have the money for more public services? During the 1998 Speech from the Throne, it all seemed to make sense once again as Ralph presented yet another version of caring, listening, and planning. The Father had talked with Albertans, and Albertans waited for the unfolding of The Agenda for Opportunity.

Déjà Vu All Over Again?

Ralph's common-sense delusions explain the relationships among education, economy, and morality as an eternal struggle for individual salvation through household renovation and the care of children. But it is within the context of the various consensus-building forums that the figure of Father Ralph is fleshed out as representative for all Albertans and where the ideological drama is given its content. At these forums, the symbol of Ralph is invested with old and new meanings that mingle in a continuous process of ideological regeneration.

Once upon a time in 1992, Don Getty was the Father. He sponsored an "arms-length" Premier's Conference on Alberta's Economic Future.[18] The meeting, and related roundtables, also emphasized what was to become "people development" at the 1997 Growth Summit. The Getty conference promoted education, scientific research, and technological development. The guiding priority, however, was resource-led, "free-enterprise" and "knowledge-based" global competition. (The potential consequences were, of course, ignored.) The process "revealed" the truth, a "common-sense" framework for the implementation of sectoral reform that Ralph Klein set in motion during his first term.

Few remember that the above consensus-building process was called Toward 2000 Together (T2T). Unlike the 1997 Summit, and events leading up to it, the 1992 Conference excluded, on principle, people from the "caring" professions. Emphatically, educators and related experts were told that "education" was not about "economics," which the conference organizers were promoting. However, education was the Conference's hottest topic for discussion. The participants, mainly Progressive Conservative admirers, received the gospel about the "profitable" and potentially private function of knowledge and education in the new economy.

Forged during the T2T consultations, the new alliance fought an election and spoke of equal opportunity, community empowerment, and educational spending to justify what were to become "unexpected" cuts to public services. As early as 1991, the PC party elite were looking for a new way to promote "free enterprise" and cuts to social expenditures.[19] The process reinforced for ordinary Albertans the belief that it was sacrilegious to question the efficiency and effectiveness of private entrepreneurship. By 1998, the central assumptions and priorities had not changed, although the reality of managing the consequences was beginning to bite.

In January 1997, hundreds of Albertans became involved once again in a consultation process with the government that had promoted the cuts in the first place. These wide-ranging consultations included more than 40 mini-summits with 170 submissions and a considerable amount of province-wide polling. In light of Alberta's burgeoning budget surpluses, the question of what to do with the growing largesse understandably caught the attention of those dealing with the consequences of restructuring. The consensus-building process filtered and disseminated views and information, including a special website.[20]

In September 1997, the Growth Summit surveyed the Alberta landscape. Unlike the 1992 Conference, the community of elite "stakeholders" had been enlarged to include the "interests" of education, health care, and social work; the Summit coincided with the absence of a fall sitting for the provincial legislature. According to Mike Percy, dean of business at the University of Alberta and co-chair with the premier of the Summit, this consensus-building forum was "a marketplace for ideas, some of which the government will like, some of which they won't."[21] But as a forum for information, the Summit was an expensive way to confirm what the government already knew. In a July 1997 poll, seventy percent of Albertans had expressed their belief that non-fiscal issues such as health care, unemployment, and education should be the government's highest priority.

Instead of ideological debate, delegates to the Summit were presented with digested information informed by the government's assumptions. Alberta's unelected leaders mulled over how to spend the budget surplus: tax cuts? debt reduction? social spending? After two days of intensive discussion, they reviewed 243 suggestions and ranked a number of issues and solutions. Two polarized views were pitted against each other: the social versus business positions.

Bauni Mackay, president of the Alberta Teachers' Association, was a delegate to the Summit (see chapter ten). Her input was incorporated into the official discourse along with others in the education and social sectors: "The vision I would like to see for 2005 is that Alberta will have the best educated and healthiest population in the world."[22] Who could disagree? The stakeholders emphasized social spending over tax cuts and recommended "people development." The meeting ended with a commitment to fiscal controls and other recommendations dealing with all sectors of Alberta society. Premier Klein promised to consider the recommendations as part of the government's future business plans.[23] The media highlighted "people development" as the government's "new" growth priority.

However, the sharing of information and a positive public-relations campaign were not the sole purposes of the Summit. As journalist Mark Lisac insightfully pointed out, the Summit process included a deluge of documentation; recommendation overload; connections among influential Albertans; the sanitizing of reform effects; the exclusion of critical perspectives; and broad goals — but no discussion of the means to achieve those goals or any way to credibly account for the past or the future.[24] Moreover, as another columnist described it, the growth conference was "a surrogate election campaign, a fail-safe attempt to liberate public wisdom without consequences and without the bother of an elected opposition."[25] These criticisms correctly identify that the ruling heights of the Summit were reserved for the assumptions of economic liberalization and public management. Thus, one might more aptly describe what happened as the "orchestration of meaning." Most importantly, the Summit incorporated the voices of the formerly excluded elites, diffused anger, and instilled hope in dealing with the consequence of economic restructuring. In total, the consultation process exemplified a new kind of governance in Alberta: "liberal corporatism."[26] Corporatist processes include the managerial elites of key corporate entities — such as business, government, and labour — who meet to plan the organization of society. Such activity subverts the legislative process and the effective mobilization of opposition.

Orchestrating the Public Mind

So far, this chapter has shown how New Right ideology is organized as both a moral drama and pseudo-consensus under the watchful eye of the premier. The Getty and Klein governments' ongoing orchestration of "non-political consultations," or "round-tables," or "summits," channels public desire — as a form of guided learning — to bring together the contradictory elements of liberal and conservative ideology. These corporatist retreats promote an ever-changing language of salvation, assimilate the leaders of various interest groups, sidestep democratically elected legislatures, predict the future, and guide Alberta's political response. But what exactly is the orchestration process and how does it work?

In this case, the government's planners, consultants, and facilitators used various rhetorical and organizational strategies to channel the desires and manage the meaning of language. During Alberta's restructuring process, including Toward 2000 Together (T2T) and the Alberta Growth Summit 97, the managers of public perception used seven rhetorical strategies to shape the categories of the public mind: classification, definition, value judgement, factual judgement, vernacular tropes, vernacular coding, and orchestration.[27] This concluding section describes these strategies and explains how they work.

Classification allows the facilitators of the process to invest facts with political values or to smuggle in political values under the veil of objective and neutral statements. In the early 1990s, T2T laid a grid for discussion which still resonates in 1998: the burden of government spending; responding to rapid global change; education and training; life-long learning and skills; sustainable development; linking economic to social policy; and implementing a new decision-making process. The facilitators of the consensus-building forums established these themes to structure the discussions. In the case of the 1997 Summit, these categories, although differently named, were also provided ahead of time: people development; health and quality of life; vision for the province; infrastructure, regulatory and tax issues; role and function of government; partnerships; and a framework for policy development and management.

Definitional strategies impart specific meanings to the classification schemes. Definitions are given ahead of time and — in the name of consensus — establish claims, which impart one particular point of view. Definitions establish what and how to talk about the themes. For T2T, the themes were dealt with according to two principles: that budgetary deficits (and resultant accumulated debts) could not be viewed as a taxation problem and that any suggestions would have to promote growth through private enterprise. Thus, not only were the themes given, the ways to deal with themes were also prescribed, further entrenching ideology.

In the Summit process, "people development" was given a particular spin. For example, the first action prescribes, "develop initiatives for building and recognizing the value of the public sector and its people, for making Alberta competitive." The other recommendations follow a similar definitional logic. Education, as in 1992, is recognized as an "investment." Furthermore, the "drive" for quality education must meet the standard of "efficiency and effectiveness in maximizing the use of existing capacity." But what does this technical goal mean? The goal remains open to definition and is implied by other statements and texts. For example, "people development" is later restricted to a context where salaries must remain "competitive."

The rhetorical strategy for value judgement defines the above standards with reference to a particular definition of what "Albertans" value. It is based on mass public-opinion polling or selective consensus-building forums with "stakeholders"; such events and knowledge are thus used to justify particular values. This strategy is politically expedient because the massive number of consultations and polling possibilities create a situation where politicians can pick and choose values as they would the flavour of the month.

The rhetorical strategy for factual judgements allows politicians to ignore the values expressed by public opinion if they contradict the intended goal. In this case, politicians draw on the factual judgements of experts to justify the plan. The government garners its expertise from a sympathetic network of neo-liberals and neo-conservatives who work for business faculties, the Fraser Institute, the Conference Board of Canada, the Canada West Foundation, and other private think-tanks in the business of promoting business. Experts validate the necessity for actions that may counter public opinion. They provide important sources for defining the problem, the explanation, and the solution. At the same time, counter-expertise or counter-ideology is denied a forum.

Special elite-stakeholder summits are also held by invitation only. In these forums, experts who might otherwise disagree in public develop a consensus about potential options that the public rarely hears about. Like manna from heaven, expert opinion is useful if it also complements public-opinion polls. By using both value and factual judgement strategies, the facilitators of elite and popular consultations produce a surplus of textual resources, values, and facts. Politicians can pick and choose from these resources whenever popular or scientific "facts" are required to legitimate policy formation and implementation.

Rhetorical strategies are required to translate expert opinion into the everyday language of ordinary Albertans. Citizens may become confused by details and recommendations, especially if they contradict each other or reveal negative consequences. Translation requires the use of two strategies to overcome complexity and contradiction: vernacular tropes and vernacular coding. Both strategies emphasize judgements based on taste or feeling rather than intellect. That is, if it feels good, "just do it."

Everyday language can be managed with turns of phrase that allow participants to make sense of the information they are asked to think about. These literary twists of meaning inform clichés, analogies, and metaphors. For T2T, the analogy was a journey without destination; references included self-reliance, predestination, and individualism. Other references included Robinson Crusoe, Voyages of Discovery, taking risks, and surviving storms. We all want to get to safe harbours, was the appeal. In the 1997, when safe anchorage should have been reached, participants in the Summit process were told it was a "starting point" and to treat the prospering economy as "a double-edged sword."[28] Presumably, double-edged swords did not exist in 1992.

Ralph's television addresses — with their references to house renovations and credit-card balances — provide exemplary cases that emphasize feelings and reduce the complexity of difficult issues in favour of clichés: short-term pain for long-term gain, anticipating trends and success, maximizing opportunities and advantage, enjoying family and community. Premier Klein co-chaired the 1997 Summit and established a personal relationship with the delegates. Together, they consented to the idea that the government should invest in infrastructure and social services related to growth. They also consented to remain committed to a vision of the future that included a knowledge-based economy and consistency with balanced budgets, economic downturns, and outcome-based management.[29] Here, too, the Father figure presided: Klein's presence symbolized order and unity as well as personalizing the government's commitment to its own ideology.

Coding expert opinion into everyday language also appears to "justify" action for action's sake without forcing participants to confront the potential irrationality of government thought or action. The coding process requires a structured approach to issues and plays on the positive feeling of agreement. In the end, everyone seems to be "really" talking about the same thing. Specific codes provide prescriptions for thinking and inscribe what is to be done within the content of the materials that participants discuss. Coding provides a grid to re-interpret everyday experiences in a way that coincides — not always completely — with the desired outcomes of the facilitators.

These six rhetorical and organizational strategies are combined in consensus-building forums with powerful effect, and facilitators organize consensus-building processes in a machine-like fashion. In 1992, the dominant code for T2T was "Government constraints are business opportunities." During the 1997 Summit process, the codes were more fluid and less specific, even though the process itself was more rigid. Delegates were asked a "fundamental question": "In the context of where we want to be in the year 2005, what private and public sector actions and policies are needed to endure sustainable and broad based growth in Alberta?" They used worksheets and answered their questions according to a set of criteria. Participants — with little time to discuss the meaning, context, or consequence of pre-supplied options — had to review themes and prescribe actions within the context of working documents provided by the organizers. They were expected to consider the issues based on the vision for Alberta already expressed in summary and background documents. The delegates "flagged" particular recommendations on the basis of concurrence (green), clarification (yellow), or contestation (red). The Summit organizers then used this information to re-translate the meaning of the discussions. Facilitators reviewed and evaluated the findings.[30] The premier stated, "The Alberta Summit brings together a diverse group of Albertans to help set the province's course and provide new ideas on how to shape the future."[31] With much of the information, content, and form predetermined and many of the criteria, goals, inputs, and outputs prescribed for discussion, there was little that this group of people could talk about that was original. Thus, the ideological code: deal with the social consequences as efficiently and effectively as possible without challenging the New Right agenda.

The last organizational strategy is "orchestration of the constellation of meaning," which requires the coordination of rhetoric with political power. In addition to what has been already touched on, facilitators and translators need strategies to reconstruct oppositional thought through the subordination, marginalization, distortion, or exclusion of competing points of view. These oppositional points of view provide evidence of "true debate," but mask the power the organizers have to include or exclude participants and to rework oppositional ideas in a controlled environment. In the 1992 T2T process, the consultations included and mediated differences between the resource sectors and the new knowledge-based and value-added sectors. Agribusiness also found favour. The process also dealt with small-business interests as a secondary claim on resources and enticed them to take the opportunity to assume potentially privatized government services. When Klein became the PC leader, he initiated a new consensus-building process, called Creating Tomorrow, to appease the small-farm sector. The election brought these special interests to power. Throughout the T2T process, most points of view representing labour, environment, education, health care, or social service were excluded. The few who did participate found their ideas fragmented, marginalized, or distorted — reincorporated into the dominant agenda.[32]

■ ■ ■

The 1997 Alberta Growth Summit did not break new ground. To be sure, the select groups of invited stakeholder-elites had been expanded, compared with 1992's T2T Conference, to include groups defined as the "social economy" (environmental, community groups, and others) and "MASH" (municipalities, academic institutions, schools, and hospitals).

As in 1992, however, membership was representative of key sectors but not of the Alberta population as a whole. Of the ninety-five appointed delegates, business and industry formed the largest group, with many presidents and vice-presidents from private-sector companies. Discussion of "government" was limited to five PC insiders. Women made up a little more than one-fifth of the participants. Although union representatives did find a limited presence, the Alberta Federation of Labour and its many affiliates, as well as the Alberta Union of Provincial Employees — the biggest union in the province — chose not to participate. Although most of Alberta's working people have no representation in unions anyway, neither did they get it at the Summit. Alberta Teachers' Association president Bauni Mackay was left "to speak for" public-sector unions.[33]

The Summit participants felt good about the exercise. They got to know and understand those who participated. They were committed to the process. Nothing new was learned, however. The often-used "people development" and other such themes had been pre-packaged and were structured into the discussions by facilitators of the process and their political advisors. The participants poured their disagreements into the mould.

The biggest accomplishment of the consensus-building process was a new language for Alberta's elites with which to justify another policy cycle. After each round of public consultations, Alberta's dominant political class speaks about reform with one voice and appeals to the concerns of average citizens in a language they understand. Whether these ideas are really right, true, or truthful is beside the point, requiring a process that distinguishes real consent from deluded conformity. Albertans retain faith in their political leadership and are committed to the process in spite of its double-edged consequences. Many people support what is happening because they like what they feel and know what they like, and even if the process is painful for others or even themselves, it reminds them of Alberta's blessing and the agenda for opportunity. For the optimist in such circumstances, it seems that there is nothing to do but grin and bear it. And besides, we're over the worst now — aren't we?

Notes

I wish to thank Trevor Harrison and Deanna Williamson for their suggestions and comments about earlier drafts of this chapter.

1 *Globe and Mail*, 9 January 1998, A1.

2 For the most part, today's conservative values are subordinated to neo-liberal economics. The "Klein ideology" also includes a "populist" appeal to small-property owners. In the West, populism is closely aligned with a radical form of liberalism called "libertarianism," which asserts that individual liberty is the primary political value and that private property is the most important institutional safeguard against state intervention. For a review of

New Right ideology see D.S. King, *The New Right: Politics, Markets and Citizenship* (London: Macmillan, 1987).

3 For a comprehensive review of the ideological assumptions and practices of this reform movement, see B. Elliott and D. MacLennan, "Education, modernity and neo-conservative school reform in Canada, Britain and the US" in *British Journal of Sociology of Education* 15:2 (1994): 165-185.

4 These ideas can be traced to specific locations and were promoted by various networks of interested parties during the Toward 2000 Together consultations. The key players were the Canada West Foundation, the Business Council on Sustainable Development, the Business Council on National Issues, national adherents to the New Learning Culture, new international entrepreneurs in Third World development, and the futurology market in business marketing. All found fertile ground within the political culture of Alberta. See J.L. Kachur, *Hegemony and Anonymous Intellectual Practice* (doctoral dissertation, University of Alberta, 1995).

5 Alberta Hansard, April 22, 1993, 2353.

6 For example see J.E. Chubb and T.M. Moe, "Politics, markets, and the organization of schools" in *American Political Science Review* 82 (1988): 1065-87. This orientation is readily identifiable in the writings of neo-liberal thinkers. R. Douglas, *Unfinished Business* (Auckland: Random House, 1993); M. Friedman and R. Friedman, *Free to Choose* (New York: Avon, 1980); D. Osborne and T. Gaebler, *Reinventing Government: How the Entrepreneurial Spirit is Transforming the Public Sector* (New York: Plume, 1992).

7 Alberta Hansard, April 22, 1993, 2353.

8 The initial consensus-building documents — produced by the Banff Centre for Management — link education to the economy. *Toward 2000 Together Moderator's Report on Conference Proceedings: Premier's Conference on Alberta's Economic Future*, 1992a. *Toward 2000 Together Summary Report: Roundtables on the Future of the Alberta Economy*, 1992b. *Toward 2000 Together Summary Report: What Albertans Are Saying About Our Economic Future*, 1992c. *Conference Workbook, Premier's Conference on Alberta's Economic Future*, 1992d. *Toward 2000 Together: Report of the Advisory Committee on Alberta's Economic Future*, 1993.

9 *Conference Workbook*, 25.

10 *Conference Workbook*, 26.

11 *Conference Workbook*, 27.

12 *Conference Workbook*, 27-28. See also recommendations arising from *Moderator's Report*.

13 See appendix K.

14 For a detailed description of funding realities in Alberta see Kevin Taft, *Shredding the Public Interest* (Edmonton: University of Alberta Press/Parkland Institute, 1997). According to Mark Lisac (*The Klein Revolution*, Edmonton: NeWest, 1995), the deepest cuts were initiated in 1993 and took effect in 1994. For the three years 1993-96, the government plan included the reduction of corporate taxes and the maintenance of personal income taxes at current levels while instituting a twenty-percent cut in program expenditures. This last cut was supposed to translate into a twenty-seven-percent reduction in provincial services in health, education, and social services. By January 1994, the journey down the neo-liberal road to prosperity had begun, not through economic and educational planning, but through funding cuts to education of more than twelve percent for education and more than seventeen percent for colleges and universities. Advanced education had to cut $135 million or 15.8 percent over 4 years, and students were expected to pick up more of the costs through tuition-fee increases.

15 The sociology of education is awash with studies repeatedly showing that human-capital variables account for less than twenty percent of the variation in social inequality while gender, labour-market demand, and ownership of property account for most of the rest. For

a short review, see R.J. Brym and B.J. Fox, *From Culture to Power* (Toronto: Oxford Press), 1989, 92-119; and Appendix K.

16 Government of Alberta, *Agenda for Opportunity* (television address) 8 January 1998.

17 *Agenda for Opportunity*.

18 For a detailed analysis of the preliminary stages of Alberta's 1990s reform and the Toward 2000 Together consultations, see Kachur, *Hegemony*, 132-251.

19 For an account, see Lisac, *The Klein Revolution*, 42-50.

20 Government of Alberta, *Alberta Growth Summit '97, Final Report*, October 1997.

21 *Edmonton Journal*, 29 October 1997, A7.

22 *Alberta Growth Summit, Final Report*, 19.

23 *Alberta Growth Summit, Final Report*, 19.

24 M. Lisac, column, *Edmonton Journal*. 1 November 1997, A18.

25 G. Laird, guest column, *Globe and Mail*, 6 October 1997, A21.

26 Corporatism is closely linked to traditional forms of conservatism because of its paternalistic ethic. It understands relationships as one of dominance and subordination and is inherently authoritarian and anti-democratic. This ideology originates in large bureaucratic organizations such as multinational corporations and government ministries. As with other forms of conservatism, corporatism believes in natural hierarchy, collective regulation, and economic planning. It combines interest representation, policy implementation, and delegated self-enforcement. Consensus-building takes on a specifically elitist form in the absence of public watchdogs. The state becomes the facilitator of policies, and "stakeholder" consultations displace the legislative process. For a discussion of corporatism in Alberta see T. Harrison, "Making the trains run on time" in *The Trojan Horse*, G. Laxer and T. Harrison, eds. (Montreal: Black Rose, 1995), 118-131.

27 See Kachur, *Hegemony*.

28 Government of Alberta, *Alberta Growth Summit '97. Setting the agenda for Alberta's future*. September 1997, 1, 3.

29 *Alberta Growth Summit, Final Report*, 6.

30 Government of Alberta, *Alberta Growth Summit Agenda*, September 1997.

31 Government of Alberta, *Alberta Growth Summit '97. Setting the agenda for Alberta's future*. September 1997, 1; other related Government of Alberta documents: *Cross-Sector Breakout Sessions; Worksheets: A, B, and C*.

32 Kachur, *Hegemony*.

33 Government of Alberta, *Alberta Growth Summit, Final Report*; L. Goyette, column, *Edmonton Journal*, 24 September 1997, A14.

6

Re-investment Fables: Educational Finances in Alberta

Dean Neu

Education re-investment part of new education plan . . . .
"The Alberta Growth Summit identified 'people
development' as the number one priority facing this
province," said [Education Minister] Mar. "First things
first . . . our children [underscore] the importance of a
quality, appropriately funded education system in
developing our youngest Albertans."
— Alberta Education, January 1998[1]

In this period of fiscal prosperity, the mantra of government ministers is "re-investment." This theme is particularly pervasive in the area of public education. But what does it actually mean to re-invest in public education? Is the amount being re-invested anywhere near the amount that was withdrawn from public education during the first three years of the Klein government's mandate? Furthermore, with all the government's talk about the importance of competing in the global economy, how do the current levels of funding compare with other provinces? After all, it seems naïve to assume that we can provide our youth with a superior education given significantly inferior levels of funding support. While the phrase "doing more with less" has a nice ring to it, most economists will tell you that there is a positive association between funding inputs and educational outcomes.

This chapter attempts to answer these questions. Starting from Alberta Education's annual reports and the three-year business plans for education, I examine changes in historical funding levels for public education and provincial per-student comparisons. Sadly, the results of this analysis suggest that, despite glowing pronouncements and adept public relations, the notion of re-investment is mostly hyperbole: per-student funding levels for public education (in constant dollars) continue to decrease. These funding facts, when juxtaposed with the pronouncements of government ministers and public-relations brochures, suggest that impression management is more important to the current government than improving public education through the provision of adequate funding. Finally, I consider how much it would cost to return per-student public education funding to its historical levels.

The Education Field of Dreams

"The best possible education for all Alberta students." This slogan, from then-Minister of Education Halvar Jonson, is taken from the cover of Alberta Education's 1994/95 Annual Report. Did he actually believe this? Or was he misquoted? Perhaps he meant to say, "The best possible education for all Alberta students *given the meagre amount we are planning to spend on public education.*" After all, as Minister of Education, Jonson presumably had access to historical data which showed that during its first term the Klein administration was the most miserly government in terms of education spending in recent Alberta history. Surely the Education Minister realized that spending on public education during the Klein government's first mandate was, on average, less than during the Lougheed and Getty periods.

Of course, if one examines Alberta Education's annual reports or its three-year education business plans, such a conclusion appears unthinkable, since the topic of spending cuts is downplayed. Like the corporate annual reports they simulate, these glossy reports deal in impressions, not facts. Following the advice of public-relations firms who counsel their clients to design their annual reports to project the "right image," these reports contain proactive, "feel-good" statements. For example, the "Meeting the Challenge III" education business plan[2] contains twenty-seven pages of narrative peppered with highlighted slogans such as: *"Meeting the needs of students in a rapidly changing world"*; *" Quality programs and high standards for all students"*; *" Students come first!"*; *"Help Students be the best they can be"*; and *"Education is everybody's business."*

It is noteworthy that *Meeting the Challenge III* contained but a single numerical table buried in amongst the text. Since this is the only numerical summary contained in the business plan, let's examine this table in more detail.

Table 6.1: Education Business Plan Funding Estimates

Fiscal Year (in $ millions)	1995/96 Budget	1996/97 Target	1997/98 Target	1998/99 Target
Public and Separate School Board Funding, Including ECS*	2,733	2,750	2,808	2,814
Private Schools and Private ECS	45	50	52	53
Departmental Operations	49	46	44	39
Other	18	17	17	17
Total Spending on Education	2,845	2,863	2,921	2,923
Less Opted-out School Boards	(140)	(164)	(165)	(168)
Total Ministry Spending	2,705	2,699	2,756	2,755

* Includes opted-out schools, contributions to the Teachers' Retirement Fund, and the Learning Resource Distribution Centre (LRDC) and Material Resource Centre (MRC) subsidies.
** Includes LRDC revolving fund and Premier's Council on the Status of Persons with Disabilities.

On the surface it appears that education spending is increasing, but what's missing from this picture? First of all, the table provides aggregate spending but does not make any sort of adjustment for enrollment increases. In a telephone conversation with the communications officer from Alberta Education, I was told that Alberta Education expects a yearly increase in enrollment of two percent. Furthermore, the inflation rate as measured by the Consumer Price Index was 1.6 percent last year. When these factors are taken into account, per-student expenditures in real dollars are actually decreasing over the 1996-1999 period! This table also promotes a form of historical amnesia since it does not provide the reader with any way of comparing these spending levels to prior spending levels. As the next section demonstrates, education spending during Klein's first term decreased from previous Lougheed and Getty periods.

Klein's First Term

"Alberta's education system has turned the corner. The reductions are behind us. Education will reap the benefits of the province's fiscal restraint policies." — Halvar Jonson, then Minister of Education[3]

As the preceding section suggests, it is necessary to examine historical education funding patterns in order to assess the current government's emphasis on education. Graph 6.1 and Table 6.2 show per-student spending on education (in constant dollars) from 1980/81 until the present. For exposition purposes, I have divided the data into four distinct periods: the Lougheed years (1980-85), the Getty era (1986-92), first-term Klein (1993-97), and second-term Klein (1998-2000). The presumption is that the Lougheed government set the spending levels until the year March 1986, Getty to the year ending March 1993, and first-term Klein to March 1997.

Graph 6.1: Per-Student Spending on Public Education[4]

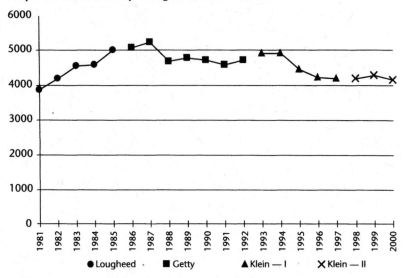

● Lougheed · ■ Getty ▲ Klein — I ✕ Klein — II

Table 6.2: Enrollment, Funding and Per-Student Spending[5]

Year (ending March 31)	Enrollment[6]	Funding (in millions)	Current $	Consumer Price Index	Constant $[7]
1981	422,370 (a)	1064 (a)	2591	67.2	3856
1982	425,011 (a)	1340 (a)	3154	75.5	4177
1983	428,865 (a)	1629 (a)	3799	83.7	4539
1984	433,616 (a)	1751 (a)	4038	88.5	4563
1985	432640 (a)	1992 (c)	4603	92.4	4982
1986	435,312 (a)	2109 (c)	4844	96.0	5046
1987	423,372 (b)	2214 (c)	5229	100	5229
1988	455,990 (b)	2223 (c)	4876	104.4	4670
1989	464,585 (b)	2408 (c)	5182	108.6	4772
1990	474,373 (b)	2536 (c)	5346	114.0	4690
1991	486,612 (b)	2661 (c)	5469	119.5	4577
1992	464,421 (b)	2810 (c)	6051	126.2	4695
1993	475,013 (b)	2979 (c)	6271	128.1	4896
1994	481,296 (b)	3074 (c)	6387	130.4	4898
1995	479,074 (b)	2779 (d)	5801	130.7	4438
1996	487,164 (b)	2733 (f, e)	5610	133.5	4202
1997	489352 (b)	2782 (f, e)	5685	135.6	4193
1998	499139 (d, e)	2875 (f, e)	5760	137.8	4181
1999	509122 (d, e)	3058 (f, g, e)[8]	6006	140.0	4291
2000	519304 (d, e)	3078 (f, g, e)	5927	142.2	4168

The figures and numbers contained in the preceding graph and table paint a grim picture of education funding during Premier Klein's first mandate. While government pundits will argue that the decision to centralize education funding during this period allowed the provincial government to eliminate funding disparities amongst rural and urban school boards, it also allowed the government to slash per-student spending on public education.

The value placed on public education during Klein's first term certainly represents a change from previous conservative governments, which appeared to value a strong public education system. Per-student spending during both the Lougheed years under consideration and the subsequent Getty years exceeded per-student spending during Klein's first term (see Table 6.3).

Table 6.3: Comparison of Per-Student Spending: Lougheed, Getty, Klein

	Average Per-Student Spending	Direction of Spending Change over Period
Lougheed Years	$4,527	+30.9%
Getty Years	$4,804	-6.3%
Klein Years, first term	$4,382	-14.6%

Interestingly, over this same period, Albertans were inundated with the message that competing in the global economy was critical and that "education for economic prosperity" was a key goal. As the actual funding levels demonstrate, however, there appears to be a disjuncture between public rhetoric and the concrete actions taken by government politicians.

The Return of Santa: "Re-investing" in Public Education

"Our first priority in education is our students. Alberta's young people must be the best-educated in Canada, able to achieve their individual potential and contribute to Alberta's prosperity and superior quality of life." These are the words of Gary Mar, current Minister of Education. On January 9, 1998, Mar held a press conference to announce the government's plan to re-invest in education. He stated that the government's re-investment plan ensured that Alberta's youngest citizens would be able to fulfill their potential and that the government would make "people development" (see chapter three) its number-one priority. Once again, however, we must ask whether this is simply rhetoric or whether the re-investment plan demonstrates a commitment to adequately fund public education?

The numbers for 1988/1999 in Table 6.3 show, as a consequence of this re-investment announcement, projected per-student spending increasing for first time since the Klein government was elected in 1993. However, this is a one-time jump! Projected per-student spending in 1999/2000 again dips below 1997/98 per-student levels. Furthermore, 1998/99 per-student levels are still twelve percent less than when the Klein government took office. In other words, these re-investment announcements do not fundamentally change per-student spending levels. Aside from a one-year blip, per-student spending levels will have declined in six of seven years of the Klein government's term in office.

In his re-investment announcement, the Minister of Education suggested that Alberta's youth must be the best-educated in Canada, presumably for reasons of economic competitiveness. But certainly the Minister was aware of provincial per-student spending comparisons (published by Statistics Canada), which show Alberta's lagging spending performance. One should perhaps ask teachers, parents, and school administrators whether Alberta's youth are likely to get this "superior" education given the depleted levels of funding in Alberta?

As Table 6.4 (below) indicates, Alberta's per-student spending on public education falls below the national average, with five of ten provinces spending more on public education than Alberta. Quebec, Ontario, British Columbia, and Manitoba spend, on average, fourteen percent more per student on public education than does Alberta. Note also that this group contains provinces with both larger and smaller populations and varied rural/urban mixes, making it difficult to argue that Alberta possesses superior economies of scale. If one believes the results of economic studies which demonstrate the positive association

Table 6.4: Provincial Per-Student Funding Levels (nominal dollars)[9]

	1993/94	1994/95	1995/96	1996/97
Quebec	6,946	7,078	7,129	7,032
British Columbia	6,509	6,504	6,817	6,882
Ontario	7,050	6,857	6,833	6,649
Manitoba	6,472	6,481	6,576	6,620
New Brunswick	5,842	5,940	5,973	6,156
Canadian Average	6,066	6,022	6,020	6,045
Alberta	5,998	5,845	5,826	5,848
Saskatchewan	5,399	5,515	5,653	5,637
Nova Scotia	5,635	5,648	5,480	5,366
Prince Edward Island	5,467	5,250	4,901	5,148
Newfoundland	5,247	5,100	5,040	5,108

between resource inputs and outcomes, it is difficult to contemplate how Alberta Education could be providing the best education of any of the Canadian provinces given the noted funding discrepancies.

■ ■ ■

"Over the coming years, we will assess the impact of these 12 initiatives to make sure they are achieving the results we expect. We will add any new ideas and adjust the priorities to build in new approaches wherever necessary. The details of this action plan will change to meet changing needs, but the simple commitment will remain — *First things first . . . our children.*"[10]

Alberta is a rich province. Our natural-resource wealth has provided us with an unique ability to invest in the health and educational futures of all Albertans. Yet despite rhetoric and hyperbole to the contrary, the provincial government continues to short-change Alberta's youth. The preceding analysis has demonstrated three incontestable facts: 1) per-student funding for public education during Premier Klein's first term was less than during the preceding Lougheed and Getty periods; 2) the re-investment initiatives announced in January 1998 do not reverse the trend of declining per-student funding; and 3) per-student funding in Alberta is below the Canadian average, making it difficult to argue that Alberta's youth will receive a superior education.

While this chapter has not examined the implications of these funding decreases at the individual school and student level, the chapters that follow detail some of the consequences of this decreased funding upon students, teachers, and school administrators. Clearly, decreased funding has affected the ability of the public education system to provide a quality education for all students.

It is true that, under the current policy of education funding, the provincial debt will be paid off quickly. It is also true that with decreased spending on public education, it will be possible to lower taxes and reward those high-income earners who tend to benefit from such policies — ironically, these are many of the same people who benefitted from Alberta's previous education system. But let's not pretend to care about the education and future of Alberta's youth. Caring is demonstrated by adequate funding, not by public-relations campaigns.

Of course, the counter-argument is always that we cannot afford such an extravagant education system. However, as the following table (Table 6.5) indicates, restoring per-student funding levels would barely dent Alberta's burgeoning surplus. Restoring per-student funding to the average level of funding during the combined Lougheed and Getty periods ($4,600 in constant 1986 dollars) would cost the province less than $300 million annually. Under such a funding regime, the actual surplus would have been $873 million in 1995/96, $2.26 billion in 1996/97, and the projected surplus for 1997/98 would be $2.41 billion. Clearly, such spending is affordable given the financial health of the province.

Table 6.5: The Affordability of Public Education[11]

	1995/96	1996/97	1997/98
Enrollment	487,134	489,352	499,139
Target per-student spending (1986 constant dollars)	$4,600	$4,600	$4,600
Target spending in nominal dollars (after adjusting for CPI changes)	$6,141	$6,238	$6,337
Target total spending (nominal dollars)*	$2.99B	$3.05B	$3.16B
Actual spending	$2.73B	$2.78B	$2.88B
Spending Increase needed	$259M	$270M	$288M
Provincial Surplus before extra education spending	$1.13B	$2.53B	$2.7B
Adjusted Provincial Surplus	$873M	$2.26B	$1.41B (e)

*Numbers in the table may not add due to rounding errors.

Would this increase in funding result in Alberta's youth receiving the best education of any Canadian youth? If we return to Table 6.4, we see that the target spending of $6238 per student still falls below the amount spent by Quebec, British Columbia, Ontario, and Manitoba. However, the difference between the average spending of these provinces and Alberta would be approximately eight percent, down from the current fourteen-percent difference. While it doesn't appear that these funding increases would result in a "superior" education, at least the education received by Alberta's youth would be "average." Perhaps that's the best that we can hope for, given the current declining public-education funding levels that I have documented. In closing, if we truly believe that our children come first, restoring funding levels would be a nice way to prove it.

Notes

1 Government of Alberta press release "Education Re-investment part of New Education Plan," 9 January 1998.

2 Alberta Education, *Meeting the Challenge III, Three-Year Business Plan for Education, 1996/97–1998/99* (Edmonton, 1996). See also *Meeting the Challenge IV, Three-Year Business Plan for Education in Alberta, 1997/98–1999/2000* (Edmonton, 1997).

3 *Meeting the Challenge IV.*

4 The figures here are taken from the constant-dollar figures shown in the final column of Table 4.2.

5 This table is constructed from several sources: (a) Decore and Pannu, "Alberta political economy in crisis: wither education" in *Hitting the Books,* Terry Wotherspoon, ed. (Toronto: Garamond Press, 1991), 75-97; (b) Alberta Private School Funding Taskforce, *Funding Private Schools in Alberta: Part 1* (Edmonton, 1997); (c) Statistics Canada, *Advance Statistics of Education* #81-220; and *Education in Canada,* #81-229; (d) Alberta Education communication officers; (e) estimate; (f) *Meeting the Challenge III* and *Meeting the Challenge IV*; (g) Alberta Education, *Education Re-investment.*

6 Enrollment numbers do not include ECS enrollments, although the funding numbers include ECS funding. As a result of this, per-student spending numbers overestimate spending by somewhere between $0 and $100. In the interests of comparability, I have not attempted to adjust for this.

7 The constant dollar-per-student spending numbers reported here differ slightly from those reported by Decore and Pannu. In reviewing the two data sets, this difference appears to be the result of differing sources of enrollment numbers. The historical per-student funding trends do not differ between the two data sets.

8 On January 8, 1998, the Education Minister announced $380M of new funding applicable to the fiscal years ending March 1999-2001. As of February 10, 1998, Alberta Education was unable to provide me with a per-year spending breakdown. Thus, in Table 2 I have assumed that thirty-three percent of this new funding is applicable to each of the three fiscal years ($127M per year).

9 Data for this table are taken from Statistics Canada, *Education Quarterly Review,* #81-003 and *Education Quarterly Review* 3:2.

10 Alberta Government, Reinvestment announcement, January 9, 1998.

11 Enrollment and actual spending numbers are from Table 2; provincial surplus numbers from the Alberta Treasury [on-line]. Available at http://www.treas.gov.ab.ca.

7

Deep and Brutal: Funding Cuts to Education in Alberta

Frank Peters

Our priority as a government is to enhance the quality of education even during these difficult financial times. Meeting the future needs of our children requires a radical change to the governance and delivery of education.
— Alberta Education[1]

In a press release on January 18, 1994, Halvar Jonson, then Minister of Education, officially presented to the public his government's proposal for restructuring Alberta education. The release reminded Albertans that the government was merely following up on the results of its extensive consultation process, while further asserting that "quality education, fiscal equity, accountability, and cost control were the essential considerations in determining future direction for education in the province." In keeping with these four aims, the government proposed considerable changes related to five different aspects of education: the governing structures, the fiscal structures, school management, school programs, and charter schools. While not unrelated, these five areas are sufficiently discrete to allow for an examination of the restructuring endeavors under one or more of the headings. This chapter examines the changes to the fiscal structures relating to education, proposed in January 1994 and since implemented.

Background

Prior to the provincial election in Alberta in June 1993, the Conservatives and the Liberals both warned the electorate that they would face either "deep" or "brutal" cuts, depending on which party was elected. The Conservatives, under Premier Ralph Klein, received a reasonably strong mandate in the election on June 15, winning fifty-one of eighty-three seats. Despite receiving only forty-four percent of the popular vote, the Tories adopted a governing style commensurate with a far bigger support base and have continued to rationalize their actions with explanations that they are obeying the wishes of the province's entire population. Public pronouncements have been, and continue to be, liberally peppered with phrases such as, "Albertans are telling us . . .," "acting on your instructions . . .," "you told us . . . we have heard you," "Talk to us . . . ." The use of such phrases reflects a government confident of its ability to manufacture the support required for all of its initiatives (see chapter five).

By 1993, the idea that social spending was completely out of control in Canada was part of the ideological platform of Conservative and Liberal parties throughout the country. More importantly, this idea was believed by many Canadians, despite the fact that, compared to the advanced countries of western and northern Europe, Canadian spending on social security (and social spending in general) falls far behind other developed countries and only slightly ahead of the United States.[2] Buoyed by this public belief, which they had a part in creating, governments at both provincial and federal levels in Canada adopted and implemented policies committed to the elimination of debts and deficits. Education, health, and welfare were the expenditure areas most easily and most forcefully targeted.

The government of Alberta incorporated the major elements of changes to the financing of education into a larger overall restructuring of the governing framework of education. Independent of the reduction in money provided to school systems, this new framework saw a reduction in the number of provincial school boards by well over 50 percent, from 141 to about 63 (see chapter twelve). Initial estimates from the Alberta School Boards' Association (ASBA) indicated that the government hoped to save as much as $20 million from this reduction. More conservative estimates, however, were put forward by Alberta Education. The ministry first suggested a possible saving of about $13.5 million, but later, in an affidavit to the courts,[3] it provided the figure of about $12.9 million per annum savings and acknowledged that these savings might come more slowly than anticipated, as contractual obligations and buy-outs were negotiated with surplus staff.

The province also removed from school boards the right to collect a component of the property tax for educational purposes, a right which school jurisdictions had exercised since before Alberta became a province. Further, significant changes were introduced related to the appointment of school-system superintendents. The government proposed a substantial reduction in the number of people employed by the ministry of education, and — as I detail in a following section — initiated a forty-percent reduction in positions over a four-year period.

There is little doubt in the minds of educators in Alberta that the compelling ideology behind the government restructuring was financial in nature and had nothing to do with the improvement of learning or the enhancement of teaching. Decisions to cap administration expenditures and to change superintendents' contracts, although justified by government announcements as responses to calls for greater accountability, were made in the context of the more sweeping decision to spend less money on education. The salary rollbacks and grant cuts, which I document later, were more obvious in their intent. But all the changes were driven not by organizational or educational imperative, but by the fundamental decision to spend less money. The government's unswerving commitment to reduce expenditures changed education's fiscal arrangements in three main areas: responsibility for funding, expenditure control, and reduction in grants.

Responsibility

The assumption of full funding of school boards by the provincial government, effective September 1, 1995, was a major departure in Alberta. In 1994, half of the provinces in Canada permitted school boards to raise a significant portion of their revenue from local taxes on property. In its restructuring, the Alberta government moved away from this system, which had been in place since 1961, and adopted a structure whereby all school boards are funded by the province from general revenue and the province applies a uniform provincial tax on residential, farm, commercial, and industrial property.

This system of funding is seen by many as providing for greater equity across the province. School trustees and ministry officials alike acknowledged that the previous system had one large and apparently insurmountable problem: the massive variation in the assessed value of corporate, residential, and industrial property in differing school jurisdictions. These variations led to substantial differences in the fiscal effort required in different jurisdictions to generate comparable amounts of money on a per-student basis. Moreover, despite these efforts — and despite the need to impose extremely high tax burdens in many jurisdictions — the amount of money available to school systems varied substantially across the province. The changes to educational funding have considerably reduced the huge differences in the amount of money available to school boards on a per-student basis and have put in place a more equitable funding system.

In 1992/93, the differences in expenditure per student in different school jurisdictions ranged from a low of $3,663 to a high of $22,582. By 1997/98, it is estimated that this range will be compacted to a low of $5,312 and a high of $12,900. Alberta Education does caution, however, that these estimated figures are generally lower than the "actual" figures produced in the audited financial statements. This last figure may in fact distort the general picture across the province. Northland School Division, by virtue of its unique circumstances, will always be required to spend more money per student than other school systems. This jurisdiction provides educational services to twenty-five isolated, and predominantly aboriginal, communities in northern Alberta. Its small schools have low teacher/pupil ratios and increased costs for maintenance and supplies. The contraction, however, is even more notable in that the highest-spending jurisdiction in 1992 was not the Northland school system but Berry Creek School Division, a resource-rich jurisdiction that is now part of a larger school division. Although the new system may be more equitable, it is not without problems, as we shall see.

When the province announced its intention to withdraw taxing authority from school boards, a number of Catholic boards, led by the Calgary Catholic School Board, claimed that they had a constitutional right to collect educational taxes from their own supporters. Rather than engage in what could have become a protracted and costly legal wrangle, the province amended its legislation to permit denominational school systems to opt out of the centralized funding arrangement and to continue to collect property taxes from their own supporters, although from a much narrower and more legalistically defined base than was available in 1993. In no case is a board permitted to raise more money by means of local taxation than it could receive from the centralized funding system. This choice of opting out was not made available to the non-denominational public school systems, which educate about seventy-five percent of the province's students.

In an unprecedented move, all school boards in the province challenged the extent of the provincial restructuring of education. They claimed that the restructurings, taken as a whole, deprived the school boards of an implicit constitutional right to a reasonable amount of local autonomy. While the initial judicial decision rejected the constitutional claim, the court did indicate that the provincial government had discriminated inappropriately against non-denominational school boards in not permitting them to collect a portion of their revenue by means of local taxation, when they had granted this option to the denominational or separate school boards. The provincial government's appeal of this decision was upheld by the Alberta Court of Appeal in March 1998, but it appears that the Public School Boards Association of Alberta will now seek leave from the Supreme Court to appeal this judgement.

Control

The provincial government increased its control over how education dollars are spent by introducing a funding scheme whereby money is provided to school boards in the form of three block grants: the instructional block, the support block, and the capital block. Each block is comprised of several components and government regulations permit only limited transfer of funds within and between blocks. This effectively prevents school boards from using the funds for purposes other than those intended by the province. The instruction block is the hub of the entire funding system. School boards receive a grant of $3,860 for each student in elementary and junior-high school in the system. (This figure will increase by one percent in 1999 and again the following year, bringing the grant to $3,937 by September 2000). School systems receive funds for high-school students in accordance with the number of credits in which the students are enrolled and considered to have completed successfully. The instruction block is also the source of money relating to home education, learning resources, early childhood education, and special instruction.

The support block consists of three components: plant operation and maintenance, board governance and system administration, and student transportation. The grant relating to plant operation and maintenance is based again on the number of students in the system, as well as on the size of the schools. The governance and administration grant for approximately one-third of the systems in Alberta is four percent of the sum of the instruction block and the two other components of the support block. This is the amount available to all boards with enrollments of over 6,000 students. If the total enrollment is under 2,000, the board receives six percent of the total mentioned above, and in jurisdictions with enrollments between 2,000 and 6,000, the administrative allocation is calculated on a sliding scale between four and six percent. Almost two-thirds of all Alberta school jurisdictions fall below the enrollment figure of 6,000. The final block provides money for capital expenditures relating to school building projects and debt servicing on existing school buildings.

In essence, a school jurisdiction can transfer monies from any component of the support block to the instruction block and can transfer up to two percent of the instruction block to plant maintenance and operations or to the transportation components of the support block. Boards cannot transfer any money into the board governance and system administration component of the support block, nor can they move money into or out of the capital block. The system of block funding severely limits a school board's discretion in allocating resources to meet identified local priorities. The money received in grants must be spent in those areas the government has identified.

Cuts

In the news release of January 18, 1994, the minister of education announced an overall reduction in education spending of $239 million, or 12.4 percent, over the 4-year period from 1993/94 to 1996/97. Given the January 1994 date of the announcement, it is interesting to see the government use the 1993/94 year as the beginning date for the decrease. By doing so, it was able to conceal the fact that the actual cut to education amounted to 15.6 percent. (As Neu shows in chapter six, the real cut was actually much worse if inflation and population growth are taken into account.) At the start of the 1993/94 school year, the government provided a 2.2 percent increase to education funding, an increase which, in practice, became part of the base from which school boards had to work in calculating the depth to which they had to cut to meet government demands. This increase was announced in the spring of 1993, just prior to the June election that resulted in the Klein government's first mandate. Within less than twelve months, however, the same government not only removed the 2.2 percent increase, but also imposed extra cuts. As much as forty-three percent of the 1994/95 cut in education was met through salary rollbacks imposed on all educators throughout the province.[4]

These rollbacks were announced in November 1993 and applied to all working in public-sector positions in the province. Their first effect was felt in education in April 1994, when a 5.6 percent reduction in School Foundation Program Fund grants was imposed on all school boards. This was "equivalent to a 5.0% reduction in salaries and benefits in education."[5] In its announcements regarding the reductions in public-sector compensation on November 24, 1993, the government indicated that it had considered four different options while trying to settle on a means of reducing the province's share of the human-resources budget by five percent. They decided to reduce funding for the various sectors by five percent and permit the sectors to determine how best to structure the specific reductions. An announcement from Alberta Education indicated that this specific intervention would reduce government education spending by $64 million in the next year. Incredibly, the announcement stated that, while the five percent cut would significantly reduce education spending, there would be minimal impact on the classrooms, education programs and students of Alberta!

These cuts to salaries have remained in place for the past four years, and it is only with the most recent contract settlements that some recovery of these forfeited monies is being realized. The most forceful protest against the delay in restoring some of the rollbacks came in the Calgary Public School District, where teachers adopted a work-to-rule position at the start of the 1997/98 school year, in an attempt to force the school board to restore some of the foregone earnings. This impasse was resolved only in December 1997, and the resolution is due, in part, to a clause in the new contract which will offer an extremely generous early-retirement package for experienced, more expensive teachers. This approach may save the board money in the long term, because it will be able to hire younger, cheaper, less experienced teachers as replacements[6] (see chapter eleven). While such a move may indicate wonderful confidence in younger teachers, it may also have repercussions on student learning, as many older, more experienced teachers will no longer be available, deemed too costly a commodity.

As threatened strikes by teachers in Calgary and Edmonton throughout 1997/98 attest, the issues of salaries, benefits, and foregone earnings will continue to occupy a prominent position for some time. Approximately eighty percent of the contracts between boards and teachers are due to be renegotiated in 1998, and a number of those that have recently been settled are scheduled to re-open immediately for another round! It is not clear that the money which the government is talking about re-investing in education will be sufficient to meet the increasing demands of the educators.[7]

The specific tactic of requiring each service sector to find ways of imposing the cuts permitted the government and its ministers to say, when the questions were asked, that they were not the ones imposing the layoffs. The decisions were being made in the hospitals or in the school systems. These sectors, as one commentator pointed out, were being given far less money but were "left free to decide what they could no longer afford."[8]

November 24, 1993 also saw the deferral of ninety-one construction projects planned for the period 1993 to 1996. The total cost of these projects was estimated to be $100.3 million, and the deferral resulted in an additional saving through a reduction of $20.8 million in debenture payments. The response that "Albertans have told us . . . " was used by the minister of education to justify the initiative. The move, he said, would enable the government to "reduce spending while maintaining the quality of education." At present, 60 percent of the province's schools are 25 years of age or older; "by 2007, 84 percent of schools" in Alberta will have reached this age. More importantly, however, "a lot of the components within these buildings have already reached their life expectancy."[9] These statements suggest that some infusion of the dollars approved under the School Capital Funding Plan for 1991-95 and withdrawn in 1993 might have been beneficial and ultimately might have resulted in lower overall expenditures than are now required to correct the drastically advanced problems evident in a large number of school buildings. In terms of capital expenditures and physical structures in our educational system, we are on the edge of a crisis. The announcement by the Minister of Education on September 11, 1998[10]that $82 million would be made available for school capital spending in 1999-2000 was greeted with both pleasure and disappointment by school boards. There was satisfaction that the government had apparently acknowledged the existence of a facilities problem but discomfort that there was no firm commitment to assisting boards to alleviate these problems. The ministerial announcement, prefaced with the comment that "we have heard Albertans' views on the future of our school facilities," accepted in principle the policy recommendations of the School Facilities Task Force. However the two fiscal recommendations from the committee were deferred "to be dealt with as part of the government's overall fiscal plan."

One of the more contentious areas from which money was cut by government edict was Early Childhood Services (ECS), or kindergarten. Here, government grants were initially to be cut in half, although school boards were permitted to continue to provide full service if they could find the money from other sources. ECS special-needs grants were not reduced as forcefully, and in some areas were increased slightly to provide for children who were "disadvantaged by socio-economic circumstances." Funding for transportation of children attending regular ECS programs was eliminated entirely. Following widespread protests over the proposed funding changes in this area, the government adjusted the depth of the cut and agreed to fund 240 of a total of 400 hours. Then in September 1996, with little or no fanfare, the government did a complete about-face on this matter. ECS again became "fully" funded. (However, the hour/ grant funding ratio in 1995/96 was $3.54 per hour, while in 1996/97 this actually dropped to $2.96 per hour.)[11] Neither the initial reduction in funding nor the subsequent restorations of grants were accompanied by any compelling pedagogical rationale. In announcing the restoration of full funding, the minister of education referred to the concern with the variation in the number of hours of ECS programming among school jurisdictions. He also indicated that "because of the high fees being charged by some boards for ECS programs, there is a risk some Alberta children would be placed at an educational disadvantage." It is puzzling that nobody anticipated these outcomes when the decision to cut in this area was initially considered.

Funds were also reduced in the area of school food services, native education programs, and general transportation, while funding for community schools was abolished entirely. There was a reduction, too, in the grants to private or independent schools.

In its initial restructuring announcements, the government indicated the intention to reduce the number of people employed by the ministry of education. This reduction has been made. There has been a considerable reduction in the services provided through the ministry to students, schools, and school systems. The total costs of all services delivered by the Department of Education have dropped from $56.4 million in 1992/ 93 to $46.5 million in 1996/97; a further decline to $39.3 million is expected in 1998-99. This overall decrease in expenditures of over 30 percent in service delivery represents a decline from an expenditure of $115 per student in 1992/93 to $90 per student in 1996/97; further declines to an estimated $82 per student for the school year 1997-98 and $81 for 1998/ 99 are expected. At the same time, the number of persons employed (on a full-time equivalent basis) by Alberta Education declined from 863 in 1992/93 to 518 at the end of March 1997 and down to 358 by March 1998,[12] a reduction of almost 60 percent! Indeed, the premier is able to boast that the government is now a third smaller than it was in 1993,[13] without saying anything about the services that it no longer provides or about those many services that have been privatized but which nonetheless operate under government mandate and regulation. At the same time as these reductions were being implemented, schools and school systems were also coping with substantial reductions in funding and consequently were unable to compensate for the decline in services that had previously been available. The government's position is that it has accomplished Goal #8 — "Alberta Education is managed effectively and efficiently to achieve government goals" — because the expenditures on department services have decreased and the number of people in the ministry has been reduced!

Schools also faced increased pressures arising out of other government initiatives. For example, many adults — parents of school students — were affected by factors such as downsizing and uncertainties in the job market and by government policies that resulted in reductions to social assistance and unemployment benefits for many marginalized families. Many of these social and work-related upheavals resulted in increased demands for services in the schools, services which the schools were incapable of providing, because of reductions in their own resources.

Commentary

One can only describe reactions to the Klein government's cuts to education as civilized to a surprising degree. While there have been protests against particular initiatives (such as the cuts to ECS) and predictable objections from the Alberta Teachers' Association (ATA) and the province's three school trustees' organizations, there has been no sustained public opposition capable of producing any significant changes in government policy. Indeed, the ATA, an organization which has assiduously refused to throw its official support behind any particular political party, has been criticized for not being more militant and more vociferous in opposing certain aspects of the government's restructurings.[14] A very large protest by teachers in the fall of 1997, following more than three years of unremitting restraint and cost cutting, was surprisingly free of bitterness or shrillness. The crowd, variously estimated at anywhere between 10,000 and 20,000, chanted, applauded, and listened, but behaved, above all, in a polite, dignified, and restrained manner. The studied, proper, patient protest by the educators of Alberta was a powerful exercise in democratic opposition. And yet it does not appear to have brought about many tangible results (see chapter ten).

The government, prior to its re-election in 1993, indicated that it intended to implement a demanding fiscal plan that would substantially cut every government-funded service in the province. It held to that plan and is now able to boast about their success. At the same time, the premier and government ministers insist there will be no returning to the apparently uncontrolled spending which they claim characterized previous governments.[15] The province, Albertans are warned, still has a debt to pay off, although this debt is supported by assets such as the Heritage Savings Trust Fund. Despite these warnings, it seems that the obsession with debt and deficit reduction, which underpinned virtually every government initiative of the past four years, may be waning. There are now plans in place to "re-invest" in those very same activities and services which only a few years ago received brutal and savage treatment in the name of putting our financial house in order.

Faced with the findings that Alberta now spends less money per student than all US jurisdictions and most Canadian provinces, Alberta Education has responded that spending and quality of education cannot be directly linked. Only the relatively low-income provinces of

Newfoundland, Nova Scotia, and Prince Edward Island (see chapter six) spent less per student in 1996/97 than did Alberta. And since 1985/86, Alberta alone among the Canadian provinces showed a decline in the real dollars spent, per pupil, in education. In terms of the 1985/86 dollars, Alberta expenditures per student had declined by 8.5 percent by 1996/97, while all other provinces had increased their expenditures by between 2.4 and 21.4 percent.[16] However, the ministry responded to these revelations by drawing attention to how well Alberta students have done on the Third International Math and Science Study tests and on the national School Achievement Indicators Program tests, where they have consistently outperformed many of their Canadian counterparts.

There is, however, one major problem with this argument. While the tests referred to were written in the 1994/95 school year, the learning the students acquired as preparation for their test performances was accumulated over their previous years in school, years when Alberta ranked notably higher than today in terms of per-student expenditures in education.[17] It is misleading to suggest — as the Department has — that the cuts to education are having no negative effects on student learning. Given the cumulative effects associated with learning and with growth, it is simply too soon to make any definitive judgements about the effect of the spending reductions to education on student learning. The cuts have resulted in a reduction of services to students, increased crowding in classrooms, and a widespread perception by teachers that their jobs are more stressful and less rewarding. On this basis, we should not be surprised if student performance diminishes in the years ahead.

The cavalier manner in which the government dismissed the findings of a 1996 ATA survey[18] gives further indication that the government holds little, if any, regard for evidence that fails to support the promulgated, official position. The study, conducted in April 1996, was triggered by Premier Klein's comment in his January 1996 "PC Talk" that education was "the good news story" of his restructuring program. The ATA survey elicited a surprisingly high response rate from more than 10,500 Alberta teachers in over 70 percent of all public and separate schools. The responses pointed to deteriorating conditions in the classrooms, more students in the classrooms, less teacher time for individual students, and a general decline in overall satisfaction of teachers as a result of the changes imposed by government. Over eighty percent of respondents felt that the changes had had a negative impact on students, while almost ninety-five percent saw them as negative for teachers. Yet the minister of education and the premier dismissed the study findings.

Alberta has been singularly successful in reducing its provincial debt and in adjusting its budget, to the degree that a surplus of $2.2 billion was reported for 1997/98. The Alberta economy grew by 5.5 percent during that time. A large part of Alberta's economic recovery is attributed by the Klein government to the steadfast manner in which it stuck to its program of cuts and expenditure control throughout 1993-97. *The Economist* told Canadians that Premier Klein was "Canada's pioneer of lean, mean government,"[19] and one author credited him with teaching Canadian politicians to "go fast, hit hard and don't blink."[20] However, some people argue that much of Alberta's fiscal success is linked to the unanticipated high price, on global markets, of the province's natural resources, rather than the slashing and chopping of the government (also see chapters three and six).[21] Given the latter good fortune, it is appropriate to ask whether the former bone-scraping surgery was really needed in order to restore fiscal control. Could it be that Albertans during this period were victims of what George Grant once termed "decisiveness . . . at the expense of thoughtfulness"?[22]

When the Klein government outlined its plan to eliminate the provincial deficit in 1993, it projected a balanced budget by 1996/97. The fanfare and high visibility associated with Premier Klein and his government's activities overshadowed the fact that, in early 1995, six other provinces projected balanced budgets for 1995/96, a year ahead of Alberta's initial projection. As it turned out, huge revenue gains in Alberta produced the balanced budget as early as 1994/95, although creative tinkering with tax and resource revenues allowed the government to postpone the announcement of this breakthrough until early 1996. Yet, even two years later, there is considerable concern about deteriorating provincial services, particularly in the areas of education, health, and social services.[23] In 1996, Alberta provided the lowest level of public service in Canada. The Alberta government spends "at least 15 percent less per person than the lowest spending 'have not' province and more like 20 to 25 percent less than the balanced budget provinces overall when provincial expenditures are placed in more fully comparable terms."[24] This level of expenditure cannot be explained by a low fiscal capacity. Quite the contrary: Alberta's tax and other revenue bases are the largest of any province, yet Alberta's per capita taxes are still the lowest in the country. Rather, one is forced to conclude that Alberta's occupation of "the basement of Canadian provincial government services"[25] have been imposed exclusively by adherence to a particular political ideology and not by present-day fiscal realities (see chapter five). Nor does the announcement of the 1998/99 budget indicate any inclination to change this situation by injecting substantial monies into service areas. As Neu shows in chapter six, the "new" money going into education will not keep up with increases in Alberta's population and the cost of living. In short, while there has been very modest "re-investment" in services in this province within the past two years, there is nothing to suggest that the government intends to remedy the injuries caused by previous cuts and which may yet lead to irreparable harm to the province's educational and social structures.

■ ■ ■

There is a growing awareness among Albertans that the deep and brutal cuts imposed on education in the last four years have done considerable harm. Among teachers, there is increasing tension related to contract negotiations, with demands that new contracts provide early-retirement incentives and bonuses — surely an indication of a desire by senior teachers to get out of an increasingly stressful, thankless, and devalued occupation. And the tension is unlikely to be lessened by knowledge of burgeoning government surpluses and financial rewards for Alberta's top public servants for "helping the provincial government achieve its financial targets."

There also is a growing realization that the popular government challenge of the last four years to "find a new way of doing things"[26] — this line, or something similar, has been thrown out nearly every time new financial cuts have been imposed — is a wholly unattainable goal unless it is accompanied by a fresh and substantial infusion of funds. The 1998/99 budget, containing spending increases of $380 million — spread over three years — falls well short of what is needed. Spending on education continues to decline in real terms (see chapter six).

Creativity alone will not solve any of the challenges presented by the ASBA Task Force on special-needs students.[27] Nor will creativity satisfy the demands of an underpaid, overstressed teaching force, which sees itself as undervalued. Creativity without resources will not repair or renew malfunctioning infrastructure. Creativity will not replace many of those services which are so essential for the support of the classroom teacher and the learning activity and which, because of the removal of financial resources, disappeared in the mists of restructuring and downsizing (see chapters eleven, twelve, and thirteen).

Unfortunately, there is no indication that the Klein government intends to take the action needed to stop the pain brought about by the brutal and deep cuts it has inflicted on education in recent years. Government announcements regarding education are akin to entrusting ourselves to faith healers, a practice many of us rightfully look on with some degree of skepticism. Likewise, we are wary of the dangers and the emptiness of faith unaccompanied by acts of good works.

Irrespective, however, of whether the cuts visited upon education were needed at all, whether they were unnecessarily severe, or whether their potential consequences were considered in any thorough manner, there is the broader question of the manner in which the changes were introduced and imposed. Some have suggested that Ontario's Harris government has used more draconian tactics than has Klein's administration;[28] this may be true. Nonetheless, any examination of the strategies used in Alberta to ensure compliance with the selected changes reveals a rigidity and a persistence that speaks more directly to power, force, and coercion than to democratic participation.

Notes

1 Government of Alberta press release, "Education Grants Announced," 18 January 1994.

2 See Linda McQuaig, *The Wealthy Banker's Wife: The Assault on Equality in Canada* (Toronto: Penguin, 1993), 15.

3 This information was provided in a factum from Alberta Education in the case of Public School Boards of Alberta v. Attorney General of Alberta, 1995 (Q.B.).

4 This information is found in R. Bosetti, *Meeting the Challenge: Alberta's Approach to Restructuring Education*, a paper presented to the Ontario Council for leadership in educational administration conference, Toronto, May 1994.

5 Alberta Education, press release, 18 January 1994.

6 See *Edmonton Journal*, 16 December 1997, A6.

7 See *Edmonton Journal*, 11 December 1997, B7.

8 Mark Lisac, *The Klein Revolution* (Edmonton: NeWest Press, 1995), 203.

9 ASBA, *Spectrum*, Fall 1997.

10 Alberta Education, press release, 11 September 1998.

11 Personal communication on May 27, 1998 with David Flower, Co-ordinator of Communications, Alberta Teachers' Association. In 1996/97, ATA staff officer Klaus Opatril used government figures and controlled for inflation and enrollments to get at the *actual* per capita ECS spending.

12 The numbers presented in this section have been taken from recent Annual Reports of Alberta Education. It should be noted that these numbers frequently create some confusion as different reports give different numbers when apparently reporting on precisely the same function or service.

13 Ralph Klein, *Agenda for Opportunity* television address, 8 January 1998.

14 V. Soucek and R. Pannu. "Globalizing education in Alberta" in *Our Schools/Our Selves*, S. Robertson and H. Smaller, eds. 48(5), Vol. 7 (1996).

15 Klein, *Agenda for Opportunity*.

16 See The Canadian Teachers' Federation *Economic Service Notes*, February 1997.

17 Alberta Education, *Alberta Education Review*, October 1997.

18 See the *ATA News*, 11 September 1996 and the ATA press release of the same day.

19 *The Economist*, 15 February 1998, 38.

20 I. Manji, *Risking Utopia* (Toronto: Douglas & McIntyre, 1997), 163.

21 See D. Cooper and D. Neu, "The politics of debt and deficit in Alberta" in *The Trojan Horse: Alberta and the Future of Canada*, Gordon Laxer and Trevor Harrison, eds. (Montréal, Black Rose Books, 1995); K. Taft, *Shredding the Public Interest* (Edmonton: University of Alberta Press/Parkland Institute, 1997).

22 The Grant quotation is found in Manji, 163.

23 For a thorough discussion of this topic see M.L. McMillan, *Leading the Way or Missing the Mark? The Klein Government's Fiscal Plan* (Edmonton: Western Centre for Economic Research, University of Alberta, 1996).

24 *Leading the Way or Missing the Mark?*, 14.

25 *Leading the Way or Missing the Mark?*, 15.

26 This particular phrase is attributed to Innisfail-Sylvan Lake MLA Gary Severtson in *Spectrum*, Fall 1997, in relation to school buildings.

27 *In the Balance . . . Meeting Special Needs Within Public Education*. Report of the Special Needs Task Force (Edmonton, Alberta School Boards Association, 1997).

28 See *Edmonton Journal*, 29 October 1997, A7.

8

From Boardroom to Classroom: School Reformers in Alberta[1]

Alison Taylor

Schools and universities are emerging as an increasingly important battleground for the struggle against corporate rule.
— Author Tony Clarke[2]

Between the fall of 1993 and the spring of 1995, Alberta was in the throes of what Edmonton journalist Mark Lisac describes as the "Klein Revolution." The government restructuring and cutbacks that characterized this revolution affected public education as much as other areas. While some of these changes were in the works before Ralph Klein took over as premier, the public became aware that something was happening when the government scheduled "public roundtables on education" in the fall of 1993. "Stakeholders" were selected to attend these meetings, held in Edmonton and Calgary, for the expressed purpose of advising the government on spending priorities and reforms. The budget was then released in early 1994 along with "business plans" for the various departments including education. Five MLA teams were established to implement different areas of the plan, including the amalgamation of school boards, centralization of funding, development of accountability and performance measures, clarification of roles and responsibilities, and discussion of business involvement and technology integration. Each team held its own "consultation process" and developed reports and recommendations between 1994 and 1996.

The re-election of Ralph Klein's government in March 1997 demands pause for thought. For those who were opposed to much of the restructuring and cutbacks, it is important to reflect on the first four Klein years and consider how the government "pulled it off." I suggest that educational reforms were not opposed to the extent one might expect largely because they were constructed as "populist," with little attention given to key players (see chapter four). Because reform groups and their proponents were not always visible, it appeared that consent for the reform agenda was won from the public rather than manufactured. In retrospect, it is important to look at who was saying what and why. The purpose of this paper is to interrupt the "common sense" by looking at some of the key players and their interests in public education.

What are the lessons for educators here and in other provinces? Several reforms in Alberta, such as the amalgamation of school boards and increased centralization through changes in funding and accountability mechanisms, have since been adopted in Ontario under the Harris government. There too, concerns have been raised about the extent of cutbacks to education funding and the potential for greater privatization of education.[3] In this chapter, I focus on certain groups and individuals who have been influential directly through their government lobbying efforts and indirectly through the establishment of brokering organizations that have facilitated greater business involvement in education at local levels and provided provincial policy-makers with reform models. I would expect that similar "business-in-education" networks have been instrumental in educational reform in other provinces.

Naming Names

In the winter of 1994, as the Klein government was releasing its first budget and restructuring plans, *Calgary Herald* education reporter Lisa Dempster wrote an unusually pointed article called "Inner circle re-draws classroom," in which she identified "individuals and groups who have helped the Alberta premier formulate the new way of thinking about education."[4] Dempster named former education minister Jim Dinning, Athabasca University business professor Stephen Murgatroyd, parent-reformer Joe Freedman, Alberta Chamber of Commerce president-elect John Ballheim, private-school spokesperson Gary Duthler, and the "parent" group Albertans for Quality Education.

I think Dempster was accurate in her documentation of influential people in educational reform. However, in this chapter, I rearrange and expand this list by focusing less on individuals and more on organizations that have arguably influenced the direction of educational reforms in Alberta since the early 1990s. Like Dempster's, my list includes Albertans for Quality Education and the Chamber of Commerce but also includes two less-visible groups: the Calgary Educational Partnership Foundation and the Science Alberta Foundation. The latter two groups arguably acted as "coordinating agencies" through which the interests of corporations could be furthered at both local and provincial policy-making levels.

Albertans for Quality Education

Dempster acknowledges the disproportionate representation of Albertans for Quality Education (AQE) in the government consultations that occurred in the fall of 1993: "[Albertans for Quality Education] represents about 325 parents, yet received four invitations to the provincial roundtables on education — twice the number as the Calgary Catholic board."[5] Furthermore, subsequent reforms introduced by the government corresponded quite closely to AQE recommendations in its 1993 position paper. The most obvious parallel is the AQE's request for the "implementation of new alternative education delivery systems such as charter schools."[6] In the spring of 1994, the government amended the School Act to allow for charter schools. AQE priorities also included increased parental involvement in schools and more accountability of schools "through the publishing of test results and other appropriate measures of effectiveness." The government subsequently mandated school councils and established an MLA team to develop an accountability framework and performance measures for schools. The three-year business plan for education also expanded the provincial testing program and required that school jurisdictions and schools report annually on student, school, and jurisdictional achievement. Newspapers in Calgary and Edmonton began reporting results of provincial tests on a school-by-school basis in the spring of 1996. The government's responsiveness to the AQE raises questions around who this group represents.

Dempster describes the AQE as "a grassroots group that advocates abandoning the current child-centred approach for a more traditional teacher-centred classroom."[7] But the AQE is more than a parent group. Their first newsletter in September 1993 describes the group thus:

> AQE was formed in March, 1993 to address growing concerns by parents, businessmen and educators that the quality of education in Alberta has declined to unacceptably low levels. One objective of this newsletter is to provide a voice for parents in Alberta.

This quotation acknowledges that members include businesspeople and educators as well as parents. It should be noted that while the AQE claimed to be a voice for parents in Alberta, approximately half of its members were located in Calgary. Further, the AQE is housed in the downtown Calgary location of a large corporation where one of the group's representatives is employed. Members of the AQE have sat on committees of the Chamber of Commerce. And finally, prominent reformer Joe Freedman is a supporter of this group.

Like the AQE, Freedman purports to represent dissatisfied parents but has demonstrated a remarkable ability to secure corporate support for his endeavours. He is the founder of the Society for Advancing Educational Research, which released a video entitled *Failing Grades: Canadian Schooling in a Global Economy* in early 1993. The financial backers for Freedman's reform video included "the Royal Bank, the Bank of Nova Scotia, Syncrude, [and] Kodak."[8] A few years before, Freedman had persuaded the Alberta Chamber of Resources (ACR) to provide financial support for a comparison of how Alberta schools rank with those in Japan, Germany, and Hungary. A report called "International Comparisons in Education" was then released by the ACR and Alberta Education in 1991.

The AQE also includes several representatives from private schools and tutorial services. The affiliation between private-school operators and the AQE is evident at conferences where speakers have included Gary Duthler, President of the Alberta Association of Independent Schools and Colleges in Alberta, and other private-school representatives. Booths at conferences advertise a variety of private-education services. Thus, the coalition represented by the AQE is by no means restricted to dissatisfied parents. With these different strands within the group, one may wonder what holds the group together. I would suggest that the notion of "choice" and the potential of public funding following each student provides the glue (see chapters nine and twelve). In advocating choice, private-school operators, dissatisfied parents, and dissatisfied employers can all potentially satisfy their demands for changes in schools that meet their needs as providers and consumers. Whether this move toward a market model meets the needs of other "stakeholders," or of society collectively, is far less certain.

The Chamber of Commerce

> If young people are to be prepared for the future and to get the education they need to be successful citizens, entrepreneurs and employees, Albertans need to know the strengths and weaknesses of the education system. As part of this process, the Minister of Education solicited the views of Alberta commerce and industry.[9]

The quotation above comes from a study commissioned by Alberta Education in cooperation with the Alberta Chamber of Commerce in 1991. As Dempster notes, Alberta Chamber of Commerce president-elect John Ballheim participated in a number of government committees looking at restructuring education in the early 1990s. In addition to being involved with the Chamber, Ballheim is the president of DeVry Institute of Technology — a private college in Calgary. A representative of the Alberta Chamber of Commerce later sat on the Advisory Group for the MLA Team on Business Involvement and Technology Integration.

Again, we ought to ask who is represented by this group and what they want. The Alberta Chamber of Commerce purports to be a grassroots organization representing various-sized businesses across the province. The Chamber has lobbied governments to eliminate the deficit without raising taxes. Members also express concerns about securing skilled labour. In terms of education, these concerns translate into funding cutbacks and a restructured education system. For example, a draft letter addressed to then Education Minister Halvar Jonson from the President of the Chamber of Commerce dated February 1, 1994 states:

> Our educational system is in the same position that the North American car industry was in during the 60s and 70s — out of date and out of touch with reality. While it is capable of producing a fairly good overall level of education, it is far from competitive with educational systems in Europe and Asia, and to an increasing extent, the United States. The educational system must be overhauled and restructured.

The influence of business groups will not cease with the educational changes announced in 1994 but rather is slated to increase. *The Framework for Enhancing Business Involvement in Education*[10] makes several references to government intentions to include more business representation on educational policy committees. Again, we might ask how the government's responsiveness to business groups such as the Chamber of Commerce narrows the goal of education to preparing students for particular jobs and limits its ability to respond to other "stakeholders" who may be promoting broader educational goals.

The Calgary Educational Partnership Foundation

While the Calgary Educational Partnership Foundation (CEPF) has less provincial visibility than the Chamber of Commerce and AQE, it has nevertheless played an important role in educational reform in Alberta. Modelled after the Ottawa-Carleton Learning Foundation, an Ontario partnership foundation supported by local business and education leaders since 1987, CEPF aims to contribute to the "fundamental restructuring of education in Alberta" and build "powerful relationships between businesses and educators."[11] Evidence of CEPF's influence on government is seen in the *Framework for Enhancing Business Involvement in Education*, where the "cooperative efforts" of the CEPF are lauded and where plans to establish a provincial Career Education Foundation are unveiled. CEPF is thus seen as a model for other public/private joint educational ventures.

So who is represented by CEPF and what are their interests? CEPF was established by the past Superintendent of Education in Calgary in collaboration with several business leaders. It is housed in Canadian Hunter Explorations Limited. The 1993 board of directors included six business people, two trustees, one administrator, one teachers' union representative, and a representative of the Science Alberta Foundation (SAF). The president and treasurer of the foundation were also businesspeople. The foundation's close association with the Conference Board of Canada is evidenced by the fact that Calgary-based Conference Board affiliates have participated in the CEPF, while CEPF representatives have participated in Conference Board activities. This connection is noteworthy because the corporate-sponsored Conference Board and its affiliates have been influential in promoting business-education partnerships and other educational reforms in Alberta and in other provinces in the 1990s.

CEPF and the science foundation, which I discuss subsequently, represent organizations that broker greater collaboration between school and business leaders. CEPF is attractive to businesspeople who want to form partnerships with one school or system-wide. It arguably represents an organization through which local corporations can increase their influence over the school system and over provincial educational reform more generally.

The Science Alberta Foundation

SAF is a non-profit organization funded by the provincial and federal governments and by the private sector; it is located in a downtown Calgary office building. It was the brainchild of Jim Gray, the president of Canadian Hunter Explorations Limited, the same company that houses CEPF. As an employer of people with science skills, Gray was concerned about the future labour pool. For Gray, SAF represents a way of developing the idea that science education is key to economic prosperity in mainstream culture:

> The SAF can form part of Alberta's response to the need to develop a more enriched, competitive economy in a future increasingly dependent on science and technology. The Foundation can be a change agent in popularizing the need to change the economy and in helping to bring about that change.[12]

Like CEPF, SAF represents a way of bringing together educators and businesspeople, and providing businesspeople with more control over their "investments" in education. SAF works with schools and the Education Ministry on science curriculum and teacher training, and provides science workshops for parents. As evidence of its entrepreneurial character, SAF has developed revenue streams based on its various products and services. In fact, SAF is similar in many respects to the education fund established by American corporate leader and financier Richard Mellon in the late 1970s. Mellon envisioned a "civic organization with top corporate leadership involvement that would work closely with the public sector."[13]

The government's response to SAF has been extremely positive. The foundation received $1 million in pilot funding for a year, and funding continued for a second year at a time when severe cuts were taking place in other areas of educational spending. The fact that educational restructuring in Alberta involved a re-ordering of funding priorities as well as overall cuts is important to note.[14] SAF is to be a model for the planned provincial "Career Education Foundation" discussed in *the Framework for Enhancing Business Involvement in Education.*[15] The MLA team obviously saw it as a good example of a public/private partnership that bridges schools and businesses within communities.

The "models" provided by CEPF and SAF are predicated on the beliefs that the interests of educators and businesspeople are synonymous and that businesses should be playing a greater role in education. Since these organizations are constructed as involving educators and other "stakeholders" in partnership, representatives are permitted to speak for all "stakeholders." In effect, businesspeople gain an institutional voice in the educational policy community of the government while the input of other educational "stakeholders" is diminished.

■ ■ ■

I have argued that the four groups named above have all had a visible effect on policy reforms in Alberta. They would support the push for increased "efficiency" in education through restructuring and cutbacks. While the Chamber of Commerce might emphasize reforms that assume that education is just another over-regulated industry, AQE members emphasize parents' right to choose schools for their children. The effects in both cases are similar: the view that market-driven forms of schooling are "the solution." CEPF and SAF are more subtle in their approaches. They promote themselves as "apolitical" organizations where stakeholders can work toward common goals. However, the effect is that activities that were once managed by the Department of Education and were controlled to a greater extent by educators (such as curriculum development, professional development of teachers, and skills development opportunities for students) are now managed also by broker institutions that arguably provide corporate sponsors with greater opportunities to influence outcomes.

The political influence of the groups discussed in this article is due to their collective and independent efforts. CEPF and SAF representatives, for example, have been invited to participate in sessions at business-education conferences sponsored by the Conference Board of Canada and have also taken part in activities of its National and Corporate Councils on Education. A number of corporate sponsors for CEPF and SAF are Conference Board affiliates. CEPF and SAF are also closely related because of their shared sponsorship from the corporate network in Calgary; they have collaborated on educational initiatives in the past. The CEPF-SAF network extends to the Calgary Chamber of Commerce, whose president sits on the board of the CEPF.

The interconnections between businesspeople and "coordinating organizations" in Calgary are perhaps not surprising. What is surprising, however, are the connections between Albertans for Quality Education and business groups. I mentioned that AQE representatives have sat on Chamber committees and that Joe Freedman has liaised with the Alberta

Chamber of Resources (ACR). These connections between dissatisfied parents and dissatisfied employers are rooted in a shared desire to achieve *private* benefits from *publicly funded* education.

I would suggest that institutional connections among reform groups have facilitated political reform efforts both locally and provincially. Therefore, while I agree with Dempster that certain individuals in Alberta have been influential, I would argue that institutional networks and the development of coordinating organizations like CEPF and SAF provide structures that ensure that reforms continue in the direction of a market model for schooling.

I expect that similar networks and structures can be found in other provinces. As educators who are opposed to this direction, it is important to make visible the "business-in-education" networks and underlying interests that are shaping reforms. It may also be useful for educators to form their own coalitions and networks in an attempt to regain a voice in the educational policy community.

Notes

1 An earlier version of this chapter appears in *Our Schools/Our Selves* 8(6) (December 1997).

2 Tony Clarke, *Silent Coup* (Toronto: Canadian Centre for Policy Alternatives and James Lorimer & Company, 1997), 159.

3 K. Dehli, "Shopping for Schools," in *Orbit* 29(1) (1998).

4 L. Dempster, *Calgary Herald*, 11 February 1994, A14.

5 Dempster, *Calgary Herald*.

6 Albertans for Quality Education, *Presentation to Government of Alberta*, Education Roundtables, November 1993, 1.

7 Dempster, *Calgary Herald*.

8 Maude Barlow and Heather-jane Robertson, *Class Warfare* (Toronto: Key Porter, 1994), 206.

9 R. Meanwell and G. Barrington, *Senior Executive Views on Education in Alberta,* prepared for Alberta Education, 1991, 1.

10 Alberta Education, *Framework for Enhancing Business Involvement in Education* May 1996.

11 CEPF, *Business Plan* (Calgary, undated).

12 SAF, *Executive Summary* in information package.

13 V. Lies and D. Bergholz, "The Public Education Fund" in *American Business and the Public School,* M. Levine and R. Trachtman, eds. (New York: Teachers College Press, 1990).

14 Wotherspoon also highlights this in his discussion of educational restructuring in Canada in *Hitting the Books: The Politics of Educational Retrenchment* (Toronto: Garamond, 1991).

15 Alberta Education, *Framework for Enhancing Business Involvement in Education,* 5.

9

Privatizing Public Choice: The Rise of Charter Schooling in Alberta[1]

Jerrold L. Kachur

Parents are entitled to choice within the public system, including alternate programs and charter schools, the choice of a private school, or the choice of home education.
— Guiding concept: Private Schools Funding Task Force 1997[2]

The Klein Progressive Conservatives promote schooling as "choice," that is, as a delivery system that unleashes the free-wheeling logic of the market. This increased freedom, however, is illusory because Alberta's ruling party has had to strengthen — not lessen — the power of government in order to restructure the province's school systems. This chapter surveys Alberta's four provincial school-systems and explores the changing relationships among private and public education systems — with a specific focus on an emerging quasi-market for charter schools in Alberta.[3] I argue that the recent considerations of "equality of opportunity" exhibit patterns that are not reflective of either meritocracy or democracy. The construction of a quasi-market requires a more authoritarian government and the promotion of an "educational parentocracy": "where a child's education is increasingly dependent on the wealth and wishes of parents, rather than the ability and efforts of pupils."[4]

Parentocracy: A Theory of Parental Choice

While the post-war period was imbued with the assumptions of progress and merit in Canada (see chapter one), recent history is marked by an emerging debate between democracy and parentocracy. The parentocratic wave has been marked by ongoing criticism of liberalism from the left and right. While the left argues that the competition for credentials undermines democracy and reproduces social inequality, the right argues that liberal education compromises intellectual and moral standards for excellence — and too much democracy is unaffordable.

The promoters of an educational parentocracy, largely a New Right coalition of conservatives and neo-liberals, have exerted increasing influence in Britain, the United States, and elsewhere throughout the 1980s and into the 1990s (see introduction, chapter eight). The conservatives defend the private rights of parents and raise the question of "morals." They identify the social and education crisis with the breakdown of traditional authority, economic leadership, and the transmission of high standards. They question comprehensive and inclusive public education as a menace to parental freedom and individual liberty. For their part, neo-liberal free-marketers have a solution that conservatives favour — the school voucher and charter market.[5]

Both neo-conservatives and neo-liberals alike disdain the social welfare state. Thus, the New Right asserts its new-found power over education in the name of individualized parental freedom, or "privatized choice." This privatized education further appeals to conservatives because elite schools with "high standards" may be preserved, as may a diversity of schools for many religious and social groups. Thus, parentocrats champion schools to become separate educational firms — like business corporations — subject to market-discipline and market-incentives, just like the already-existing "independent" schools. The major advantage of this kind of educational organization, according to its proponents, is that it maximizes variety and choice in the name of individual freedom while rejecting attempts to impose "uniform service" or "public monopoly" as a kind of slavery to the welfare state, special interests, or the democratic horde.

Neo-liberal theorists and a narrow constituency of parents and business backers assert two important changes by giving new meanings to old words (see chapter eight). Rather than equal access or outcome, "equality of opportunity" now means that all parents are free to move their children to whatever school they so desire and can afford. Rather than a rational public process, "economic and bureaucratic efficiency" now means that every school has a strong financial incentive to attract customers or be disciplined by economic failure. Failure to recruit students (that is, consumer parents) should result in school bankruptcy. Thus, parentocrats call for removing the fetters on supply and demand; independence, parentocracy, and privatization go hand in hand, along with financial delegation to schools, open enrollments, and fees for school services. This open competition among schools is supposed to raise standards for all.

Furthermore, adherents to parentocratic ideas intend to destabilize ("shake up") locally controlled boards and public systems and to push all education systems toward greater privatization and differentiation (see chapter twelve). Monitoring occurs at "arms-length," thus requiring the introduction of formalized and standardized assessments and the imposition of a centralized and core curriculum to raise and evaluate standards. Thus, paradoxically, the promoters of parentocracy want both a variety of schools and a strict uniformity in curriculum. This rhetoric of "choice" is seductive: who can disagree with freedom of choice? This promotion, however, occurs at the same time as the diversifying changes to the education system exhibit more centralized control by state authorities.

Public or Private Schools in Alberta?

Alberta has four different kinds of schools: public, Catholic, private, and charter.[6] The public system was founded as a Protestant system under the Constitution Act of 1867 and the Alberta Act of 1905. Although it still retains some Christian programming, it is now primarily secular as a result of assimilating non-Christians into the system. The acts also established religious-minority education and the necessity for a separate form of public education. The Catholic system accounts for about thirty percent of all students enrolled in public education. During 1996/97, 489,352 students were enrolled in public programs in Alberta, with total spending of $2.86 billion or $5,848 per student — just below the Canadian provincial average of $6,045 per student.[7]

Another kind of schooling is home education, which can be considered public or private. In 1996, about 1.5 percent of Alberta students (approximately 8100) were registered in home study (a 10-percent increase over 1995/96). Students must register with either a supervising school board or a private school, which receives a $990 grant and potential supplements for another $990 for each student.[8]

On the other side of the public-private divide are private schools, which are publicly regulated but retain some autonomy from provincial control. The School Act allows religious denominations or private groups to run schools and receive money from the government — as long as they hire certified teachers, follow a government-approved curriculum, meet the provincial standard for student achievement, and undergo ongoing assessment and monitoring. These schools can teach religion and to some extent select students on the basis of their own exclusionary criteria. From 1986 to 1996, private enrollments increased from 13,275 to 20,327, and now constitute about 4 percent of total school enrollments in the province.[9]

There are basically two types of private schools in Alberta: registered private schools and accredited private schools. Registered private schools are not required to hire teachers with Alberta teaching certificates (although many do). They do not have to teach the mandatory requirements for K-12 programs and courses, but they must follow government-approved curricula for students to get credit. They currently receive no funding from the province and cannot grant high-school course credit. Alberta's twenty-six registered private schools operate in religious communities, primarily Mennonite, and are monitored by Alberta Education. Accredited private schools offer programs approved by the Minister of Education and their teachers have valid teaching certificates. Some of these schools focus on special education and heritage languages, but most provide religious education. Students at accredited private schools must write provincial achievement and diploma exams and are expected to meet the same standards as students in public systems. There are 187 accredited private schools.[10] In 1996/97, the majority of these schools charged tuition fees in the range of $3,000 to $5,000 per year and received, on average, $1,815 in funding per student from the province.[11]

Private-school users are not all cut from the same cloth. Private schools face the same challenges as public education systems, and issues related to special needs, cultural retention, and economic competition cut across the public-private spectrum. Some parents have children with special physical and intellectual needs, while others, many rural parents, want the same kind of choices offered in the major urban centres. Yet, for other parents, their use of private schools may well be an attempt to escape the "anti-intellectualism" of mass education. High economic status may be a factor in some cases, but Alberta's private schools are readily accessible to middle-income groups and are not the domain of the rich and famous, as is usually the stereotype. Privatized education may allow money to speak with a louder voice, and provides another way for weaker middle-income children to escape academic assessment in proximity with brighter working-class or poor children. These economic inequities, however, are also endemic to Alberta's class stratified and differentiated public systems. For the most part, private schooling in Alberta serves those people who want to preserve the distinctiveness of their culture, usually religious or linguistic in nature. Of the roughly 200 private schools in Alberta, approximately three-quarters are affiliated with or operated by a religious denomination. At issue for many private-school promoters and users, however, is the notion of "choice" or "independence." They are convinced that if governments could provide more funding, the idea of choice would become more meaningful and real.[12] In the words of one parent displeased with the public schools, "basically, the only choice we're given is to take it or leave it but we still have to pay for it."[13]

In 1998, the Minister of Education and other public-school supporters hesitated to extend more public money for private education. Even in conservative Alberta, the ideology of radical individualism or cultural separatism finds only partial government support. In 1946, the Social Credit government changed the Department of Education Act to recognize private schools formally. Provincial funding for private schools began in 1967 at $100 per student. In 1974, the Lougheed government increased the amount to $246 and matched the basic per-student grant provided to the public system.[14] While public education had access to a number of additional grants, capital funding, and property taxes, private schools were limited to their basic grant. Over the next two decades, the government's basic instruction grant rose to fifty percent. By 1997/98, the government had taken over the collection of all education taxes and their redistribution. During 1994/95, the Klein government awarded private schools eligibility to a number of specific grants, including special and home-based education grants. In the same year, the province assumed responsibility (from local school boards) for setting and distributing education property taxes and introduced a new funding framework which linked rate increases to increases in grants to public schools.[15] The per-student funding rate for private schools is 50 percent, compared to the $3,686 per-student grant for public education. When compared to other provinces, the rate gave Alberta's private schools one of the highest provincial funding rates for 1996/97, Quebec (sixty percent) being in first place and some private schools in British Columbia (fifty percent) also being funded more generously than in Alberta. By the year 2000, the Alberta government intends to increase the per-student grant for private-school students to $2,362, or 60 percent of the public per-student grant.[16] The proposed increases from 1997-2001 (without accounting for inflation) would mean a 30.1 percent increase in funding for private schools, while public education would get a 6.8 percent increase over the same period.[17]

On March 6, 1998, Education Minister Gary Mar announced increased public funding for private schools of $7.2 million (or 22 percent) over two fiscal years and ended a year-long speculation about the government's position on the private-school funding issue. In the spring of 1997, a contingent of Klein's rural back-benchers (supported by some key cabinet ministers) introduced a private members bill (Bill 209) that proposed to increase funding by about $14 million for Alberta's private schools. At the 1997 PC fall convention, however, party delegates split on the issue. A majority voted to eliminate private-school funding altogether. The government immediately proposed hearings before proceeding with the divisive issue. In February 1998, before the results of the Private School Funding Task Force were announced, the Minister of Education ruled out any plans to pull taxpayer funds from the private schools, but he also would not endorse full funding. Instead, he called for "a compromise," leaving the window open for increased funding. In response, the Liberals claimed that private schools should end exclusionary practices and establish transparent financing with elected school boards. The New Democrats asserted that private funding occurs at the expense of the public system.[18] But the Tory caucus ignored public sentiment, opposition critics, and a PC-party resolution to approve the higher funding — one of twenty-six recommendations arising from the government's task force. The government also acceded to some recommendations regarding private-school exclusions and transparency.[19]

The anti-private-school lobby's response to the decision was swift and angry. One PC constituency executive resigned her post in protest, and others questioned their commitment to the Conservative party.

Alberta Teachers' Association president Bauni Mackay called the decision a sad day for public education and a large symbolic step towards privatization and a two-tiered education system. The president of the Calgary Council of Home and School Associations, Colleen Connelly, called it a denial of a majority of spokespersons who wanted the task force to recommend reduced funding. The Liberal education critic, Don Massey, said it represented the Tory government's love affair with private enterprise, and Pam Barrett, the leader of the New Democrats, described it as money "stolen" from public schools.

The pro-private-school lobby was cautiously supportive of the government's decision. The president of the Canada Family Action Coalition, Roy Beyer, was concerned that private funding support remained only sixty percent of public funding support. Private-school spokespersons and supporting parents saw the decision as a confirmation of religious tolerance, special needs, and alternative choice.[20] Gary Duthler, executive director of the Association of Independent Schools and Colleges in Alberta and member of the task force examining private-school funding, stated, "They [private schools] threaten the monopoly of the public education system, not its existence . . . . But does the public school system have to be a monopoly in order to be effective?"[21] In challenging the monopoly of the public system, Duthler clearly understood private schools as *important mechanisms to increase the responsiveness of the public system.*[22]

Public-education advocates believe private schools are less accountable and accessible than public and separate schools, and worry that the spread of private schooling endangers the public system. Those who favour private schools call for "funding fairness" and do not see private schools as a threat to public education.[23] Public-school defenders of access, transparency, and accountability, and private-school defenders of funding fairness and independence, actually converge at a point already envisaged by the Klein government's proposal for charter schools as *privatized public choice* for parents. While it may be too early to identify conclusively what might happen, we may expect a growth in charter schooling and the "choice" system; that is, a convergence of public and private forms of schooling toward the charter model and the increasing responsiveness of the public system to the quasi-market for education services.

Privatizing Public Choice: Charter Schooling

The majority constituency for private schools are religious denominations. But if the new charter schools cannot be denominational — by law — then what is the point in drawing similarities among charter, private, and traditional public forms of schooling? Charter schooling is primarily a political answer to educational policy differences between economic liberals and cultural conservatives. Charter schooling is also part of the neo-liberal solution to the dilemmas facing many governments throughout the Western world. The problem, as defined by many Western governments, is how public schooling can help a nation develop a competitive edge in the global market, reduce governments' expenditures on the social welfare state, *and* provide government services to an increasingly diverse group of "clients."

In the pre-Klein era, the Conservative government, under the leadership of Don Getty, scripted two parallel and contradictory answers to the above dilemma. The first proposed solution was more rhetorical than real and involved the drafting of an explicit pre-election strategy laid out in the 1992 Dinning Report.[24] For public relations, this compromised document seemingly committed the government to the progressive direction established in the 1972 Worth Report.[25] The second proposed solution, becoming more real each day, involved the logic of liberal corporatism and the careful orchestration of stakeholder consultations on the economy — not education (see chapter five). The most recent consultation, the 1997/98 Private Schools Funding Task Force on Private Education, is the latest government response to a breakdown of consensus in the PC party on the issue of public and private-school funding within the broader political agenda to retrench the social-welfare state and enhance corporate profitability. Charter schooling is just one piece of a larger education and economic puzzle.

For the right, "charter schooling" may be a solution to the breakdown of consensus within and between public and private-school supporters because its major advantages are the maximization of school variety and choice and the rejection of uniform service through a public-education monopoly. Charter schooling also allows the PC government the option to retain the support of a traditional political base, the private-school constituency, while still defending public education. The rhetorical defense of public education in the charter-school debate is important for the government because Alberta parents, both inside and outside the party, are committed to "public" education. A majority of parents see no reason for using public money to pay for a private system that does not provide universal access; in fact, they are not quite sure whether private schools should be receiving any funding in the first place — especially in light of cuts to the public system. Simply stated, parents support public education.[26] But what does this commitment to public schooling mean when talking about "charter schools"?

While private schools are considered distinct from public education, the School Act now allows for the Minister of Education to grant private societies (as corporations) the right to run charter schools that are fully funded by the province and provide alternative public schooling. Charter schools have proven to be one vehicle to introduce market competition between diversified and specialized forms of educational provision for Alberta. The schools must be approved by the Minister of Education directly or in conjunction with a school board. They are created and run by parents or non-profit societies as registered companies or corporations. They cannot deny access to any students, except given limited space and resources. Unlike private, independent, or home schooling, charter schools are public institutions funded by government on a per-pupil basis. They are allowed to charge fees only if they are in keeping with those fees charged by the public boards of education. Religious or denominational schools are not permitted unless affiliated with already existing Catholic districts.[27]

In 1995/96, 224 students were enrolled in charter schools ($978,646 for operations). For 1996/97, enrollment numbers for 11 schools were estimated at 1843 students.[28] The charter-school market, however, has already become somewhat unstable. The Alberta government announced in May 1998 the closing of its flagship charter school, the Global Learning Academy.[29] Another charter school, the Science Alberta Foundation Charter School, is slated to open in Calgary by the end of 1999.[30] A proposed Charter School for Commerce in Calgary was rejected.[31] Near Edmonton, Mundare Community Charter school was re-incorporated into Elk Island Public School District — leaving the total number of charter schools hovering at around ten. So even though charter schools *were* growing in number and enrollment in the initial stages of development, their expansion has been sporadic.

With so few recruits and so many difficulties, charter schools seem hardly a threat to the organization of Alberta public education. As a unique hybrid, however, they play a pivotal role in the debate about public funding for private schools. Neo-liberal theorists for an educational parentocracy paint charter schools as a halfway house on the way to a completely privatized voucher system of educational delivery, a system where the government provides funding directly to parents as tokens for the purchase of services in an educational quasi-market.

The restructuring of Alberta's education system around market-based provision and the subsequent emergence of charter schools owe their existence to an overwhelming deference to neo-liberal thought. The rationalization of education services and the marketization of education has resulted from the strategic choices of Klein's conservatives as envoys of privatization to take a leap of faith that will supposedly let the market work its magic. The vision of charter schools promoted by Klein's government is part of Alberta's preparation for entry into untrammeled global competition.

Potential Consequences of Chartering for Public Schooling

What are the implications of privatized public choice for Alberta education and society? The provision of education services through quasi-market mechanisms in Alberta has two major potential effects on schooling: increased diversity in the public system and increased challenge for teachers. Not only is the charter-school variant of public schooling state subsidized, but it remains a form of "privatized education," as the neo-liberal theorists of parentocracy highlight. This increasingly private-like education in the public system is not based on a voucher system as the theorists imagined but rather on conditional "funding envelopes."[32] Money follows the student and is tied to specific state requirements and parental demands, thus fostering the expansion of the most marketable programs. The province now has a new kind of schooling based on parental choice, which increases the differentiation and specialization of existing school practices. Its effects go beyond the designated charter schools.

The market for charter schools has had a diversifying effect on existing public programming. "Traditional" public school boards have responded by increasing the permeability of their school boundaries and intensifying the delivery of alternative programming, including a further accommodation to cultural diversity. The new engagement by public boards in more aggressive marketing of their already diverse programming allows them to compete directly with charter schools, private schools, and each other (see chapter twelve). The importance of the charter-school effect is not so much about the modest number of students who attend charter schools as about how public-school boards have responded to the new competition. Some public boards have responded to the increasing importance of private schools and the appearance of charter schools by increasing their alternative programming in an effort to attract clientele from the province's independent, private, and home-schooling community. For example, the Edmonton Public School Board (EPSB) has long promoted a variety of programming choices to meet the diverse interests of parents and students. In addition to their "regular" and "special" programs for students with special learning needs, EPSB offers more than twenty "alternative" programs. EPSB has even gone so far as to develop its own form of "charter choice" in 1995 by offering new alternative programs, including the religious-based Logos Program.[33] And in 1998, EPSB announced its newest addition to its sports-alternative program, the Hockey Academy, a school for hockey players who will hone their skills and scholarship for a substantial tuition fee under the guidance of qualified instructors and professional athletes. The Calgary Public School Board, however, has not adapted either to "charter schools" or "alternative programs." Similarly, for rural communities, delivery of any new programs is risky, given the financial cost of maintaining existing programs and the declining rural student-population base.

Canadian educational practice has always accommodated cultural diversity. Moreover, the search for market share has also pushed public-school boards to accommodate further lay-mediated denominational interests, as in the case of the Logos Program, and, unlike the Alberta charter school regulations, to allow more chartering of religious schools. Implementation of the Logos Program has resulted in strong resistance from the Alberta Teachers' Association (ATA) and has proven to be the most controversial program. Unlike charter schools, the Edmonton Logos Society and a lay board of directors operate a program that is both publicly funded and religion-based. In the Logos alternative program, instruction is grounded in Christian principles and taught from a Christian viewpoint. Teachers are also expected to adhere to the curriculum prescribed by Alberta Education and to respect the established standards of assessment for each grade level. Parents are asked to sign a commitment of support for the objectives of the program.[34] In the non-Catholic public system, this resulting new mix of denominational and non-denominational programming goes against the grain of Canadian nationalism, yet is in keeping with Alberta's multicultural history and provincial interests.[35]

As a second effect, the emerging quasi-market challenges teachers' income and professionalism. The quasi-market puts downward pressure on teachers' income and status.[36] Since charter schools do not require teachers to be active members of the ATA, the potential use of non-union labour has created a mechanism that could be used to weaken the collective-bargaining power of teachers or to pressure the traditional public sector to adopt similar practices. An expansion of private schooling would have a similarly depressing effect on teacher income. Thus, Alberta teachers may have to respond to the quasi-market proposals as an increasing threat to their livelihood and status.[37]

Moreover, the emerging quasi-market may compel teachers to re-evaluate their role as professional public servants and identify themselves as managers of students and technology. In this case, professionals may no longer see themselves as public servants promoting the public good, but rather as selling products to the highest bidder. At best, professional status is constrained by the logic of business and, at worst, teachers' professional organization is confronted by a new division of classroom labour and more part-time labour (see chapter eleven). Marketization of educational services also includes the possibility for the "McDonaldization" of education services through the expansion of corporations into profitable areas of consumer service and technology transfer.[38] For example, Telus is committed to investing people, money, and technical support in the development of at least seven community-sponsored learning programs.[39]

Market Choice and the Stronger State

Deregulation at the local level has been accomplished at the cost of increased state re-regulation at the provincial level, as well as centralization of financing and policy-making at the ministerial level. Thus, the consequences of more "choice" is not what its promoters intend — less government. It is important to remember that the new charter market in education services has required the interventions of a more powerful executive arm of government to create the conditions for this quasi-market education system.

Fundamental restructuring has been accomplished through the exercise and enhancement of managerial power. In 1994 and 1995, the Klein government established, in a highly interventionist manner, the charter-school market.[40] The School Amendment Act was given assent on May 25, 1994. Thereafter, Alberta Education released the Charter School Handbook and established the target of fifteen charter schools for the fall of 1995. On January 1, 1995, the Department óf Education Act was replaced by the Government Organization Act, and sections of the Department of Education Act were added to the School Act. In addition, the School Amendment Act included legislation to regionalize school districts, thus shifting more power from locally elected officials to provincial "educrats." In the decisive year of 1994, this province's so-called "anti-interventionist" government also orchestrated a five-percent rollback of teachers' wages. However, it failed to follow up its challenge to the ATA and deliver Bill 210, the Teaching Profession Amendment Act, intended to undermine union solidarity by increasing the pressures on teachers to form self-regulating bodies.

But even more controversial than the process of centralization of control was legislation in Bills 41 and 57. Bill 57 was intended to allow every minister to hand over power for government programs to private corporations without legislative debate, thus rendering ministerial and corporate connections invisible and undermining democratic accounting. After stirring up controversy by prematurely tipping its hand to the opposition, the government withdrew the bill and proceeded with Bill 41. This bill allowed for a similar transfer of power, enabling the government to proceed to contract out services to private providers at the discretion of the minister.[41]

Finally, the charter-school market has been facilitated by a plethora of new statutes, school regulations, and policy interventions that affect the whole system of educational choice — public, private, and in-between.[42] From 1989 to 1994, twenty regulations directly related to schooling were repealed, and in 1995 alone, nine regulations under the School Act were repealed and twenty-seven related regulations went under review.

This deregulation, and the implementation of new regulations, as part of the government's three-year business plans, redefined the roles and responsibilities of educational actors, regionalized and amalgamated school boards, established a new framework for funding school boards, identified and encouraged business involvement and technology integration, and developed the accountability framework and created the performance measurements and means of assessment for the system.[43] Moreover, the implementation of this managerial and technocratic tendency has led to the increasing use of policy-based lending which ties funding envelopes to the implementation of specific programming goals and the initiation of a centralized program of evaluation through standardized testing, polling, and the publication of performance indicators. While implementation and delivery of educational services remain at the local level, conception and evaluation of these same services have shifted to the offices of a smaller educational bureaucracy consolidated more tightly under ministerial control (see chapters seven and twelve). The Government of Alberta and the Ministry of Education justify this enhanced control in the name of "effective internal administration of the government of the province."[44] If the issue is control in the name of choice, then the Alberta government has more of both.

■ ■ ■

Since the mid-1970s, increasing polarization between rich and poor — credentialed and less credentialed — has become the rule in Canada (see Appendices F and K).[45] Alberta is not exempt from this trend. Further, given the nature of Canada's existing political economy and educational systems and the consequences of quasi-marketing, the province of Alberta can anticipate a further increase in existing educational and social inequalities.[46] The logical implications of the research into quasi-markets for education are clear: more diverse and separatist programming, an increasing hierarchy of credentials, enhanced inequities in economic rewards, and a smaller but stronger state.[47]

More importantly, as the market re-regulates education, increased consumer *choice* ironically brings less citizen *voice*. Once power is removed from citizens, monopolized by technical experts, and assessed by the market's "invisible hand," an ethical and political debate about educational goals simply does not — *cannot* — arise. Democratic participation is stifled. Society is reduced to a collection of atomized consumers whose freedom consists in making consumer choices based on unequal purchasing-power. The political currency is no longer language but its debasement through advertising and the dollar. Concurrently, the market does not "evolve" but is built by a government administration which cannibalizes institutions of democracy in favour of instrumental controls. Education in Alberta is thus reconceptualized as a "delivery system" with a "bottom line" that subordinates the democratic decision-making processes of the citizenry to the "quality control" of "outputs." The smaller and more powerful state bypasses local and school-based democratic decision-making mechanisms. Consumer choice supersedes citizen voice, and educational administrators are compelled to perform as strategic managers in search of market niches under the guidance a more encompassing and anonymous state. Promoters of educational markets assert that, given new opportunities, those parents from non-dominant cultural groups and social classes will exercise more choice over their child's schooling, but what will really happen is that those families who already possess cultural and economic resources will simply add to their existing advantages, further enhancing socio-economic polarization. In addition to the new demands placed on schools to deal with this polarization, the promoters of privatization and many others will have to confront the unintended consequences — a more intrusive state and the decline of democratic freedom.

Notes

I wish to thank Frank Peters, Trevor Harrison, Deanna Williamson, and Derek Briton for their suggestions and comments on earlier drafts of this chapter.

1 There are two related versions of this chapter: see J. Kachur and D. Briton, "Alberta education: retooling through deschooling" in *The Ethics of the New Economy: Restructuring and Beyond*, L. Groarke, ed. (Waterloo: Wilfred Laurier University Press, 1998), 261-72; and J. Kachur, "Quasi-marketing education: the entrepreneurial state and charter schooling in Alberta" in *Citizenship and Social Policy: Neoliberalism and Beyond*, D. Broad, ed. (Halifax: Fernwood, forthcoming).

2 One of eight guiding concepts for answering questions supplied for respondents to the task force. Government of Alberta, "Erratum to Private Schools Funding Discussion Paper" in *Funding Private Schools in Alberta: Part 2: Addressing the Questions: Private Schools Funding Task Force, 1997*, 3.

3 A quasi-market is almost — but not quite — a free market. For a review of quasi-markets and education from a international perspective, see B. Elliott and D. MacLennan, "Education, modernity and neo-conservative school reform in Canada, Britain and the US" in *British Journal of Sociology of Education*, 15:2 (1994): 165-85; J. Le Grand and W. Bartlett, *Quasi-Markets and Social Policy* (London: Macmillan, 1993); G. Whitty, "Creating quasi-markets in education: a review of recent research on parental choice and school autonomy in three countries" in *Review of Research in Education* 1996: 22.

4 P. Brown, "The 'Third Wave': education and the ideology of parentocracy" in *Education: Culture Economy Society*, A.H. Halsey, H. Lauder, P. Brown and A.S. Wells, eds. (Oxford: Oxford Press, 1997), 393.

5 The classic statements on choice are found in M. Friedman and R. Friedman, *Free to Choose* (New York: Avon, 1980); and J.E. Chubb and T.M. Moe, "Politics, markets, and the organization of schools" in *American Political Science Review* 82 (1988): 1065-87. Also see also R. Douglas, *Unfinished Business* (Auckland: Random House, 1993); D. Osborne and T. Gaebler, *Reinventing Government: How the Entrepreneurial Spirit Is Transforming the Public Sector* (New York: Plume, 1992).

6 I do not look at schooling under the jurisdiction of the federal government — for example First Nations or Department of National Defence schools. Technically speaking — and according to the legislation — Roman Catholic and charter schools are public schools. I use the popular designations for these public schools (see *Edmonton Journal*, 26 July 1997, G1). I attempt to clarify the differences whenever possible by using the term "public education" when I mean public and Catholic or separate schools. Moreover, most public systems in Alberta, Saskatchewan, and Ontario are *denominational schools*, meaning Catholic *and* Protestant, yet most public schools, for historical reasons, are Protestant. Usually the designation "separate" means "separate public" and is usually Catholic; however, Alberta provides key exceptions to the rule. Where Catholics are in the majority, the Protestants are treated as "separate," as in St. Albert. (Undoubtedly clear now?)

7 All numbers are unadjusted for inflation. Newfoundland spent the least at $5,108 and Quebec the most at $7,032 per student during 1996/97. Statistics Canada *Education Quarterly Review*, 3(2) — as cited in 92nd Annual Report of Alberta Education; Government of Alberta "Erratum to Private Schools Funding Discussion Paper" *Funding Private Schools*, 1997.

8 Government of Alberta [on-line]. Available at http:ednet.edc.gov.ab.ca/news/.

9 Government of Alberta "Erratum to Private Schools Funding Discussion Paper" *Funding Private Schools in Alberta: Part 1: Setting the Stage for Discussions: Private Schools Funding Task Force, 1997*.

10 *Funding Private Schools*, 6-7.

11 *Funding Private Schools*, 12.

12 F. Peters, "Perspectives on private schools" in *First Reading: Fundamentalisms — Search Out Truth* (Edmonton Social Planning Council, 1996), 17-18.

13 *Edmonton Journal* 26 July 1997, G1. Statement by a mother who took her son out of the public system and placed him in a private school.

14 Catholic separate jurisdictions are part of "public education" but discussion of "public schools" assumes that it excludes them if understood as separate schools.

15 *Funding Private Schools*, 5.

16 *Edmonton Journal* 6 March 1998, A1, A16. Private school students with special needs will receive 100 percent of the public per-student grant.

17 The Alberta Teachers' Association, *Backgrounder*, 17 March 1998.

18 *Edmonton Journal*, 10 February 1998, B5.

19 Government of Alberta, Setting a New Framework: Report and Recommendations of the Private School Funding Task Force, February 1998. [on-line]. Available at http://ednet.edc.gov.ab.ca/news/newsreleases/1998nr/mar98/privrpt2.htm; *Edmonton Journal*, 6 March 1998, A16. Private schools will still choose their student population but will be responsible for children expelled during a school year. Parent councils will be required for schools where parents do not make up the majority of members on the board of a society. Each school will be required to do more reporting, to conduct regular on-site monitoring, and to designate a principal who has an approved teaching certificate.

20 *Edmonton Journal*, 6 March 1998, A1, A16; 7 March 1998 A1, A16; 16 March 1998, A1, A12. *Globe and Mail*, 6 March 1998, A6.

21 *Edmonton Journal*, 16 March 1998, A1.

22 CBC Radio, *Edmonton A. M.*, interview with Kathy Daly, 6 March 1998.

23 Mark Lisac, column, *Edmonton Journal*, 15 November 1997, A18.

24 Alberta Education *Revisioning the Nineties: Some Thoughts on the Urgency for Educational Change* (The Dinning Report), 1992.

25 The Worth Report established the goals for comprehensive school reform in Alberta which affected educational reform in the 1970s and 1980s. It established an ethical liberal ideal of education as person-regarding. For a detailed discussion see R. Manzer, *Public Schools and Political Ideas: Canadian Educational Policy in Historical Perspective* (Toronto: University of Toronto Press, 1994), 153-54.

26 See *Edmonton Journal*, 8 September 1998, A1.

27 Alberta Education *Charter School Handbook* (revised February), 1996.

28 Alberta Education, Information Services Branch, Educational Information Services, "Authority student population summary," 17 November 1997. These numbers tend to vary depending on actual and projected enrollments as well as on the source. As of February 1998, charter schools exist in Medicine Hat, the Centre for Academic and Personal Excellence (CAPE) for gifted students grades K-9; in Fort McMurray, Moberly Hall Charter School specialized in alternative learning styles for grades 1-9; in Mundare, Community Charter School specialized in student centered education for grades K-9 [incorporated in Elk Island District]; and in Strathcona, New Horizons School operated by the Education for the Gifted Society for grades 1-9. Edmonton operates three schools: (1) the Suzuki Elementary School, specialized in music for grades K-7; (2) the Aurora school, focussing on high academic expectations for grades K-8; and (3) the Boyle Street Community Services Co-op for inner-city students grades 8-10. Calgary operates four schools: (1) Action for Bright Children (ABC) for gifted students grades K-3; (2) Almadina school specialized in English as a Second Language for grades 1-9; (3) Global Learning Academy, specialized in independent learning for grades K-8 [no longer operating]; and (4) Foundations for the Future specialized in "back to the basics" for grades K-9.

29 A. Mitchell, "Alberta shuts flagship charter school." *Globe and Mail*, 23 May 1998, A1, A7.

30 Government of Alberta [on-line]. Available at http:ednet.edc.gov.ab.ca/news/. Alberta Education, Information Bulletin, 26 November 1997. The school focusses on science and math for grades four to six.

31 *Edmonton Journal*, 6 March 1998, A2. The proposal to Calgary Public School Board was for a school, grades three to nine, that would emphasize business philosophy in all subject areas and require students to wear compulsory ties and white collars, to tote briefcases, and to hit the links with the school's golf club.

32 Educational administrators might be more familiar with the idea as "conditional grants" based on specified policy outcomes. Decentralized control is related to "site-based management" (see chapters thirteen and fourteen).

33 EPSB [on-line]. Available: http://www.epsb.edmonton.ab.ca/, 10 September 1996. The Logos program potentially includes at least five schools. Other schools are the Nellie McClung Alternative Junior High Program for girls, premised on the belief that girls will achieve better academic results in an all-female environment, especially in mathematics and science; the Edmonton Public Professional School of Ballet, for grades seven through twelve; and the Sports Alternative Program, for grades four through twelve. The latter two provide flexible scheduling for students involved in extensive training and competition. The Cogito Alternative Program, for kindergarten through grade six, is defined according to basic educational values and traditional approaches.

34 Edmonton Logos Society, "Logos School — a program with a difference," 1996.

35 For example, the history of Jewish religious schooling in Edmonton. For a review of pitfalls of multiculturalism see Kas Mazurek, "Multiculturalism, Education and the Ideology of the Meritocracy" in *The Political Economy of Canadian Schooling*, T. Wotherspoon, ed. (Toronto: Methuen, 1987), 141-63.

36 For a survey of the effects of choice on teacher organizations in other places, see G. Whitty, "Marketization, the state, and the re-formation of the teaching profession" in *Education: Culture Economy Society,* A. Halsey, H. Lauder, P. Brown, and A. Wells, eds. (Oxford: Oxford Press, 1997), 299-319.

37 Canadian Teachers Federation (CTF) "National issues in education." [on-line]. Available: http://www.ctf-fce.ca., 1997.

38 See R. Dale, "The McDonaldisation of schooling and the street-level bureaucrat," in *Curriculum Studies* 4(2) (1994): 249-62.

39 Such as its "Bright Futures Foundation" and "Learning Connections." Telus has spent $8.5 million on its "World Learning" initiative (TWL) to link elementary and secondary students via the Internet to global information. While Telus — or one of its programs — has not received charter school status, the definition of charter schools as legal corporations does not rule out the possibility. Telus Community Initiatives [on-line]. Available at http://www.telus.com/corporate/community/index.html, February 1998.

40 Alberta Education, *90th Annual Report 1994-1995,* 1995.

41 S. Robertson, V. Soucek, R. Pannu and D. Schugurensky, "'Chartering' new waters: the Klein Revolution and the privatization of education in Alberta" in *Our Schools/Our Selves* (March 1995), 103, footnote.

42 Alberta Education, *Regulatory Reform Action Plan,* 1995.

43 *Alberta Education Annual Reports*: 1994/95, 1995/96, 1996/97, 1997/98.

44 Alberta Education, *Regulatory Reform Action Plan,* 1995, 1.

45 Also see J.L. Kachur, "Northern dreams: society and schooling in Canada" in *Schooling and Society in Today's World: Comparative Studies*, K. Mazurek, M. Winzer, and C. Majorek, eds. (Boston: Allyn and Bacon, forthcoming).

46 Much of the literature in the sociology of educational inequality is devoted to explaining why and how contemporary schools reproduce middle-class privilege. There is no debate as to whether this privilege exists. See Terry Wotherspoon, *The Sociology of Education in Canada* (Oxford: Oxford University Press, 1998); C. Lessard, "Equality and inequality in Canadian education" in *Social Change and Education in Canada*, R. Ghosh and D. Ray, eds., third edition (Harcourt Brace: Toronto, 1995), 178-95.

47 See M. Dobbin, *Charter Schools Charting a Course to Social Division* (Toronto: Ontario Secondary School Teachers' Federation, 1996); S. Ball, "Education markets, choice and social class: the market as a class strategy in the UK and the USA" in *British Journal of Sociology of Education* 14(1) (1993): 3-19; A. Green, "Educational achievement in centralized and decentralized systems" in *Education: Culture Economy Society*, A.H. Halsey, H. Lauder, P. Brown, and A.S. Wells, eds. (Oxford: Oxford Press, 1997), 283-97; H. Lauder "Education, democracy, and the economy" in *British Journal of Sociology of Education* 12 (1991): 417-31; S. Ball, R. Bowe, and S. Gerwitz, "Circuits of schooling: a sociological exploration of parental choice of schools in social-class contexts" in *The Sociological Review* 43 (1995): 52-78; A.S. Wells, "African-American students' view school choice" in *Who Chooses? Who Loses? Culture, Institutions, and the Unequal Effects of School Choice*, B. Fuller, R. Elmore, and G. Orfield, eds. (New York: Teachers College Press, 1996); S. Waslander and M. Thrupp, "Choice, competition, and segregation: an empirical analysis of a New Zealand secondary school market, 1990-93" in *Journal of Education Policy* 10 (1995): 1-26; L. Gordon, "'Rich' and 'poor' schools in Aotearoa" in *New Zealand Journal of Educational Studies* 29(2) (1994): 113-25.

10

Challenging Restructuring: The Alberta Teachers' Association

D.J. Flower and H.L. Booi

Angry teachers jammed the legislature grounds Saturday in one of the largest demonstrations in Alberta history, to demand more spending in education.
— Headline in the *Edmonton Journal*, Fall 1997[1]

Estimates of the crowd of teachers and supporters at the Alberta Legislature on October 4, 1997 exceeded 20,000; the Alberta Teachers' Association (ATA) distributed over 30,000 "Get the Message" scarves at the rally that afternoon. Why did so many teachers converge on Edmonton on that Saturday, some driving in buses for over six hours each way from the remote corners of the province? The reasons are reflected in the comments of teachers at the rally. Don Flaig, who travelled from Lethbridge, stated, "My vocation is with the children in the classroom. We need a minimum of material, adequate funding and a place to do it. These are under threat." Sandra O'Flaherty from Calgary said, "We are overworked and underpaid and children are suffering because of it. Burnout rate is unbelievable in our boards." Rachelle Morris from Riviere Qui Barre stated, "I'm here for the kids. They are the ones losing out because of the cutting." According to Don Totten of Calgary, "It's about time big class sizes were cut down . . . it's high time the government knew how we felt." Katherine Anselmo of Edmonton offered another commonly stated reason: "I'm here because I'm proud to be a teacher."

The combination of pride and frustration was reflected in a speech by Susan Szewaga, a teacher at Magrath Junior and Senior High School in Lethbridge: "Many of us became teachers because we wanted to help students. Under current classroom conditions this is becoming more of a dream than a possibility." ATA President Bauni Mackay offered the participants a blunt summary of the purpose and "message" of the rally: "We want Albertans to get the message that teachers can no longer hold together an excellent public education system under increasingly deteriorating conditions."[2]

Alberta teachers do not have a strong tradition of systematic political involvement, let alone of high-profile mass demonstrations. To understand the forces that led so many thousands of teachers to express themselves in such a dramatic fashion requires an examination of a number of factors: a long series of government actions going back to the 1980s, culminating in the Klein government's program of restructuring; profound changes in classroom conditions; mounting frustration and anger on the part of teachers; and an increasingly systematic program of action conducted by teachers through their professional organization, the ATA.[3] This chapter explores how the ATA confronted the government's neo-conservative agenda through a systematic program of rebuilding support for public education.

Background: Expectations, Resources and Discontent

A casual observer of the political and educational scenes in Alberta might hold the view that cutbacks and "restructuring" began with the so-called "Klein Revolution" of 1993/94. The reality is quite different. For most of the decade preceding the Klein government's decision in January 1994 to cut $239 million from the education budget and to reduce teachers' salaries by 5 percent, Alberta's teachers and classrooms had to contend with the increasingly negative effects of government actions (see chapters six and seven).

By the end of the 1980s, teacher representatives from around the province were hearing stories of mounting frustration from teachers at all levels. The core of their concerns centred on a combination of rising expectations and shrinking resources, which were occurring in the context of social changes that were having profound effects on classrooms. They felt bombarded by a host of developments and "imposed innovations," such as increased external testing, a fixation with accountability, "measurable outcomes," integration of students with special needs, "program continuity," "portfolio assessment," and "individual educational plans" — all of which contributed to constant pressure to "do more with less." Because children's needs in other areas were not being met, there also were growing concerns that teachers were being put in the position of having to act as social workers, psychologists, and nurses. Increasingly, they were expected to engage in activities for which they had no training.

Schools "were no longer just sites for promoting pro-social values, their purpose became to prevent social collapse."[4] They were expected to provide for more children affected by social, emotional, and intellectual problems as a result of mounting social problems; at the same time, schools were expected to provide a level of excellence for the children of parents who have benefitted most from the education system. These increased expectations related to "the assault on schools."[5] A coalition of forces led by the business community promoted a series of myths, such as "our schools have failed us . . . and our kids" (see chapter eight). The coalition alleged high levels of dropouts, illiteracy, and disappointing performances in international competitions. The publication in October 1991 of *A New Vision for Education* by Alberta Education, focusing on "goals, results and accountability," contributed to the pressure for "improvement." Ironically, however, teachers found they had fewer resources than ever to meet these ever-increasing demands.

Fiscal Realities

The funding of Alberta's education system was also under attack. Educational expenditures in Alberta had started to decline after the oil bust of 1980/81.[6] In constant-dollar terms, Alberta's per-pupil spending declined between 1985/86 and 1990/91 by 1.5 percent during a period when every other province in Canada showed increases — as high as 21 percent in the case of British Columbia.[7] But the opposite view was promoted in the summer of 1992 by Education Minister Jim Dinning, who asserted that, if expenditures were allowed to continue to rise without control, health, education, and social services would, by 1996/97, be using up almost the entire government revenue.[8] Dinning proposed improving the efficiency and effectiveness of the education system by recognizing fiscal reality; identifying and implementing short and long-term strategies; improving education for students within financial constraints; placing a greater focus on results to improve effectiveness; being more efficient; and doing better with the funds we have.[9]

Dinning's actions signalling a combination of emerging directions and mounting teacher frustration prompted the ATA's provincial executive (PEC) to embark on the first steps of what ultimately was to develop into an increasingly urgent struggle to preserve and enhance public education. At its September 1992 meeting, PEC decided to produce materials to "counter the myths" and to begin preparations for a long-term campaign based on creating a willingness to pay for public education.

The ATA had already decided to establish a Committee on Public Education and Professional Practice at its 1992 Annual Representative Assembly (ARA) to look into the impact of the factors which were "imposing unsound practices on teachers and creating conflicting and unreasonable expectations of public education." The committee received 200 submissions, representing input from some 3000 teachers. The resulting report, *Trying to Teach,* was released in January 1993 and "helped define the future political action of the ATA."[10] A columnist described it thus: "if politicians and business people read only one educational document this year, the passionate and disturbing 27-page report should be the one."[11] The report identified the combined effects of integration, special-needs students in regular classes, results-based curriculum, program continuity, continuous progress, individual education plans, increased external testing, and portfolio assessments. It included submissions by teachers and expressed much of the frustration that was building within the profession. The following statement exemplifies how some teachers felt:

> I decided to take early retirement because of the new policies. Although I enjoyed teaching I could not stand to see the disadvantaged not receiving the help they needed. I exhausted myself trying to fill the gap, and I felt that expectations of teachers were so high as to be impossible and therefore I received little feeling of success in the last few years.

Roundtables, Consultations — and Cuts

The government called for a possible twenty-percent reduction in funding over the next three years to an already over-burdened education system. Following the election of Ralph Klein's government in June 1993, the ATA agreed to participate in the regional stakeholder meetings hosted in September by Alberta Education. This participation continued despite the threat involved in the tabling of a private member's bill aimed at making membership in the ATA voluntary, thereby permitting teachers to opt out of membership of the "union."[12]

Many of the stakeholders present at these regional meetings wondered "if the whole process was a charade" and if "the government had already made up its mind."[13] It soon became evident that indeed the government had a plan to restructure education in Alberta fundamentally (see chapter five). In his budget address, provincial treasurer Jim Dinning stated, "the outcomes of those roundtables [planned for this fall] will set a new course for education in this province. That new course will involve fundamental change: change in the way we organize and deliver education, change in how we define basic education, change in how we fund the process and the results."[14] Dinning's remarks supported his earlier statement on August 19, 1993, when he indicated that all government departments had been directed to prepare a plan based on a minimum of a twenty-percent reduction in each department. The Association calculated that this 20-percent reduction in education would remove $369 million.

Although the ATA agreed to send delegates to the two Education Roundtables scheduled for October in Calgary and Edmonton, it felt that the meetings were contrived and that the outcomes might prove meaningless. The ATA organized a response to the Alberta Education's workbook *Meeting the Challenge*, by producing its own workbook, *Challenging the View*. The Association distributed 18,500 of these workbooks. Forty-seven of the ATA's eighty-one locals sponsored their own public roundtables throughout the province and, unlike Alberta Education's formula, made them open to any member of the public.

But the Alberta government was not interested in developing education policy consultations. Following the provincial roundtables, there were demonstrations about the impending cuts to education, particularly in Calgary, involving students who left the classrooms in protest. Several MLAs cited the ATA as promoting these disturbances and accused it of spreading "misinformation to the public." In one case, a principal was accused of sending out a school newsletter that was "highly political, very inflammatory, and factually incorrect."[15] The ATA's president stated that "teachers do not condone students leaving classes to protest proposed cuts to education funding" and urged students to stay in school.[16] Nonetheless, on October 30, 1993, "2,000 students, teachers and parents met in Calgary to protest the proposed government cuts to education. Calgarians at that meeting complained about the manipulated consultative process."[17] At the same time, the ATA combatted the cuts through a four-week, $210,000 media campaign based on the theme, "Don't cut my future," with advertisements in provincial daily and weekly newspapers; billboards in Edmonton, Lethbridge, and Calgary; signs on public transit in Calgary and Medicine Hat; and some radio advertising.

Before the results of the government's roundtables were released, on November 24 the premier made the dramatic announcement of a "one-time reduction in funding" equal to five percent of the human-resources budget of the provincial government: in other words, a salary rollback that would include teachers. The ATA advised its negotiators to ignore the reduction for the remainder of the current contract year, since most school boards would be able to absorb those costs. Instead, the ATA focused on the impact of the rollback on negotiations for the 1994/95 school year.

Almost as a back drop to the real action, the ATA and the government released the results of their respective roundtables early in December. Both looked at efficiencies and recommended a reduction in the number of school boards and in the role of administration. But differences remained. The government's recommendations centred on increased accountability through measurement and evaluation, decision-making at the local level, new ways of providing classroom instruction, and re-examining curriculum. The ATA's recommendations included the sharing of the delivery of services by separate and public school boards, reducing or eliminating funding to private schools, reducing or eliminating achievement tests, and acknowledging public education as an investment in Alberta's future.

Restructuring and Cutbacks

Premier Klein dispelled any lingering doubts about the government's determination to slash education with his announcement on January 17, 1994, that he would reduce education spending by 12.4 percent over the term of the new fiscal plan. The atmosphere of privatization, deregulation, and "smaller government" pervaded the general direction.

Halvar Jonson, the minister of education, presented the details of the grants for 1994/95 on the following day. In addition to cutbacks, the changes altered fundamental elements of the education system in the province (see chapters seven and twelve). The government consolidated funding so that school boards could no longer requisition local resources, and the provincial government became entirely responsible for the redistribution of education funding. Other changes included:

- reducing the number of school boards from 141 to 63;
- Alberta Education appointing all superintendents;
- increasing school-based decision-making;
- increasing choice by parents and students in the selection of school within the public-education system;
- introducing charter schools;
- expanding achievement testing and diploma examinations;
- reducing and restructuring Alberta Education;
- reducing home-education grants by fifty percent
- reducing the early childhood services (ECS) grants on September 1, 1994;
- providing only 200 hours of ECS, half of the previous requirement.[18]

Decisions and Directions

Teachers faced an overwhelmingly negative situation: a powerful, fast-moving, determined, and aggressive government fresh from an election victory, with a mandate to eliminate the deficit; government hostility toward unions in general; the threat of substantial cuts to classrooms that already were stretched to the limits; and the demand for a five-percent salary cut. While some teachers took cold comfort in the fact that their actions had probably played a role in reducing the proposed twenty-percent cut to around twelve percent, most focused on the further erosion of public education. Most teacher representatives believed there was an extremely limited chance of success for dramatic actions, such as a province-wide strike, given the prevailing political winds the government's "deficit hysteria." They instead chose to combat the government's agenda through a long-term program of building support for public education.

On January 31, the ATA launched a $500,000 public-relations campaign entitled "KnowMore." The campaign had two goals: to maintain and enhance public education and to enhance the image of the teaching profession. Just two weeks into the campaign, the president of the ATA met with the premier and proposed that the premier "delay funding cuts and declare 'three hundred days for kids'." The plan intended to examine the system and build "a vision of where they [Albertans] want education to be and, together, find cost-effective ways of achieving that vision."[19]

The premier rejected the ATA's request two days later, indicating that the steamroller restructuring was not to be slowed.

During the course of the spring, the ATA released a follow-up to *Trying to Teach* entitled *Trying to Teach: Necessary Conditions*, which outlined the profession's views of the direction essential for education, and worked with a Common Front fighting to "save our public services." It invited, with the Alberta Federation of Labour (AFL), the assistant national secretary of the New Zealand Educational Institute to explain the impact of the neo-conservative actions in education and health that had occurred in New Zealand. It also provided support for groups promoting a return of 400 hours for kindergarten.

On the issue of salary rollbacks, teachers faced a difficult dilemma. In jurisdiction after jurisdiction, boards told their teachers that, if they refused to negotiate a five-percent salary cut, the jobs of younger teachers would be eliminated and class sizes would increase. By September, all of the bargaining units had negotiated a rollback in order to protect classroom conditions and their colleagues' jobs.

"Public Education Works"

The ATA established a task force to develop a proposal for a long term program to build support for public education in the province. At its meeting on October 27-28, PEC approved the task force's recommendation to establish a Public Education Action Centre (PEAC) with a member of executive staff assigned full-time to its operation.

PEAC began its activities in January 1995 by outlining the threats to public education in Alberta and in Canada; it planned to preserve and enhance public education by influencing the public, governments, and teachers through the development and implementation of an ongoing, proactive campaign. PEAC approved twenty principles, which included mobilization of teachers in grassroots activities, making clear the threat to public education, promoting positive changes in education, building effective coalitions, and making use of assistance from public-relations professionals. The action centre called on ATA members in the schools and locals to promote public education in their own settings; during the spring, forty of the ATA's fifty-one locals started local programs. The action centre also produced pins, buttons, posters, notepads, letterhead, and stickers with a graphic of an apple in a check mark and the slogan "Public education works." In March 1995, the action centre organized a tour of the province by Heather-jane Robertson, co-author (with Maude Barlow) of *Class Warfare: The Assault on Canada's Schools*. At the same time, the ATA produced and distributed a document entitled *A Framework for Educational Change in Alberta*, which outlined the profession's view of the desired approach to educational change and promoted a very different view of education from the technocratic and privatizing vision of the government. Instead, it emphasized public education as the central element in the development of individual potential and the foundation of democratic society.

School Councils

On April 24, the government introduced Bill 37, the School Amendment Act 1995, which introduced a legislative framework for the existence and operation of school councils. It established a clear mandate for the role of the school councils and allowed parents greater opportunity to become involved in their children's schools. It also clarified that principals were responsible for the operation of the schools (see chapter thirteen). The ATA supported school councils as an important initiative in school improvement. With the assistance of other stakeholders, in particular the Alberta Home and School Councils' Association (AHSCA), and with funding from Alberta Education, the ATA developed a manual for school councils, the *School Council Resource Manual*, which was distributed to all schools in November. The ATA further collaborated with the AHSCA and the Council on School Administration to develop a series of workshops aimed at assisting parents, teachers, and administrators to set up school councils. In 1996, the ATA produced and distributed to all schools *Partners in Learning*, a resource guide "to assist educational partners."[20]

The Impact of the Cuts

In a summary of activities for the school year September 1994 to June 1995, a report from the ATA to the Canadian Teachers' Federation (CTF) suggested that the cuts to the education budget were beginning to take their toll on Alberta's teachers.[21] Teacher morale was decreasing, stress was increasing, and pupil-teacher ratios were beginning to increase significantly. The loss of teachers and teacher aides had a serious impact on classes with special-needs children. But the government did not share this view.

On December 19, 1995, the premier of Alberta officially declared through the Edmonton media that "the deficit is dead" and that he was now looking to Albertans for help in finding ways to re-invest or "reap the rewards" of their perseverance and sacrifice.[22] In his New Year's interview, the premier stated, in response to the comment "changes to education seem to have been accepted well," that education was "the good news story."

Educators did not support the premier's comment that education was a "good news story." The announcement of money for re-investment in the 1997/98 budget indicated to the ATA that the decision-makers needed to be told that some of that re-investment needed to be in education. Accordingly, at its February meeting, the ATA executive approved spending $65,000 on an advertising campaign in all weekly and daily newspapers across the province over an eight-week period. The campaign urged all involved to "choose children" when suggesting to the politicians where the money should be re-invested.

At the same time, Edmonton Public teachers released *Classroom '95: time to reinvest . . .* , a qualitative study of the impact of educational funding cuts on teachers in Edmonton public schools. Teachers had been asked only two questions: "What has been the impact of funding cuts on your work as a teacher?" and "What has been the impact of funding cuts on your school?". Some 650 teachers and 60 school staffs responded, providing a picture of increased workloads, declining morale, overburdened classrooms, unmet needs, intensification, and frustration:

- This has been an extremely stressful year for all of us. Both students and staff are exhausted, demoralized and frustrated . . . instead of dealing with approximately 180 students per year, I have to deal with 260. This increase alone prevents me from dealing with students as effectively as I have in the past.

- Overall, the biggest impact has been on the support services that enable me to do my job as a teacher. These services have declined substantially, and have reduced my ability to deliver quality education.

- Simply put, I do less interesting work with my students. They get less lab work in science because I have no assistance with lab preps and we have no money to provide resources.

- I often contemplate leaving the profession, but I love teaching children. I can't imagine that any other job could be that satisfying. But . . . this job is getting less satisfying each year. When will it all stop? . . . Does anyone care? Is anyone listening?

With talk of re-investment, and with the deficit well under control, the possibility of improvement seemed more realistic — if the public became aware of the conditions in the province's classrooms. The ATA decided to seek teachers' assistance in preparing *A Report Card on Education*, a simple document tabulated by constituency that would give MLAs a picture of the local classroom situation. The report card was a valuable tool, first because it gave a snapshot of conditions across the province, and second, because of the size of the response.[23]

The results of the survey provided the ATA with a focus for a possible provincial election in 1996: (i) class size, (ii) support staff and resources, and (iii) per-pupil spending. When the election was called in February 1997, the ATA made education a central issue. It de-emphasized the five-percent salary roll back. The Committee on Education Issues argued that increasing public support for public education could be mobilized and that salary issues should be pursued through collective bargaining and lobbying after the election. The ATA campaign involved both locals and individual teachers and supported activities with radio advertisements. The overall assessment in the ATA was that education was indeed a key issue — but would the government respond by re-investing some of its enormous budget surpluses in education? It would be unwarranted for the ATA to claim sole responsibility for the measure of re-investment in education eventually announced in the Alberta government's 1998 budget. By raising and promoting the issues in a clearly focused election campaign, however, the ATA did address concerns that were quickly supported by parent groups and others.

The Growth Summit

After the election, Premier Klein's announcement of his decision to hold a "Growth Summit" presented teachers and the ATA with a dilemma. On the one hand, there was general agreement that most previous "consultations" were seen as manipulated and unproductive (except in giving a measure of credibility to the government's claims of listening to the public). The constraint on the debate, that participants had to agree to operate within the current "fiscal framework," contributed to doubts. The AFL announced that it would not attend the Summit, adding to the pressure to boycott the event. On the other hand, teachers could use the Summit to as an opportunity to promote the urgent need to support public education; to present the case to influential Albertans in a public forum was arguably worth the risk of aiding government credibility. There was significant debate among members of the ATA's PEC before the motion to accept the invitation to attend the Summit was finally passed. The motion included a rider that insisted on ATA being included in the Municipalities, Universities, Schools and Hospitals section, and not simply in the Labour section. In the end, the ATA, represented by its president, agreed to participate in the Summit (see chapter five).

Meanwhile, as a backdrop to the Growth Summit ,the teacher-bargaining situation deteriorated particularly in Calgary Public, the province's largest jurisdiction. Frustrated teachers worked to rule, that is, "withdrew voluntary services," in an attempt to restore salaries and improve classroom conditions.

Participation in the Growth Summit involved attendance at a host of "mini-summits" (in different regions, with the various summit "sectors," and on specific topics such as education and post-secondary education.) The ATA vigorously promoted the idea that Growth Summit participants "come to terms with the fundamental dilemmas related to growth in our society and do so in a manner that establishes the human condition as central to their task." It argued that "the right of every child to an education is non-negotiable and is, in itself, the single most important factor in the creation and maintenance of a vibrant society." It emphasized the need to preserve and enhance public education for all children, and warned that "the guise of choice is being used to foster the private good at the public expense." The ATA submission concluded by quoting the Delors Commission's description of education as "an expression of affection for children and young people, whom we need to welcome into society, unreservedly offering them the place that is theirs by right therein . . . " and made this request:

> the young are entitled to a vision of growth that takes into account their rights and aspirations. The crucial role that education fulfills in both their individual and collective futures must be supported by government policies that permit teachers and students to realize these things.[24]

The Growth Summit concluded and many teachers were encouraged by its rejection of a proposal for broad tax cuts, its emphasis on "people development," and the consensus that education is a top priority. According to the co-chair, Mike Percy, "the overarching issue was a focus on education." The ATA's decision to attend appeared to have been vindicated. The premier said that he had heard the message of the Summit — but a question remained: would words be followed by actions on the part of the government?

From the Growth Summit to the Rally

The two-day Growth Summit ended on Tuesday, September 30, and a teachers' rally was scheduled for Saturday of the same week. The momentum supporting public education seemed to be building. The huge turnout at the rally put to rest any lingering doubts about the seriousness of the issues in the eyes of most of the province's teachers. The logistics of working with so many thousands of participants were daunting for the ATA staff who organized the event, but the weeks of planning paid off. As the bus-loads poured in, traffic was tied up for blocks, but dozens of marshals directed the crowds while others passed out scarves and buttons. The crowd was described as "enthusiastic and good-natured," and the messages were reflected in the sea of signs carried by thousands of teachers: "Public Education Works," "Restore Salaries," "Reinvest in Children," "Smaller Kids," "Teachers Are the Alberta Advantage," "It's About Fairness," and "Proud to be a Teacher." The rally concluded when Bauni Mackay led the crowd in a march of solidarity around the legislature building, with the final chant, "Get the Message — Support Our Schools!"

But the *Edmonton Journal* raised the crucial question a few days later in an editorial entitled, "Did government get education message?" The editors concluded, "The message has been sent, both by the Growth Summit and by the mass rally of teachers on the weekend: our education system needs help. Is the provincial government listening?" The editorial essentially endorsed the views of teachers at the rally that the province need to rebuild the public school system after a decade of cuts.[25]

After the rally, Education Minister Gary Mar raised hopes. He asked to meet with teacher representatives in order to discuss education funding. The ATA presented a proposal outlining the profession's view of the need for an infusion of over $500 million to address concerns in five key areas:

teacher salaries, class sizes, special-needs students, coordinated delivery of services for children, and early intervention. But hopes fell in the light of the eventual announcements on funding by Premier Klein and Education Minister Mar in January 1998, described by ATA President Bauni Mackay as "a disappointment" and "an exercise in financial gymnastics." Much of the proposed expenditure of $379 million over three years was required, she said, because the government was legally obligated to fund additional students due to population growth. The money, however, would not "relieve the pressure on our classrooms." Of the $379 million proposed expenditure, the $155 million new-money package fell far short of meeting most of the needs. She concluded: "Not only will the extra funding fail to patch the cracks in our public education system, our teachers are not even mentioned, despite the premier's rhetoric about wanting to make sure Alberta has the best education system in Canada. Teachers will still be forced to choose between learning conditions and their families' financial health."

■ ■ ■

It should not be a surprise that, despite some successes, the struggle continues. Some of the factors that contributed to the cutbacks, such as the "deficit hysteria," have disappeared with successive budget surpluses in the billions of dollars, but the government's general orientation has not fundamentally changed. Until teachers and others who value public education can rally even more support among the public, their message is unlikely to influence those in power. Journalist Linda Goyette, in a column reviewing the "manufactured crisis" that triggered the "Klein Revolution," described the opportunities in the emerging situation and the lessons to be learned from our recent experiences: "Preoccupied with Alberta's riches, the government is no longer obsessed with an invented crisis or a phony revolution. That leaves room for the rest of us to talk about reconstruction and repair. We should never again suspend our right to doubt and question."[26]

Notes

1 *Edmonton Journal*, 5 October 1997, A1.

2 President's speech at Provincial Teachers' Rally, 4 October 1997.

3 The Alberta Teachers' Alliance, established during World War One, held its first annual meeting in Edmonton in 1918. By 1920, it had its first general secretary-treasurer, John Walker Barnett, who held the position until his retirement in 1946. Under Barnett's direction, the Association grew from an "Alliance" with a membership of 700 to an "Association," legally constituted under the Teaching Profession Act 1935, to which all teachers in public and Catholic schools belonged. The Teaching Profession Act clearly lists

the objectives of The Alberta Teachers' Association (ATA), which are "to advance and promote the cause of education in Alberta; to improve the teaching profession; to arouse and increase public interest in the importance of education and public knowledge of the aims of education, financial support for education, and other education matters; and to co-operate with other organizations and bodies in Canada and elsewhere having the same or like aims and objects." The ATA has a membership of 29,500 active full-time and part-time teachers in public and Catholic schools across the province. However, its total membership, including life members, student members, substitute teachers, and associate members, comes to 44,900. The Association represents both the bargaining and professional activities of Alberta's teachers in a single organization. The business of the Association is transacted by an executive committee of twenty persons known as Provincial Executive Council (PEC), including a president and two vice-presidents. All are elected by member votes for two-year terms; policy and budget are determined at an Annual Representative Assembly of approximately 450 delegates. As a result of its mandate under the Teaching Profession Act, the Association plays an active role in promoting and defending the cause of public education in the province.substitute.

4 Maude Barlow and Heather-jane Robertson, *Class Warfare* (Toronto: Key Porter Books, 1996).

5 Barlow and Robertson, *Class Warfare*.

6 A.M. Decore and R.S. Pannu, "Alberta political economy in crisis: whither education?" in *Canadian Journal of Education* 14(2) (1989): 150-169.

7 Figures produced by the Canadian Teachers' Federation in *Economic Service Notes*, February 1997.

8 Jim Dinning, *Fiscal Realities*, August 1992.

9 Dinning, *Fiscal Realities*.

10 V. Soucek and R.S. Pannu, "Globalizing education in Alberta: teachers' work and the options to fight back" in *Teacher Activism in the 1990s*, S. Robertson and H. Smaller, eds. (Toronto: James Lorimer. 1996), 35-69.

11 *Globe and Mail*, 26 March 1993, A24.

12 Bill 212, Teaching Profession Amendment Act, 1993.

13 D.J. Flower, report to ATA staff on Regional Consultation meeting, Red Deer, 28 September 1993.

14 Jim Dinning, *Budget Address*, 8 September 1993.

15 H. Forsyth, Question period, *Alberta Hansard*, 1 November 1993. 1153.

16 "Teachers urge students to stay in school," ATA *News Relearse*, 27 October 1993.

17 L. Decore, Question Period, *Alberta Hansard*, 1 November 1993. 1150-1151.

18 Alberta Education, *In Focus* 6(3) (Winter 1994).

19 "Klein says no," ATA *News Release*, 17 February 1994.

20 Letter from president Bauni Mackay to all school council chairs, ATA, 20 December 1996.

21 The ATA worked with CTF and other provincial teachers' organizations to develop a national campaign to support public education.

22 *Edmonton Journal*, 19 December 1995, A1.

23 Approximately 10,500 teachers returned the report cards, over one-third of all the teachers in the province.

24 J. Delors, *Learning: The Treasure Within* (Paris: UNESCO, 1996).

25 "Editorial," *Edmonton Journal*, 9 October 1997, A16.

26 "Column," *Edmonton Journal*, 5 November 1997, A16

Re-organizing Schools: Scenes from the Classrooms

11

Is It Just A Matter of Time? Part-Time Teaching Employment in Alberta

Beth Young

In order that people may be happy in their work, these three things are needed: They must be fit for it. They must not do too much of it. And they must have a sense of success in it.

— John Ruskin[1]

In teaching, as in many other occupations, the number of Canadians who are employed part-time has increased substantially since the early 1980s.[2] During the 1990s, the number of Alberta's teachers employed part-time has increased by over forty percent. By the 1995/96 school year, fifteen percent of Alberta's teachers — including one of every five women — were part-timers.[3] In one recent survey, several of Alberta's public-school districts reported that more than twenty percent of their 1996/97 teaching staff were employed part-time.[4] Meanwhile, the results of another survey indicate that only half as many of the University of Alberta's 1993/94 graduates in teacher education had obtained full-time teaching jobs as had 1987/88 graduates.[5] Why has this shift in employment opportunities and patterns occurred, and what does it mean for Alberta's teachers and schools? Do these numbers signal not only a weak job market overall for teachers, but also the potential "re-casualization"[6] of employment for teachers? Drawing on data from ongoing research,[7] this chapter examines the links between organizational responses of Alberta's school districts to the legislative and fiscal environment of the 1990s and trends related to part-time teaching employment.

Flexible Workforce, Flexible Workplace: The Situation in Alberta Schools

In discussions about the overall restructuring of employment, many people today talk about the need for a flexible workforce or, perhaps, a flexible workplace.[8] There are important distinctions between these two terms, although both refer to the general trend away from "standard" jobs — that is, employment by one employer, involving full-time work with an expectation of being employed indefinitely — and toward various forms of "non-standard" employment — such as job sharing, part-time, and/or contracts. Two different but overlapping aspects of this trend are pertinent here.

A flexible work*force* reflects employers' efforts to increase staffing flexibility and lower their fixed staffing costs as an organizational response to the pressures of financial restraint and escalating competitiveness. This is market-driven, "casual" employment in which employees have little influence on the conditions of their employment. Certain forms of non-standard employment arrangements thus provide employers with a "buffer zone"[9] for responding to fluctuations in demand for their products and services without increasing the core of employees who are guaranteed full-time continuing employment. As a result, there are reduced opportunities to obtain (or regain, in some cases) the traditional sort of full-time continuing employment.

A flexible work*place*, however, reflects greater societal acceptance that there should be opportunities for a range of optional employment arrangements that do not necessarily involve standard, full-time employment. Such arrangements afford individual employees more flexibility to tailor their paid work arrangements to complement other dimensions of their lives, because they have some control, or at least influence, over their working conditions. The individuals who opt for these arrangements are most often women seeking some flexibility to reconcile the multiplying demands of their professional and domestic responsibilities, as they — and their significant others — interpret those responsibilities.[10]

Recent research suggests there are more flexible workforces than flexible workplaces to be found in Alberta schools. However, the pertinence of these two aspects of employment restructuring for Canadian public schools and their teachers has not yet been fully explored.[11]

The *Alberta School Act* gives employing school districts and their administrators considerable freedom to "vary the amount of time that the teacher is required to teach" from semester to semester and from one school year to the next.[12] In short, by legislation, part-time teachers have no right to expect similar hours of work from year to year, no matter how much seniority they have. Nor do they have any right to move from part-time to full-time status, even when full-time teaching contracts are being offered. As of 1997, school boards have been unwilling to bargain away any of their administrative discretion. Until quite recently, the

Alberta Teachers' Association (ATA) also has not paid much attention part-time employment and related issues.

The available statistics on part-time teaching in Alberta show that the most substantial annual increases in the number of part-time teachers, both male and female, occurred in the first two budget and school years after Ralph Klein was named leader of the Alberta Progressive Conservatives in December 1992. From 1992/93 to 1993/94, the number of part-time teachers rose by eight percent; from 1993/94 to 1994/95, the number rose by an additional eleven percent.[13] These increases (accompanied by a decrease in the number of teachers employed full-time) can be linked to certain policy initiatives of the Klein government.

Although the cutbacks to the public sector had already begun while Don Getty was premier[14] (see chapters six and seven), a flurry of policy edicts requiring immediate implementation followed the election victory of Klein's Tories in June 1993. Some elements of the restructuring initiatives in education[15] had especially immediate and strong effects on staffing policies and practices in schools. These elements were the fifteen-percent reduction in funding to schools between 1993 and 1996; the involuntary five-percent salary reductions for all public sector employees; mandated school-site management and parent advisory councils; a fifty-percent cut to funding for early childhood education (kindergarten). It is not mere coincidence, for example, that the number of full-time early childhood education teachers has plunged by fifty percent since 1992/93, while the number of part-time ECE teachers has dropped by only fourteen percent.[16] Nearly all of the teachers affected by the cuts to the traditionally female domain of early childhood education are women. Some of them seem to have found employment as day care workers,[17] a lower-paid, lower-status, and frequently insecure form of work with young children.

In the face of severe reductions in public funding for schools, some school districts have introduced policies that allow for a different sort of part-time arrangement (see chapter twelve). Teachers with regular full-time contracts may shift to part- time employment for an agreed-upon period, while retaining their full-time, continuing contracts. Administrators then hire new, lower-paid teachers on more flexible part-time contracts[18] to fill the gaps in their staffing needs. This cost-saving measure is helpful to administrators in the new era of reduced funding combined with school-based budgets, which must be finely tuned. Each part-time agreement is negotiated individually, usually between one teacher and one principal. The agreement usually lays out some of the specifics of the teaching assignment as well as the duration of the part-time agreement. For example, a principal may agree to accommodate a veteran teacher's wish to teach specified grades and subjects, only in the mornings, for one school year. Policies that allow arrangements of this sort are now being bargained into some collective agreements in the province.

The statistics, however, make no distinction between those who work part-time on a new optional arrangement or the long-standing arrangements established under Section 84 of the *Alberta School Act*. Responses to our recent survey of Alberta's school districts suggest that the vast majority of part-time teachers are found in the second category, but not likely by their own choice.

Flexible Who, Flexible What?

Interviews with part-time teachers and with principals who supervise part-time teachers offer some surprising views, as well as some predictable views and experiences related to part-time employment. The administrators' reasons and the teachers' reasons for offering or agreeing to part-time teaching arrangements in their schools are sometimes, but not always, the same or complementary. Not all principals support all of the motives the teachers have for wanting to teach part-time. This support is important because the principals not only have the power to select teachers but also to decide on their teaching assignments. These decisions have an impact on part-time teachers' salaries and benefits, as well as affecting their sense of satisfaction and professional opportunities. Both principals and teachers are seeking strategies to minimize the uncertainties of their respective situations. Both groups are also concerned to create as much flexibility as they can in order to address their various — and sometimes conflicting — professional/personal needs and standards. The one-to-one negotiation between principal and teacher of this complex of motives and strategies expands and intensifies the work each does individually, while avoiding more institutional forms of labour negotiation.

Managing Uncertainty. Many new and re-entry teachers accept part-time employment because it is the only teaching available, even outside the large urban areas.[19] These teachers hope Section 84 part-time contracts provide a route to the apparent security and benefits of traditional full-time teaching appointments. Meanwhile, they live with annual uncertainty about their assignments and, as a result, their pay. Some high-school teachers have found that their appointments vary dramatically from one semester to the next and on very short notice. While principals see these shifts as necessary adjustments related to changes in student enrollments, at least some want to minimize their teachers' uncertainty. Still, a teacher's sense of vulnerability to shifts in program priorities and funding never really goes away.

Some of these new and re-entry teachers develop strategies to reduce their vulnerability. Recruiting more students is one such strategy. The idea is to attract adequate enrollment, so that the accumulated per-pupil funding for the school will be sufficient to justify the teacher's salary. These part-timers, thus, find themselves marketing the school and its spare course offerings. They also have to market themselves, their courses, and their programs to students and their parents, because their very employability depends on it.

A second strategy is to impress the principal. Principals themselves comment that most new teachers would "do anything" (e.g., "wash your car for you if you'd let them") to distinguish themselves as desirable employees. These teachers will also take on responsibilities well beyond those the principal assigns. Indeed, many principals observe that part-timers are "working time-and-a-half for part-time pay." This eagerness and dedication has been carried to such an extreme that some principals speak of urging the newcomers on staff to curtail their activities. These teachers, however, are trying to use various forms of influence where they know they have no power to control the conditions of their employment.

Meanwhile, principals acknowledge that the well-travelled pathway from part-time contracts to full-time continuing employment may not be open to very many teachers in the foreseeable future. Given the pressures they have been facing, principals value the staffing flexibility that can be achieved through the use of part-time teachers. They are freer to respond to fluctuating program needs, student enrollments, and funding. For example, administrators can bring in well-qualified specialists chosen to meet specific program needs that change according to variable and somewhat unpredictable enrollments. Using part-time contracts allows the principals to incorporate new teachers on staff who, in turn, contribute fresh ideas and energy to the life — and work — of the school.

Employing part-timers also increases the overall number of staff in the school available to help with various out-of-classroom duties from supervision to coaching and clubs. This is an important consideration when the full-time continuing staff are overburdened because of large class sizes and the expectation that they will participate in everything from school-based budget meetings to school councils. Principals often observe that most part-timers contribute proportionately more as professionals than do most full-timers, because they have more unassigned time to give to their work. Part-time teachers concur with that view. So while part-time teachers work harder for an uncertain employment future (and income), the schools they are employed in gain many advantages.

Several principals are troubled because they have not felt able to reward their hard-working, cooperative part-time staff members with the secure full-time positions those teachers are seeking. Others see the full-time continuing contract as a dinosaur about to become extinct. This range of opinions is equally apparent in district-office responses to a recent province-wide questionnaire survey.[20]

At the school-sites, principals report a range of strategies related to staffing with part-timers. Some are using highly technical-rational approaches to solve their staffing puzzles, while others are trying to be caring and creative but are clearly frazzled by the additional demands this places on them. A few are thinking about very different ways of organizing schools using lots of computer technology, teachers as coaches, and para-professionals. Some — but not all — of these strategies and attitudes suggest that the use of a flexible workforce may be taking hold in Alberta's public schools.

For over a decade, there has been an apparent over-supply of qualified teachers seeking employment in their field. In these circumstances, attracting and keeping a well-qualified teaching staff was accomplished without great difficulty. Ironically, in the current environment of financial constraints, although there is still a surplus of teachers, the challenges related to staffing have increased.

One elementary school principal provides this example of life in the new, "flexible" school organization. The principal had sought the services of a qualified elementary-school specialist, but could only afford to buy those services for a few hours each week. As is typical in these situations, the specialist is "shared" by several schools, each paying for a few hours. However, the number of hours that the schools can afford to pay for such services has been decreasing. Thus, schools find that they are also "sharing" the specialist with a private business, because she needs more income than the schools can offer, even in combination. Therefore, the principal and the specialist negotiate a rather complex schedule. They attempt to accommodate this part-timer's need to put together several jobs in her specialization, thus providing the equivalent of one full-time income. Because the principal is committed to having a qualified specialist on staff, she negotiates away some of her usual employment conditions for part-timers, such as regular attendance at staff meetings and a share of supervision duties. When other staff members contest that agreement as special treatment, the principal then has to negotiate an understanding with them.

As this principal points out, some teachers do have considerable negotiating power, but the story also illustrates the uncertainty, complexity, job enlargement, and intensified demands that are realities for both school principals and many part-time teachers today. Is it just a matter of time before these demands overwhelm our most conscientious educators?

Buying Time, Making Space. Some teachers see part-time teaching as a voluntary option they exercise in order to have more time in and control over their lives. Some want the time for professional activities, while others use the time for domestic responsibilities and recreation. Principals differ in their support of these various motives related to teachers' efforts to make space for their own priorities, except when women teachers' priority is child care.

Being Professional. Given the ever increasing (and increasingly complex) workloads related to the combination of cutbacks and decentralization, some part-timers — both veterans and novices — have indicated that teaching part-time helps them create the "space" (in the form of unassigned time) to do their jobs without compromising their own standards of professionalism. "Buying prep[aration] time" also has the effect of reducing stress, according to some teachers. Even so, some

— not all — principals dismiss teachers' efforts to define and maintain quality teaching through part-time employment.

One principal, for example, strongly disputes the motive of "buying prep time," while admitting that work loads were increasing because class sizes were growing. This principal sees the workload as a predictable consequence of an individual's (informed) choice to teach in particular subject areas, such as language arts, which involve marking many written assignments. Another principal dismisses the stress-reduction motive, commenting that anyone who finds full-time teaching stressful probably isn't suited to teaching at all. But even in the early 1990s, how many of Alberta's educators would have predicted this much more pressured and stressful teaching environment in a province where progressive public education, well supported by oil royalties, had long been a source of pride? Why shouldn't individual teachers attempt to gain some control over these demanding and deteriorating working conditions, using whatever means are available to them in order to maintain the quality of teaching they believe in?[21]

Unfortunately, according to the new "90s" viewpoint expressed by some principals, the truly "professional" teachers are the ones who demonstrate "flexibility" and resilience by compromising as a means of coping with today's changing demands. Either they work more out-of-class hours, or they adjust their expectations of themselves and their students downward. Is it just a matter of time before those who respond by working harder leave teaching and we are left with public schools staffed by "flexible" teachers with equally "flexible" standards of professionalism?

By contrast, when veteran full-timers opt for (carefully defined) part-time arrangements, with a stated motive that includes sharing the available employment with new teachers, they are applauded for their professionalism. This phenomenon is an interesting variation on the theme of exercising personal choice in favour of professional generosity. In these cases, the generosity is very concretely directed toward other people — junior colleagues — rather than to more ambiguous or controversial notions of professional space. What is a sign of undesirable inflexibility when associated with one stated motive becomes noteworthy flexibility when a slightly different motive is attached.

The Good Mother. Buying time to make space for family responsibilities is another widely applauded motive. However, both part-time teachers and principals generally take for granted that it is married female teachers who will (and perhaps should) choose part-time employment in order to accommodate domestic responsibilities, usually child care. It is a motive that many principals are clearly anxious to accommodate. The result is a very "large part-time lady workforce," as one teacher put it. This model in turn reinforces gender stereotypes and assumptions through the staffing patterns in the schools.[22]

Many teachers and principals have articulated the assumption that women teachers who were employed on full-time continuing contracts would forfeit them in exchange for Section 84 part-time contracts if they wanted to continue teaching once they became mothers. The teachers express gratitude to their employing district for this "option" of teaching part-time. It is their only way of combining their professional work and the demands of child care.

The women who made the shift from full-time to part-time (Section 84) contracts are now stuck there, even if they would like to return to full-time employment. Other women — in some districts — can now take advantage of new part-time policies and retain the option of returning to full-time employment. Under the new provisions, these women are generally able to negotiate and guarantee the details of their part-time assignments at a much earlier stage in the timetabling process than the women who are on the old part-time contracts. Some principals, as well as the teachers, are quick to note this ripple effect on the veteran Section 84 part-timers. The contrast underscores a type of career penalty that many of Alberta's women educators have paid for taking on traditional "family responsibilities." Not only are these women working in the margins of their profession today, but they face long-term disadvantages related to pensions and other benefits.

Those teachers who were, nonetheless, happy with the specifics of their arrangements — under either type of contract — were quick to credit their principals for making those arrangements possible. In return, the teachers worked very hard to justify this consideration. This personalized and *ad hoc* exchange implicitly reinforced the power difference between principal and part-time teacher concerning the conditions of the teacher's worklife.

So What for Students and Schools?

According to both principals and part-time teachers, students benefit because their "part-time" teachers are more energetic, humane, and creative educators than "full-time" teachers can be these days. In addition, principals argue that, with a flexible, part-time teaching staff, they can give students the benefit of learning from the best-qualified subject specialists in each subject, even in elementary schools. However, the voices of colleagues with standard, full-time teaching contracts have not yet been heard — and need to be — on this subject of "more for less."[23] What are the implications for full-time teachers in this environment? How much effort, how many hours is enough? And whose professional judgment rules?

There are many other unanswered questions and concerns. Part-timers may (understandably) not always be on-site and available to students, parents, and colleagues. Does limited availability inhibit spontaneous out-of-class consultations and, perhaps, collaborative activity among teachers? Some principals even wonder if having too many part-timers may fragment their students' learning environments, particularly for very young students. By contrast, there is evidence that teachers who undertake a job-sharing arrangement effectively do engage in collaborative activity throughout the school year. They assert that students benefit from being involved with different teachers who have complementary skills and philosophies. As one principal notes, even primary students in most schools today have several teachers.

Many principals, as well as part-time teachers on new-style contractual arrangements, emphasize that committed efforts on everyone's part to communicate and coordinate can overcome the potential drawbacks of staffing with part-timers. This attitude offers hope — but not certainty — about the extent to which employment arrangements might enable greater flexibility for *both* individual teachers *and* school organizations. But at present, one important question remains unanswered: What impact will these "flexible" staffing patterns have on students' learning environments?

■ ■ ■

Both for schools as organizations and for individual teachers and principals, the extensive use of flexible, Section 84-style part-time staffing institutionalizes uncertainty.[24] This situation has unknown and potentially negative implications for building and maintaining cohesive school cultures and learning environments. That may be the trade-off for spreading the ever-increasing workload around by having "more (new, but part-time) bodies in the building," as one principal put it. Coordinating and supervising all of the "bodies" also makes the principal's job more complicated. This challenge is one among many for today's principals (see chapter thirteen). Financial and managerial pressures, the moral dilemmas of a "market choice" environment, and the politics of devolution to school-sites are making the principal's job very unattractive to some educators.

There also are implications for teachers' personal and professional prospects in the longer term. For those employed on part-time contracts, pay, benefits, and future professional opportunities are endlessly under negotiation. This is especially true for those newer teachers who have little choice except to seek and accept one temporary, part-time contract after another.

At the same time, some school districts have turned fiscal restraint into an opportunity to introduce enlightened policies that are making their schools more flexible workplaces for at least a few fortunate teachers. Those policies could have wide and constructive application for both women and men through varying life and work situations and may serve both teachers and schools well. They may, that is, unless such policies allow politicians and administrators to gloss over the relentlessly unrealistic workload-expectations for teachers by invoking only the most demeaning and exploitive notions of "professionalism."[25] They may, if the policy and financial means are found to compensate for the inequities between part-timers that have been created by the introduction of the new alternatives to Section 84 part-time employment. Otherwise, public schools in Alberta may yet become another illustration of an increasingly female-dominated occupation in which flexible *workers*, not flexible work*places*, become the norm.[26] As the premier's 1998 television address put it: "What's next?" Is it just a matter of time?

Notes

1 John Ruskin, *Pre-Raphaelitism*, 1851.

2 Canadian Teachers' Federation, "Part-time teachers more than double since early eighties" in *Economic Service Notes* April 1996, 4; H. Krahn, "Non-standard work on the rise" in *Perspectives on Labour and Income* 7(4) (1995): 35-42; G. Schellenberg, *The Changing Nature of Part-time Work* (Ottawa: Centre for International Statistics at the Canadian Council on Social Development, 1997).

3 These statistics have been calculated from aggregate data provided by Alberta Education and based on teachers' self-reported information.

4 Unpublished aggregate data provided to the author in a recent survey of all public and separate school districts in Alberta. See note 6 below for details.

5 A.M. Decore and S. Belcher, "The Klein Cuts and the Market for Teachers in Alberta." Unpublished manuscript. Edmonton: University of Alberta, 1996.

6 D. Broad, "Global economic restructuring and the (re)casualization of work in the center, with Canadian illustrations" in *Review* 14 (Fall 1991), 555-94.

7 Unless otherwise noted, the survey and interview data discussed in this chapter are drawn from a continuing, multi-year program of research exploring the phenomenon of part-time teaching in Alberta. That study was funded by grants from the Alberta Advisory Committee for Educational Studies and from the Supports for the Advancement of Scholarship Fund, Faculty of Education, University of Alberta. For a detailed report of findings, see B. Young and K. Grieve, "Changing employment practices? Teachers and principals discuss some 'part-time' employment arrangements for Alberta teachers" in *Canadian Journal of Educational Administration and Policy* 8 (1996): 1-14; [online] available at www.umanitoba.ca/publications/cjeap. Thanks to Kathy Grieve for her assistance with this study.

8 A. Duffy and N. Pupo, *Part-Time Paradox: Connecting Gender, Work & Family* (Toronto: McLelland and Steward, 1992); C. Negrey, *Gender, time and reduced work* (New York: State University of New York Press, 1994); G. Schellenberg and C. Clark, *Temporary employment in Canada: Profiles, Patterns, and Policy Considerations* (Ottawa: Centre for International Statistics at the Canadian Council on Social Development, 1996).

9 M. Sparke, "A prism for contemporary capitalism: Temporary work as displaced labor as value" in *Antipode* 26(4) (1994): 295-322.

10 S. Acker, "Gender and teachers' work" in *Review of Research in Education*, volume 21, Michael Apple, ed. (Washington, DC.: American Educational Research Association, 1995-96), 99-162; Michael Apple, "Work, gender, and teaching" in *Teachers' College Record* 84(3) (1983): 611-628; B. Young, "On careers: Themes from the lives of four western Canadian women educators" in *Canadian Journal of Education/Revue Canadienne de l'éducation* (17)2 (1992): 148-161.

11 Saskatchewan Teachers' Federation, *The Workload and Worklife of Saskatchewan Teachers: Part-Time Teachers, 1996-1997*, October 1997.

12 Section 84, *Alberta School Act, 1994*.

13 Alberta Education (see note 2 above).

14 Kevin Taft, *Shredding the Public Interest* (Edmonton: The University of Alberta Press/ Parkland Institute, 1997).

15 F. Peters and D.M. Richards, "Restructuring education Alberta style." Paper presented at the annual meetings of the Canadian Society for the Study of Education, Montreal, June 1995.

16 Peters and Richards, "Restructuring education Alberta style."; see also Decore and Belcher, "The Klein Cuts."

17 Decore and Belcher, "The Klein Cuts."

18 Section 84, *School Act, 1994*, as described early in this chapter.

19 See also Decore and Belcher, "The Klein Cuts."

20 See note 6 above. Six of the forty-seven responding districts (out of sixty-five districts in the province) reported that fewer than ten percent of their teachers were part-time and seven other districts reported that more than twenty percent of their teaching staff were part-time. The other thirty-four districts (or about half the districts in the province) reported that between ten and twenty percent of their teaching staff were employed part-time.

21 E.g., Alberta Teachers' Association, *Trying to Teach*. Edmonton: ATA, 1993; Edmonton Public School Teachers, Local 37, *Classroom '95: Time to Reinvest . . . . A Study of the Classroom Impact of Educational Funding Cuts* (Edmonton: EPST, January 1996).

22 See also M. Morrison, "Temps in the classroom: A case of hidden identities?" in *The Supply Story: Professional Substitutes in Education*, S. Galloway and M. Morrison, eds. (London: Falmer Press, 1994), 43-65.

23 Schellenberger and Clark, *Temporary Employment in Canada*.

24 A. Hargreaves, *Changing Teachers, Changing Times: Teachers' Work and Culture in the Postmodern Age* (New York: Teachers College Press, 1994).

25 S. Acker, "Teachers, gender and resistance." in *Gendered Education* (Toronto: OISE Press, 1994), 90-104; A. Hargreaves and I. Goodson, "Teachers' professional lives: Aspirations and actualities" in *Teachers' Professional Lives*, I.F. Goodson and A. Hargreaves, eds. (London: Falmer Press, 1996), 1-27; S.L. Robertson, "Teachers' work, restructuring and postfordism: Constructing the new 'professionalism'" in *Teachers' Professional Lives*, I.F. Goodson and A. Hargreaves, eds. (London: Falmer Press, 1996), 1-27; V. Soucek and R. Pannu, "Globalizing education in Alberta: Teachers' work and the options to fight back" in *Teacher Activism in the 1990s*, S. Robertson and H. Smaller, eds. (Toronto: James Lorimer, 1996), 35-69.

26 G. Dacks, J. Green, and L. Trimble, "Road Kill: Women in Alberta's drive toward deficit reduction" in *The Trojan Horse: Alberta and the Future of Canada*, G. Laxer and T. Harrison, eds. (Montreal: Black Rose Books, 1995), 270-85.

12

Board Games: The New (But Old) Rules

Judith Evans

Things are seldom what they seem;
Skim milk masquerades as cream.
— Sir William Gilbert[1]

The Klein government's restructuring of Alberta's education system profoundly impacted school boards' abilities to exert a meaningful influence on the local quality of education. In what might have been described as a hostile takeover, had it occurred in the private sector, the government used the province's constitutional jurisdiction over education to reclaim powers previously granted to school boards. When the process of system restructuring was complete, school boards had been reduced to subsidiaries of a kind of "Government Incorporated."[2]

According to the government, the overhaul of the education system was necessary in order to bring costs under control and to make the system more efficient, effective, and accountable (see chapters six and seven). The government also emphasized the benefits that the reforms would bring in terms of giving Alberta parents more power to influence their children's education (see chapter nine). In reality, however, it was the Klein Conservatives who gained the most power. By granting themselves sole jurisdiction over public funding-related matters, they acquired an unprecedented ability to direct the education system. It was like acquiring a remote control that allowed them to steer the education system from a distance.[3]

This chapter examines the impact of the educational reforms on the province's school boards as well as their implications for school boards' organizational behaviours. In the environment of constrained resources that has characterized the first phase of the Alberta reforms, the strategies that enable school boards to achieve the greatest success in meeting the government's expectations also have the greatest potential to increase inequities in the educational opportunities of students. The ability of the reform package to deliver improved educational outcomes is questionable.

The chapter also considers the school boards' chances of continued organizational survival, given pressures on the Klein government to level the playing field to allow "fair" competition between public and private schools. When the current political context is considered as a whole, it appears unlikely that the Klein government will implement radical structural reforms aimed at changing the relationship between public and private education. Nevertheless, the government's current approach to education funding, which has seen private schools achieve an increased public subsidy and encourages public schools to top up funding shortfalls with money from private sources, may gradually undermine the public system.

Background

Alberta's educational reforms involved a number of initiatives that changed relations between school boards and other players of the education game. These initiatives included measures aimed at increasing provincial control over fiscal matters, creating a "quasi-market" to encourage school boards and schools to compete with each other, introducing new formal accountability requirements, and transferring responsibility for operational decision-making from the school boards to the schools.

Fiscal control. A key element of fiscal control was government-imposed cuts to public-education spending. School board spending was reduced from $29.53 per student per day in 1992/93 to $28.03 in 1994/95, a decline of five percent over the period, not considering the effects of inflation. In 1996/97, the most recent year for which actual figures are available, average per-student spending by school boards had increased by a mere twenty-five cents per student per day over 1992/93 levels.[4] By stripping school boards of their property taxation powers and implementing a uniform education property tax rate throughout the province, the government was able to block the school boards from responding to provincial funding cuts and continued fiscal restraint with property tax increases.[5]

In addition, the government forced smaller rural school boards to merge. Citing the need to increase the efficiency of the education system, between 1993 and 1995 the government decreased the number of school boards from 141 to 63. The number of locally elected school trustees declined from 1,184 to 435 over the same period.

Beginning in 1995, the province began funding school boards based on the number of students they served, with only a few needs-based formula adjustments (e.g., for students with severe disabilities).[6] School boards were instructed to allocate operational funding "fairly" to their schools, meaning, for the most part, on a per-capita basis. How school boards spent their money was restricted by government guidelines. The government argued that guidelines were required to ensure that funds were targeted to where they were needed.

The education quasi-market. The government induced competition among school boards and schools through the introduction of a "public choice" funding model.[7] Alberta parents were allowed to choose any publicly funded school for their child (subject to the availability of space) with funding following the child to the school. The government also amended the province's *School Act* (1996) to allow for the entry of new, independently governed but publicly funded competitors, charter schools (see chapter nine).

The education market that resulted, however, was anything but "free" with regard to continued government intervention. In addition to funding, the government controlled the supply of school space by determining which schools were built and which were renovated. It also attempted to stimulate choice by publicly releasing the comparative provincial achievement test results for school boards and schools.[8]

Formal accountability. Although local school trustees were still elected, the school boards' loss of taxation powers decreased their democratic accountability to communities. The government countered this loss in democratic accountability with requirements that the school boards demonstrate increased formal accountability through goals, targets, and measured performance. The *Government Accountability Act* (1995) now mandates all school boards and individual schools to produce three-year business plans and annual-results reports. These documents must include data on government-specified measures — for example, achievement test results and parent and student satisfaction ratings. Given this legal requirement, school boards have little alternative but to comply. However, their staff have raised concerns about how this information is interpreted and used by the public. School board staff are also concerned with the additional time demands associated with generating the plans and reports required to meet the province's accountability expectations.[9]

Devolved responsibility. The government told school boards to give principals control of their school budgets and responsibility for most operational decisions at the school level (see chapter thirteen). It also mandated that school councils, consisting of staff, community representatives, students (at the high-school level), and parents (who must be in the majority), be formed at each school. Most schools already had a voluntary parent-advisory body and, in making them mandatory, the government did not change their fundamental role of advising the principal. But it is noteworthy that school councils appeared to substantially increase their fund-raising efforts in response to the government's funding cuts.

In 1997, Alberta's public schools raised a total of $124 million dollars, through private donations, parent fund raising, and sales to staff and students (e.g., cafeterias and student stores), not including amounts raised through course-related materials fees.[10] In terms of their fund-raising ability, however, the statistics reveal that all school boards and schools are not created equal. The relatively well-off Elk Island Public School District east of Edmonton raised more than ten times as much per student as the Peace-Wapiti Public School District in 1997/98. So far, the government's response to the growing opportunity gap being created by school board and school council fund-raising has been to deny that the gap exists.[11]

The Promises and Mixed Messages of Reform

According to the Klein government, the new education system will produce better results than the old one. In 1996/97, the government's goals for the education system included increased focus on — and communication of — what students need to learn; improved student achievement relative to provincial standards; increased opportunities for parents to select schools and school programs of their choice; greater parent and community involvement in education; improved coordination of services for children with special needs; improved teaching; increased system efficiency and effectiveness (through restructuring and downsizing school boards and the ministry of education); adequate and equitable funding of all school boards; an effective and efficient department of education; a cost of education that is "reasonable and under control"; and an open and accountable education system.

The government evidently views its re-engineering of the education system as highly successful. Based on its own performance measures of progress toward its goals for the education system, the government judged its results for 1996/97 to be, on average, "very good" (on a five-point scale from "poor" to "excellent"), with "excellent" results in the areas of ensuring that school boards and schools were adequately funded, managing the department of education effectively and efficiently, and ensuring that the cost of education was reasonable and under control. It gave itself the lowest grade, "fair," in the area of improving the coordination of services for children with special needs.[12] So far, no comprehensive external evaluation studies have been conducted either to confirm or refute these self-congratulatory ratings.[13]

However, the logic of the government's goals contains inherent contradictions, which suggest that the performance of reforms is unlikely to match their promise. On the one hand, for example, the goal of focusing education on what students need to learn along with the requirement that individual school results be publicly available implies greater standardization of the delivery of education. On the other hand, parents must be provided with greater opportunities to select alternative programs and schools of their choice. This implies that school boards should further differentiate their programs.

But simultaneously standardizing and differentiating school programs on a reduced budget is a lot like trying to maximize the length and area of a rectangle when the value of the perimeter has already been fixed. Clearly, the assignment is impossible. School boards must decide which of the goals are the most important and which can be compromised, all within the constraints of the rules set by the government.

What gets measured gets done. When obtaining rewards that depend on measured performance, the rewards can become valued ends in themselves, displacing the original goals.[14] There are a variety of strategic maximization games that the government's rules and rewards encourage school boards to play. The following sections describe two of these games and analyze their implications.

Getting the Spending Numbers Right

In theory, educational reforms were supposed to give schools and school boards greater management flexibility in exchange for greater accountability on the government's performance measures. In practice, the Klein government has gained the most management flexibility. Having obtained total control over the education system's public funding, opportunities for micro-managing the school boards abound. The government has not hesitated to use these opportunities in areas as diverse as staff compensation, kindergarten programs, student transportation, school construction, and the adoption of computer technology.[15]

School board central administration spending, where the government couched a budget directive in performance-measurement terms, is a case in point. Given administrative spending targets of four to six percent of their total operational spending, school boards responded in a variety of ways. Some of the required spending reductions were achieved by downsizing and flattening their central administrations and by contracting out services. Others were achieved by shifting budgetary responsibility for designated support services from the central administration to the schools, with or without an accompanying transfer of funds.

Although costs were shifted to the schools, school board central administrations often continued to act as the service providers. The school boards established transfer prices and billed schools according to the amount of the services they used. This change in the method of accounting for services allowed them to get their administrative spending numbers right and avoid the unwelcome gaze of the government. Expenditures that were formerly classified as "administration and governance" were now classified as "instruction in schools." The actual objects of expenditure were unchanged and were no more or less "educational" after budgetary responsibility was off-loaded to the schools than before. Still, cost shifting through internal transfer-pricing likely was *not* neutral in terms of its impacts.

Requiring schools to pay for services previously provided by the school board central administration "free of charge" was meant to reduce school-level demand for these services. From an economic perspective, this practice seems reasonable. Forcing schools to pay for the amount of the services they use will make them aware of the cost of providing the services and will reduce frivolous use. But ethical dilemmas arise when schools are forced for budgetary reasons to reduce their demands for services below their actual service needs.

Consider a service such as educational diagnostic testing, previously funded out of school administrative budgets but now generally funded as "school-user pay." A school's relative need to access this service fluctuates from year to year and is seldom exactly proportional to the number of students it serves. Principals of schools with comparatively large budgets whose students have a low amount of need for the service can ensure that all students who need to be tested or assessed receive the service. They may even have a "windfall" left over to spend in other areas. But principals of schools where the level of need for the service exceeds the school's ability to pay for it must ration access, based on some eligibility criteria. Some students who would potentially benefit from the service — whose educational program may depend on the outcomes — must go without. If the students denied access are more likely to come from economically disadvantaged family backgrounds than those receiving it (because they tend to be concentrated in particular schools), inequities will increase.[16]

User-pay central services mean principals may place budgetary considerations ahead of professional judgment. In the process, the goal of increasing the equity of educational opportunities is displaced. As this example illustrates, changes that look harmless or even beneficial at the policy level can cause hardship and stress at the school level.

One way around the problem is to continue to fund key support services like testing, counselling, and curriculum consulting out of the central administration budget, and to let professional values guide decisions regarding access. However, the government's central administration spending target rules this option out, unless other administrative cuts are made or other costs can be shifted. A more cumbersome alternative is to have school principals re-allocate funds among themselves through a process of mutual negotiation. But as money gets tighter, competitive incentives mean school principals are likely to become increasingly protective of their own resources and decreasingly willing to share them with other schools, even if sharing would be in the best interests of students.[17]

Cost-shifting strategies such as internal transfer-pricing have enabled Alberta's school boards not only to meet but to exceed the government's expectations with regard to their administration and governance expenditures. Judged by the government's administrative spending performance measure alone, school boards *look* more efficient.[18] But data that show how school boards actually achieved these spending reductions, and the implications of their strategies for the other stated goals of reform, are neither collected nor reported. There is no evidence that the school boards *are* more efficient or that classrooms *have* benefited.

How have school boards responded to the government's competitive funding incentives? From the perspective of encouraging school boards to behave like private sector corporations, they are a success. Success, however, comes at a price. Once again, it is the economically disadvantaged students who seem to be paying the greatest amount.

To Market, To Market

Regardless of how efficient they look (or actually are), school boards still need money to run their schools. And with the level of their public funding now entirely dependent on the generosity and allocation rules of provincial politicians, the school boards' options for raising revenue are severely restricted.

One option involves raising money privately. In exchange for signing up staff and students' parents and relatives with a long-distance telephone provider, for example, school boards can receive a percentage of the long-distance revenues these subscribers generate.[19] At the individual school level, some schools partner with the Klein government's growing casino industry, the easiest way for them to raise a large amount of money quickly. School boards can also set policies that allow schools to charge parents for various items, such as required supplies in "optional" courses. However, depending on the family incomes of students, some proportion of these fees will be uncollectable.

A second revenue-generating option is to increase school enrollments. The growth in Alberta's student population is now relatively slow, although subject to "mini-booms" when the economy attracts families to an area. A school board desiring to grow at a rate faster than the natural increase in the student population must find a way to attract students from competitors. Depending on the intensity of competition in the particular area, the school board may decide to risk some of its limited administrative resources in order to engage in the strategic positioning and marketing of its school programs.

School boards who take an aggressive approach to competition, for example, actively raiding the students of another board, may provoke retaliation. Not surprisingly, therefore, public and separate school boards with overlapping territories generally do not engage each other in head-on competition. The rivalry tends to be of a softer, gentler kind. For example, "brand awareness" advertising, in the form of side-by-side billboards promoting the two school boards, suddenly appears in strategic locations at prime student-recruiting times, in the spring and during the first few weeks of the school year.

There are a number of other methods school boards can use for increasing enrollments while avoiding confrontations with each other. One method is to acquire a bigger territory by joining with other school boards. Government restructuring has already made small school boards bigger. Merger activity, however, may also continue for voluntary reasons. A second method is for boards to market their surplus school space to fee-paying parents in other countries. For example, both the Edmonton Public School Board and the Edmonton Catholic Regional School Division joined the 1997 "Team Canada" trade mission to Asia for the purpose of attracting foreign students to their district schools.[20] A third method is to pick on smaller competitors — private schools, charter schools, and the home-schooling market — rather than picking on each other.

The school boards' strategies are reminiscent of those used by the large players in the Canadian beer market, Molson and Labatt.[21] Faced with a flat domestic demand for beer and growing competition from foreign companies and domestic micro-brewers, but generally unwilling to compete with each other in ways that would benefit consumers,[22] Molson and Labatt have turned to two specific strategies to expand their revenues: first, they have sought out foreign markets and second, they have diversified their product lines. Given that much of the difference between beer brands is perceived and not real, marketing efforts around this second strategy are aimed at convincing consumers that a particular beer *really does* taste different or that drinking it confers special attributes or status. Even if advertising a new brand does not "win" new customers, and merely induces the brewery's own customers to switch from an old brand to the new one, the new brand will be judged a success, as "cannibalization" (as it is affectionately known to marketers) is preferable to losing one's market share to a competitor.

In a similar way, the old "public" and "separate" brands no longer seem to satisfy parents' educational tastes. Changing customer demands and new market entrants are forcing school boards to differentiate their products. For example, Edmonton Public has become a "district of choice." It emphasizes student achievement and has implemented a "zero-tolerance" discipline policy — things which seem to sell well to a wide range of parents. In addition, when threatened by the actual or potential erosion of its market share, Edmonton Public creates a similar program in an effort to pre-empt the competition or win back lost students (see chapter nine). It is now operating more than twenty alternative programs at various school sites,[23] including a home-schooling centre; the Christian-based Logos program; sports-alternative programs, where school hours are flexed to meet the needs of athletes' training and competitive schedules; two all-girl junior high schools, where the students are required to wear uniforms; and two high schools targeted exclusively to high achievers. According to the chairman of the school board, the only kind of school Edmonton Public will *not* consider opening is a Catholic school.[24]

The smaller Edmonton Catholic Regional School Board has also gotten into the positioning and marketing game. Faced with declining enrollment at inner-city St. Joseph Catholic High School, Edmonton Catholic has decided to revamp the St. Joseph program by turning it into a self-paced learning centre. The new St. Joseph program is modeled after a highly successful program at Bishop Carroll High School in Calgary. However, Bishop Carroll is located in a wealthier neighbourhood. Edmonton Catholic is hoping that St. Joseph will double its enrollment by attracting students from across Edmonton.

The "new St. Joe's" was launched at an elaborate ceremony and press conference, followed up with a billboard-advertising campaign. The school's alternative program will not serve the needs of some of the students who are currently enrolled, but according to the principal, these students can "choose" to transfer out.[25]

This cannibalistic competition, pitting schools affiliated with the same school board against each other, raises some troubling issues for public education. Many parents seem to like the idea of having greater choice of school programs. However, the alternative programs select and segregate students on the basis of a variety of student characteristics including gender, religious beliefs, academic ability, athletic ability, motivation, and income. Given the incremental costs of choice that must be borne by parents (e.g., transportation-related costs), the opportunity to choose is not equally available to all. And sometimes, it is not the parent who chooses a school but the school that chooses to leave the students.

What happens to the educational opportunities of students in the cannibalized neighbourhood schools? The experience of the Edmonton Public School Board suggests that their opportunities are diminished. When parents move children from one school to another, the school that loses enrollment acquires a "reputation" among parents in the community. The reputation, once acquired, leads to further enrollment losses. The principal and staff typically have great difficulty turning the situation around unless the school is itself chosen as a site for an alternative program.[26]

Currently, Edmonton's Catholic and public school boards are under pressure from parents who live in the suburbs (who have apparently not all enthusiastically embraced the concept of choice, particularly when available choices do not include a local school) to close older schools which are not being used to capacity in order to improve the chances of getting money from the province to build new schools in their neighbourhoods. But surplus space exists in most of the older schools. Many would have to be closed in order to get the school boards' space utilization performance numbers right.[27] Paradoxically, if all public schools operated at 100 percent of their student capacity, economic theory suggests education would become a producers' market as it was in the post-war baby boom years, when school boards' resources were stretched to the limit simply accommodating the demographic bulge. There would be little incentive for the school boards to develop and market alternative programs.

Program choice may help a school board to keep students in the district and make better use of its under-utilized school space, but does it really improve the achievement of students? In this regard, it is interesting to note how few of the newer alternative programs seem to reflect new insights into the process of teaching and learning. Indeed, many of them seem to appeal to parents precisely because they are traditional.

To date, neither the district-wide achievement test results for the Edmonton Public School Board (which has been releasing comparative school results since 1990) nor the province-wide results show evidence of a strong upward trend.[28] School boards and schools seem to have considerable difficulty producing and maintaining substantially improved achievement results over a period of time unless they resort to the use of goal-displacing strategies like selecting the best students in the first place (i.e., "creaming").[29]

In Alberta, educational reforms are still in their early days. It remains to be seen whether requiring school boards to be accountable on performance measures and linking their funding to their success at retaining and attracting students will make a difference to academic achievement, whether narrowly or broadly defined. But warning flags have been raised by policy researchers in other countries where similar reforms have been in place for a longer period of time. Just as businesses will focus more resources on the most profitable segments of the market, schools and school boards who are forced to compete will do the same. The result is an education system stratified by income, ability, and ethnic origin.[30] Few students will be well served by such a system. But economically disadvantaged students, who rely most on the public-education system as a means of improving their life circumstances, are probably the least well served of all.

■ ■ ■

What is the future of school boards? At the public meetings of the government's Private School Funding Task Force, held in October 1997, private-school supporters argued that the province should adopt an educational voucher system to allow parents to choose between private and public schools without financial penalty. If adopted, such a proposal could set off a second round of government education system reforms. Restructuring (Phase Two) would be aimed at further reducing the powers of the school boards (the "public monopolies") in order to "level the playing field" for public and private school competition. This could be accomplished in one of two ways: by providing public schools with incentives to encourage them to break away from school board control (the UK approach) or by abolishing school boards altogether (the New Zealand approach).

Is this likely to occur, however? Are Alberta's school boards doomed? Probably not. True, the government did accept every recommendation of its private-schools funding task force, including the recommendation to increase the amount of per-student funding provided to private schools.[31] However, a vote by delegates to the Conservative Party's 1997 policy convention in Edmonton in favour of a resolution calling upon the government to *eliminate* public funding to private schools suggests that the window of opportunity for restructuring the school boards out of existence — if there ever was one — has closed.

There are other good reasons to believe that school boards will survive, at least for the time being. First, Alberta's Conservative Party wants to remain in power. Steering education policy further to the right could jeopardize the party's support from the political center and give the opposition Liberals a welcome political boost.[32] Second, abolishing the school boards would suddenly drop a whole set of problems squarely on the government's doorstep. The government needs the school-board subsidiaries to keep its education division running. Equally important, it needs them to share in the political risk — although some government members do not seem to appreciate the advantage of having another group of elected officials to blame when education policies go awry. Third, Alberta has a strong tradition of supporting public education. Nearly half a million — or ninety-six percent — of the province's kindergarten to grade twelve students are enrolled in public schools.[33] Some of their parents, themselves graduates of Alberta's public-education system, are currently school-council members. These parents perceive that the situation at the school level is worse than they can remember. Schools are short of textbooks and learning resources, classrooms are crowded, and buildings, many of which were built during the 1950s, are starting to fall apart.

Thus far, however, the concerns of these parents have not translated into a rejection of public education. While some parents are dissatisfied with the current conditions and are lobbying for change (see chapter eight), parents are not an ideologically monolithic group and are fragmented by a multiplicity of interests. Nevertheless, they do appear to have a common sentiment that is supportive of public education. They are asking, as members of school councils, why the education system of a comparatively well-to-do province seems to be going backwards into the future. Increasingly, they are voicing their discontent with the situation: rallying with teachers in Edmonton (see chapter ten), marching in support of education in Calgary, making submissions to the government task forces on private-school funding and school construction, circulating petitions, writing letters, sending faxes, making phone calls, and meeting with their MLAs.

In the process, grassroots coalitions have formed[34] and leaders have emerged. School council members — even in light of inadequate spending on education in the 1998 spring budget (see chapter six) — realize that the future of their children's education depends on their resolve to continue to press the government for increased funding and other policy improvements. In an otherwise bad deal from the province, school councils may prove to be the school boards' wild card.[35]

Notes

1 From Gilbert and Sullivan's *H.M.S. Pinafore*, act 2.

2 See Alberta Legislature Office of the Auditor General, "Government Accountability," 14 October 1994. Although governments were meant to fill a different role in our lives than multi-divisional corporations, Alberta's auditor general shares the Klein government's enthusiasm for the corporate model.

3 For a discussion of the weakening and residualizing of local government by "steering at a distance," see S. Ball, "Policy sociology and critical social research: a personal review of recent education policy and policy research" in *British Educational Research Journal* 23(3) (1997): 258-59,

4 Alberta Education, *93rd Annual Report and 4th Annual Results Report, Part I, 1997-1998*, 53.

5 Catholic school boards still have the right to levy property taxes as a result of a successful constitutional challenge. However, there is no incentive for them to do so because the government lowers their funding by any excess amount they raise through levying their own taxes. Other public school boards hope to regain their lost property taxation powers through a Supreme Court of Canada appeal. If successful, this would considerably change the dynamics of educational reform in Alberta.

6 Concerned over the fiscal implications of the growing number of children classified as high special needs, the government recently decided to cap special-needs grants for children with severe emotional/behavioural problems at the 1997/98 levels. The government also capped the number of these children for whom school boards are eligible to receive funding. Consequently, the amount of additional funding school boards receive for these students is no longer connected even by head-count formula to the level of assessed need in their student populations. See Alberta Education, *First Things First...Our Children: Agenda for Opportunity, Education Highlights*, January 1998; and *Edmonton Journal*, 29 April 1998, B2.

7 The public-choice funding model is based on neo-classical liberal economic theory. See, for example, M. Friedman, *Capitalism and Freedom* (Chicago: University of Chicago Press, 1982).

8 The government was evidently worried that parents would not make the right school choices without a government-supplied indicator of school quality.

9 Alberta Government News Release, "Calgary Board of Education Review Team Releases Report: Highlights of Findings," 5 June 1998.

10 Alberta Education, *93rd Annual Report and 4th Annual Results Report, Part II, 1997-98*, 23.

11 *Edmonton Journal*, 10 October 1998, A6.

12 See the results analysis in Alberta Education, *92nd Annual Report and 3rd Annual Results Report, 1996-97*, 23-25, and *93rd Annual Report and 4th Annual Results Report, Part I, 1997-98*, 20-23. In 1997/98, the average self-rating of the government's progress toward goals was similar to 1996/97, although some goals and measures were dropped, new ones were added, and the category "poor" disappeared from the rating scale. The government viewed its goal attainment in the areas of special needs service coordination, information-technology integration, and education system openness and accountability lower than in other areas, although it still considered its progress in these areas worthy of a "good" rating. Once again, the government was most proud of its performance in the area of education funding, judging it to be "excellent."

13 The Auditor General's Office reviews the education performance measures, but the audit is confined to an examination of the accuracy of the data collection and reporting procedures as opposed to their appropriateness or their comprehensiveness.

14 The phenomenon of goal displacement has been documented in organizational literature for at least forty years. See, for example, P. Blau, *The Dynamics of Bureaucracy: A*

Study of Interpersonal Relations in Two Government Agencies (Chicago: University of Chicago Press, 1955).

15 To date, the government has avoided using legislation to intervene directly in collective bargaining between the school boards and their ATA locals. While there has been some labour unrest as a result of the funding cutbacks (e.g., strike votes taken by several teachers' locals and a work-to-rule campaign mounted by Calgary teachers), so far Alberta teachers have not resorted to strike action. This sets the Klein government's reform tactics apart from those used by the Harris government in Ontario, where provisions in collective agreements were recently set aside by Bill 160 and teachers expressed their anger by withdrawing their services both before and after the passage of the bill.

16 A five-member task force, headed by Dr. John Paterson of the University of Alberta Faculty of Education, was struck by the Alberta School Boards Association to hold public hearings into the status of special needs education in Alberta. The task force, which reported in the fall of 1997, concluded that inadequate funding due to government cutbacks has led to inadequate support services for special needs students and in many cases, long waits for the assessments required for extra program funding. See the Alberta School Boards Association publication, "In the Balance — Meeting Special Needs Within Public Education Task Force Findings," September 1997.

17 According to the Edmonton Regional Catholic School Division presentation to the Alberta Task Force on the Funding of Private Schools, 13 November 1997, this method of re-allocating funds among schools is used by the Edmonton Catholic Regional School Division. Edmonton Public School District principals have also engaged in a voluntary re-allocation of funds to support early literacy initiatives and special-needs programming for children with severe emotional/behavioural problems, who would otherwise be left in limbo by the government's recently imposed funding cap on this category of special needs grants (see footnote 4).

18 Alberta Education, *93rd Annual Report and 4th Annual Results Report, Part I, 1997-98*, 51.

19 Some school boards connect with the provincial telephone company, Telus; others, with rival AT&T (*Edmonton Journal*, 31 May 1997, B3; 1 June 1997, B2).

20 Ralph Klein, *Proceedings of the Alberta Legislative Assembly*, 9 December, 1997.

21 A. Inkpen and P. Killing, "Molson Breweries of Canada" in *Strategic Management*, A. Bakr Ibrahim and K. Argheyd, eds. (Toronto: McGraw-Hill Ryerson, 1992), 431-55. See also *Maclean's* 17 June 1996.

22 They have, however, fought each other in court over who owns the rights to ice beer.

23 *Edmonton Journal*, 19 January 1998, B3.

24 Edmonton Public School Board presentation to the Alberta Task Force on the Funding of Private Schools, 13 November 1997.

25 *Edmonton Journal*, 8 November 1997, B1.

26 *Edmonton Journal*, 17 June 1996, A1 and A12.

27 *Edmonton Journal*, 28 September 1988, B1.

28 *Edmonton Journal*, 13 September 1996, B1-B2; *Edmonton Journal*, 14 September 1996, B1.

29 B. Levin, "The lessons of international education reform" in *Journal of Education Policy* 12(4) (1997): 253-66, notes the underwhelming volume of evidence that competition "causes" improved achievement results. J.D. Maxwell and M.P. Maxwell, "The reproduction of class in Canada's elite independent schools" in *British Journal of Sociology of Education* 16(3) (1995): 309-26 discusses the creaming techniques that private schools use to perpetuate their academic standing.

30 See S. Ball, "Education markets, choice and social class: the market as a class strategy in the UK and the USA" in *British Journal of Sociology of Education* 14(1) (1993): 3-19. See also L.

Gordon, "'Rich' and 'poor' schools in Aotearoa" in *New Zealand Journal of Educational Studies* 29(2) (1994): 113-25.

31 See Alberta Education, *Report and Recommendations of the Private Schools Funding Task Force*, February 1998, and the Government of Alberta News Release, "Government Accepts Private Schools Funding Task Force Recommendations," 5 March 1998.

32 In the spring of 1998, Nancy MacBeth (formerly Betkowski) became Liberal leader in Alberta. MacBeth, who previously held the education and health portfolios in the Getty Conservative government and placed second to Ralph Klein in the 1992 Conservative leadership race, may pose a legitimate alternative to the Tories.

33 Alberta Private Schools Funding Task Force, *Part 1: Setting the Stage for Discussions* (Edmonton: Alberta Education, 1997), 5.

34 For example, Elk Island's "Council of Councils," Calgary's "Support Public Education — Act for Kids" (SPEAK), and Medicine Hat's "Citizens for Public Education."

35 On the one hand, if parent councils were able to coordinate their activities at the provincial level, they might gain some influence. In this scenario, councils would have to change their focus from local fund-raising and administrative advisement to become full-fledged political organizations that could lobby the Alberta government. On the other hand, if councils remain local and limited in their focus, their influence will be probably minimal. While detailed research about the effect of parent advisory councils on schooling in Alberta is lacking, some research concerning the outcomes of school-based management is available. For example, see B. Malen, R. Ogawa, and J. Kranz, "Site-based management: unfilled promises" in *The School Administrator* February 1990: 30-32, 53-56, 59. After reviewing 200 reports that describe attempts to institute school-based management, Malen et al. found that site participants rarely influenced policy, power relationships remained the same, school-council members supported the status quo, staff loads were increased, participants experienced role confusion, proposed instructional changes were rarely implemented, and there was little evidence of change in student achievement. (Thanks to Larry Phillips for this information.)

13

The Principalship at the Crossroads

Norm Yanitski and David Pysk

"Would you tell me, please, which way I ought to walk from here?"

"That depends a good deal on where you want to get to," said the Cat.

"I don't much care where . . . ," said Alice.

"Then it doesn't matter which way you walk," said the Cat.

". . . so long as I get somewhere," Alice added as an explanation.

"Oh, you're sure to do that," said the Cat, "if you only walk long enough."

— Lewis Carroll[1]

Not unlike Alice, Alberta's principals have come to many crossroads in the past few years. Current societal pressures that demand a new global competitiveness have placed additional demands and obligations on all public institutions, including schools. The role of the school principal has changed drastically since educational restructuring began in Alberta in 1994. Not only have principals' duties and responsibilities increased, but remuneration has decreased and job prestige has diminished. Politicians continue to criticize administration and its value to the educational endeavor. The impact of this massive change and uncertainty has resulted in difficulty attracting qualified individuals to replace positions vacated by stressed and retiring principals.[2] Further, as many principals look about and see their position at the crossroads of educational reform, they often wonder if they are on the right road and where it is taking them. Like explorers venturing into uncharted territory, principals are building a collaborative educational pathway that is emerging somewhere between the old bureaucratic system and the free-market movement.

The 1990s buzzword for both private and public organizations is change. Like death and taxes, change has become one of life's certainties, and the educational domain is not immune to change and its effects. Around the world, business and government have called for a massive restructuring of education (see introduction, chapter one). Governments everywhere are committed to educational restructuring so as to make the best possible use of resources, while at the same time recognizing pressures from global competitiveness, changing demographics, and a greater demand for parental involvement in educational decision-making. These pressures have created major inconsistencies for school principals everywhere. In Canada, every province has initiated discussions and introduced changes that will affect the method of delivery, management, accountability, fiscal responsibility, and quality of education. Ontario, through its controversial Bill 160, reduced the number of school boards from 129 to 66, eliminating up to 10,000 teaching positions, lengthening the school year, and cutting approximately $500 million from its education budget.[3] Quebec has recently tabled a bill that proposes major decentralization of the educational decision-making process.[4] Newfoundland has moved to abolish the church's role in education.[5] Almost all other provinces in Canada have restructured their school governance models in the 1990s, and Alberta is no exception. The purpose of this chapter is to set out the changing roles and responsibilities of school principals and present some of the current issues and concerns facing the position.

New Directions

In January 1994, Halvar Jonson, then Alberta's Minister of Education, announced a major restructuring plan for basic education in the province. The announcement outlined the implementation of a number of policy and directional changes (see chapter seven).[6] Central to the implementation of most of the new directional changes is the role of the principal. The reduction and refocussing of the governing structures has reduced the number of support services for schools at the provincial and regional level. This leaves the principal with the task of providing for a variety of support services for schools and their local communities. The reduction in educational funding and change in fiscal distribution on a per-pupil basis to a school-based budgeting model has put the principal in the added role of plant manager and school accountant. School leadership and management is being transformed into a community effort. School councils, community, and business partnerships have demanded a new, collaborative decision-making process that means more discussion, meetings, planning, evaluating, and political involvement for principals. This translates to more time being allocated to process and less time spent with students. Changes to the delivery of programs, new teacher evaluation policies, and an increase in evaluation and reporting procedures have also placed additional pressures and responsibilities in the hands of principals. All of these changes have occurred simultaneously as wages, compensation, staff, and support have been reduced. Principals are being asked to do more with less.

For today's new and redefined principals, much of their time is now turbulent, exhausting, confusing, political, and often made up of sheer administrative wizardry. On the one hand, principals are expected to restructure, transform, retool, and revolutionize the business of education and all those associated with it. On the other hand, they are being asked to reestablish and maintain an era and a standard that reflects a traditional view of basic education, comprising the three Rs, strong values, and strict discipline. All of this is occurring at a time when social, political, and economic changes are happening at an unparallelled rate. Educators are no longer the sole architects of education and schooling. Business and society are now demanding a say in shaping the purpose, responsibility, standard, and role of schools and principals.

Questions need to be asked. Are these demands based on improving education for students or are they based only on a new "bottom line"? More broadly, do we really know where we are going? Have we identified what end product we want, or are we simply following Alice's footsteps and trying to get somewhere fashionable and contemporary? In answering these questions — and as the people in the middle — principals must deal with students, parents, school councils, teachers, superintendents, school boards, the business community, business partners, support agencies, the media, police, health agencies, post-secondary institutions, and the department of education. All of these social, business, and educational stakeholders place demands on the principal and school staff.

As administratively encompassing and confusing as the role appears to be, the key component for the principal must be the stewardship of public education. The principal must be seen as receptive and responsive, and must attempt to satisfy concerns and deliver an exceptional product. At times, expectations may be consistent; at other times they may be in conflict. As the involvement and demands of various interest groups increase, so to will the role of the principal expand.

The current round of restructuring of education in Alberta has greatly transformed and expanded the role of the principalship. The restructuring of the department of education; reduction of school boards; changes to funding; introduction of site-based decision-making; increased choice for parents and students; increased involvement by parents, community, and businesses; and increased testing and reporting by schools have all lead to a dramatic role change for the principal. The principal can no longer be the sole decision-maker at the school: he or she must function more as the key facilitator, leader, communicator, and agent of change.

Because of increased demands, today's principals need to be well educated, resourceful, politically aware, financially responsible, exceptional communicators, and superior leaders. Leadership has become a complex phenomenon with implications for many aspects of the principal's personal and professional life. The principal's role involves leadership in group situations and in an organizational context. To ensure success at the school level, leadership means securing performance from all educational stakeholders, which in turn should lead to effective results. Principal leadership is a key ingredient in school success. In group situations, the leader's relationship with followers is an integral component of effectiveness.

The leadership dimension of the principal's role requires balancing several differing priorities. The principal can be increasingly seen as a servant of both the traditional and transformational needs of the school organization. The principal manages the hierarchy to the extent necessary, but leadership is focused on guiding, balancing, and supporting an empowered staff's and community's quest for effectiveness. Issues related to student attendance, discipline, and even the inclusion of fine-arts programming all require the principal to balance the needs of the students with demands from teachers, parents, and community groups. In their thinking and leadership styles, principals need to be simultaneously both big and small, centralized and decentralized. Big to realize the economies of scale and provide for a full range of educational services, and small to allow individual parents a voice in the decisions that affect their children. Centralized to provide consistency and efficiencies, and decentralized to ensure community input, support, and responsiveness to local issues and individual student needs.[7]

The Road to Leadership

The present development of the principal's role as the school leader may be traced to the mid nineteenth century.[8] The essential components of the principalship were largely defined by the end of the nineteenth century and have not undergone substantial change until recently. Over time, the duties and responsibilities have grown in quantity, significance, and complexity. The main role and functions of providing instructional leadership, school management, and educational stewardship have been expanded from the more specialized positions that existed in the past.

In the early beginnings of North American schools, there was no need for the position of head or principal teacher. Schools were small, usually one room, with a single teacher who served a small community or rural area. As communities began to grow and school enrollments increased, the need for more teachers and classroom spaces grew. With the development of student grading and the departmentalization of services, someone was needed to function as the head of the school and make decisions on behalf of the board of education and the department regarding curriculum, instruction, grading, and general operations of the school. Thus, the role of the principal-teacher was created. By the late 1800s, the responsibility of the principal began to shift from the maintenance of records and reports to school organization and general administration. By the early 1900s, the principal had become the directing manager rather than the presiding teacher of the school. The role was further expanded to include the daily management of schools and the area of instructional supervision. Administrative functions increased with principals conducting teacher meetings, teacher supervision and professional development, pupil services, grading and student progress, and instructional methodology. The role evolved to include many day-to-day administrative services from school operation to record-keeping. (Finances, plant maintenance, staffing, policy, and politics were functions usually performed by school boards and superintendents who had the time to provide this specialized leadership.)

By the mid-1970s, Alberta had developed an extensive educational system that comprised the Minister of Education, the Department of Education, regional offices of the department, local school boards, superintendents and central offices, and schools that were run by principals. This system of policy development and educational support remained in place until the early 1990s, when a complete reorganization and restructuring of the system and constituent responsibilities was introduced. This overhaul has dramatically affected the role of today's public school principal.

Data collected by Alberta Education for the 1996/97 school year[9] indicate there are over 2000 principals in elementary, junior high, and high schools employed in public, separate, private, and federal schools. The schools operated by these principals range in size from under 100 students to over 2500 students. Of the teachers who provided data to Alberta Education for certification purposes, just over thirty percent of principals were women and almost seventy percent were men. The average age of women principals was about forty-five years, for male principals, forty-eight years. (Data on the average level of education and experience in the role of principal were not collected by Alberta Education.)

Today, some four years after Alberta's educational restructuring plan was unveiled, the educational bureaucratic structure has been radically reorganized. The organizational structure is still headed by the Minister of Education, but the Department of Education has radically downsized all bureaus, except the evaluations and testing branch. Regional offices have been eliminated, and school boards have been reduced from 141 to 63 (see chapters seven and twelve). All of the work, resources, and support that was available through these various departments has virtually disappeared, but commitment, responsibility, and obligations to students and taxpayers have not. Accountability for budgeting, special-needs programs, and resource acquisition have been downloaded to the schools and the office of the principal. Funding cuts, salary reductions, downsizing, and inflation have further eroded the capacity of schools and the principal to maintain service levels for students. Individual student instruction has been reduced as the pupil-teacher ratios have increased, and program choice has been drastically reduced as funding cuts dictated programming for a basic education.

Highway '94: The Road to Change

One of the initial changes, and probably the most difficult to accept and undertake, was the reduction in funding. Schools and principals were asked to re-evaluate all of their services and programs and eliminate or pare down those deemed least effective and efficient. Many hours were spent with staff and parents before programs were reduced. Teachers and support personnel were cut, and all but the basic, essential services eliminated. Class sizes increased, extracurricular programs were terminated or began charging user fees, field trips were drastically curtailed, and non-"core" programs like the arts were cut back. Maintenance and renovations were greatly scaled down and capital expenditures put on hold. These cutbacks and structural changes were occurring while provincial enrollments were growing, buildings were aging, and demands for technology, individualized instruction and student choice in programming were high. Principals had to become more creative and offer quality programming with diminished resources. Many schools revisited their missions and specialized their program efforts.

The second biggest challenge to the role of the principal was the implementation of a site-based decision-making (SBDM) model. Most principals and school districts had been using a centralized decision-making model where decisions relating to staffing, capital, maintenance, and programs were made at the district level. With the implementation of SBDM, discussions, decisions, and responsibility fell on the local school and the principal. There was no increase in staffing or time provided for the new responsibilities.

Principals were required to develop an education plan for the school and outline every program and budget item. This education plan meant endless meetings with the staff, parents, school councils, students (in high schools), community, business associates, and central office. The principal became the central player trying to balance the educational needs and standards of his students with the requests and demands from the various stakeholders. This meant constantly revisiting goals and directions so they would satisfy those involved and still meet the budget targets established. Many evenings, weekends, and holidays were taken to complete the task. Principals who had previously received instructions, staffing, and budgets from central office and run their own schools now had to incorporate a collaborative decision-making format. Some found it easy to adjust. Others, however, took early retirement packages, while still others left the administrative realm and went back to the classroom. The politics of trying to please everyone, while doing a job limited by policy and funding restrictions and carrying the burden of responsibility, made a difficult job even more demanding.

A further change that occurred was the elimination and reduction of school boards by nearly sixty percent. This change realigned boundaries, created new school divisions, and changed a large number of superintendencies. New policies were created, organizational structures changed, and the old way of doing things was abandoned. With cutbacks to central administration to a four-percent level, support services and personnel for schools were reduced. This meant that, at a time when principals and schools needed the most help for a transition to SBDM, help was limited.

Additional demands for greater accountability came in the form of provincial assessment and testing. All grade three, six, nine, and twelve students now write year-end achievement exams. The exams are intended to be diagnostic indicators of how well students are doing relative to the curriculum at each of the grade levels. One consequence of this development is that the exams have become a public and media rating scale of the "best" schools. Pressure has been placed on principals to have their schools and students do consistently better than other schools and achieve better than the provincial average on these tests. But averages, being mathematical expressions, mean that, generally speaking, half of the students and schools must always be below the mean. Politicians are crafting definitions for student "success" that make no sense. For example, some politicians have indicated that they would like to see *all students above the provincial average* — by definition a statistical impossibility.

Civil Culture or Education Street?

As the head of the school, the principal's job has become a many-faceted enterprise. Principals have to deal with a greater range of concerns and problems than their predecessors. Ten years ago, major problems in the schools were smoking, skipping classes, and talking out in class. Today, the principal deals with students on parole, custody and guardianship issues, foster family placements, social services, police, and an endless array of concerns from demanding parents.

Principals often have to deal with issues related to educational priorities. Parents regularly come into the school to see the principal and discuss their viewpoints about homework. Some parents of students who play hockey believe that there should be no homework: school work should happen in school, not at home because after-school is home and family time. The value of education and the policy on homework often create conflicts between parents and the principal. Some parents appear to be more interested in assisting their child with their sports interests than in helping with school-assigned homework. At the other end of the spectrum, some parents want more homework assigned.

Even the most trivial of issues can create conflict between parents and schools. Many parents have come into a principal's office demanding an explanation to the letter or phone-call home about the inappropriate language being used by their child. As soon as the parent opens his or her mouth, and every second word uttered is a choice four-letter idiom, the principal knows where the conversation is headed. The parent usually explains that this is the everyday conversation used at home and work. An explanation of school rules, policy, and acceptable language seldom wins over such parents, who often state that it's their child, it's a free country, and only they can tell their child what they can and cannot do.

In recent years, more and more teenage students have taken on part-time or full-time jobs. These jobs often interfere with class schedules and homework time. Students end up skipping classes while they work and do not complete assignments, usually resulting in a failing grade. Students and many parents often see money, work, clothes, cars, and freedom as more important than school. Trying to get these students to come to school and succeed is often a difficult task for the principal and teachers.

Family break-ups can sometimes lead to chaotic scenes at the school. Custody is often in question, and one parent may request that the school and principal ensure that the other parent has no contact with the child. Arguments, fights, tears, lawyers, and police are often part of these situations. Principals usually do not have legal information as to who has custody rights and often get trapped in the middle of a family feud.

When parents perceive that the whole world is against them and their child, they often take things into their own hands before discussing the issue with the principal or other authorities. Parents have come to the school and barged into classes threatening teachers or other students. Violence is sometimes the result. One mother was so angered that a group of boys was picking on her son that she drove onto the school grounds during lunch break and intimidated this group of students. Police are also frustrated with the public's general lack of respect for authority and social institutions.

In today's fast-paced world, where families are trying to survive, principals have had to extend their roles from teacher to that of caregiver. Many schools have set up child-care services at the school to look after children from early morning till late at night. This program often includes meals, clothes, and love. Many principals feel that if the schools did not provide these services, many students would not have the opportunity for a quality school program. Such programs require additional time, resources, and funds.

One of the most challenging problems that the principal has had to deal with recently has been issues related to drugs, alcohol, and violence. Although these incidents are rare, increasing numbers of students come to school under the influence of drugs or alcohol, or are bringing knives and other weapons to school for protection or intimidation purposes. In a 1996 Alberta Teachers' Association (ATA) survey, fifty-six percent of teachers reported an increase in disruptive classroom behavior.[10] Violence and abuse related to drugs and alcohol are on the rise. Racial tensions have caused various violent outbreaks that have involved the use of dangerous weapons.[11] Trying to educate students who see survival as their primary objective is not an easy job. The principal is responsible for ensuring the safety of these students and all others at the school. Some principals have taken firm yet innovative positions when it comes to bullying and violence.[12] Society often points a finger at the school and says fix the problem. This is when many principals ask themselves whether they are supposed to be educators or social physicians. Social problems are multi-faceted, often the result of a rapidly changing world and changing moral values, and are beyond the control of any one principal or community. But at the provincial level — where something might be done for all schools in Alberta — demands have increased, resources have been reduced, and expectations are over-stated.

Restructuring, decentralization, and changing social values have changed the role of the principal considerably. The principalship has become the focal point for students, parents, teachers, the ATA, business, trustees, superintendents, government, and the community at large to express their views and influence decisions at the local school level. With this pluralistic perspective, it is extremely difficult to defend the public interest as leaders of the common good, since each individual or group wants to be at the forefront with their point of view. These views are often diametrically opposed. The parent may want smaller class sizes, while the government wants to control spending and keep class sizes at a level it deems appropriate. This places the principal in a dilemma, because parents are told that education dollars are decentralized to the school, based on student enrollment, and that the principal has the flexibility to organize the school according to the specific needs of the community. Parents may not understand the limiting factors that define parameters a principal cannot change. The principal cannot simply re-allocate funds to hire additional staff or free up more time for additional option courses. The funding allocated to schools is usually sufficient only to run the school with the lowest number of staff required. A principal cannot pull money out of thin air. And while the increase in educational funding contained in the 1998 budget is welcomed, it still does not go far enough in meeting the pressures faced by principals.

The Next Intersection

Aside from the limited and decreasing resources they administer, principals also have less power to make autonomous decisions based on the best interest of the students in an extremely complex world. The recent reforms have forced principals to become managers of the public purse instead of stewards of education. Furthermore, principals are severely and increasingly limited in spending their time as instructional leaders. Recent changes have completely overturned the role of the principal. An over-abundance of stakeholders with limited responsibility are drawing the principal away from student-centered issues into the political realm of "satisfactoriness."[13] The principalship has become a contested position for political maneuvering and the site of interaction between multiple players. This interaction has increased the principals' workload, time commitments, and stress levels.

In spite of the massive role change, however, most principals would prefer not to go back to the centralized management system. "With all its challenges, they [principals] seem to prefer the choices and autonomy that the new system provides over the limitations that are inherent in complex bureaucracies."[14] As much as business and government would like to encourage public education to compete in a free-market system, principals are responsible to serve all students in a publicly funded education system. Principals are guiding the education system along a road somewhere between bureaucracy and free enterprise. Today's principals have become transformational leaders, moving the organization from "past practices" to new "future practices," a movement must be accomplished for the institution to survive.

■ ■ ■

How will the role of the principal evolve over the next decade? A significant factor will be the degree to which the provincial government initiates policy that places school councils in positions of influence at the school site. If school councils become more like "mini-school boards," principals will become more like superintendents. The issue here is how governance of schools will be managed over the next decade. Many school councils have indicated that they are not interested in evolving into *de facto* school boards. If the provincial government listens to these councils, governance will remain the domain of the school boards. Given current trends, the multi-faceted position of principal may evolve into an executive administrative position, outside the teachers' association, with the principal's role a blend of educational leader and business manager.[15]

At today's crossroads, principals have to be ever optimistic and are to be commended for their dedication and service to students and the community. They truly are a special type of leader, steering their schools between the old and the new roads. The role of the principal is essential to restructuring in today's political climate. We have travelled a long way since 1994, and successful schools are becoming more responsive to their stakeholders. Principals offer efficient and effective programs that are accountable to a diverse student population. This is a tremendous accomplishment, given the magnitude of restructuring that has occurred within the Alberta education system.

Notes

1 *Alice's Adventures in Wonderland* (New York: William Morrow and Company, Inc., 1992), 89-90.

2 J. Gray-Grant, "Few stepping forward to fill jobs of retiring administrators" in *Education Leader* 9(11) (1996): 1-8.

3 *Globe and Mail,* 24 October 1997, A1 and A5.

4 R. Seguin, article, *Quebec Bureau,* 14 November 1997, A1.

5 *Globe and Mail,* 2 September 1997, A5.

6 Alberta Education, press release, *Restructuring Education.* Edmonton: Government of Alberta, 18 January 1994.

7 M. Reddyk, *Managing the Process: School Division Amalgamation/Restructuring* (doctoral dissertation, University of Saskatchewan, Saskatoon, 1996).

8 P.R. Pierce, *The Origin and Development of the Public School Principalship* (Chicago: University of Chicago Press, 1935).

9 Alberta Education, *Alberta Principals — School Year 1996/97* (Edmonton: Government of Alberta, 22 August, 1997). Given the unconsolidated state of the data as it now exists, note that the data shown here and its interpretation represent teachers who have provided information to Alberta Education for certification purposes and does not necessarily represent the total principal population.

10 K. Virag, *ATA News,* 11 November 1997, 4.

11 *Edmonton Journal,* 5 July 1996, A20.

12 David Staples, column, *Edmonton Journal,* 6 July 1997, B1.

13 *Satisfactoriness:* An attitude or response of "it's good enough," that will include suggestions and solutions from all parties in an attempt to appease everyone. Not necessarily the most effective or efficient solution or approach.

14 R. Williams, B. Harold, and G. Southworth, "Sweeping decentralization of educational decision-making authority." *Phi Delta Kappan,* 78(8) (1997): 626-631.

15 Norm Yanitski, *Site-Based Management: Its Impact on School Decision-Making* (doctoral dissertation. Edmonton: University of Alberta, 1997).

Conclusion

Trevor W. Harrison and Jerrold L. Kachur

For me education is simultaneously an act of knowing, a political act, and an artistic event.
— Paulo Freire[1]

Clearly, much has changed in Alberta since the government of Ralph Klein came to power in 1993. Nowhere have these changes been more apparent than in education, at both the K-12 and post-secondary levels. Educational funding was slashed; corporate sponsors were invited into the schools and universities; charter schools were encouraged; teachers were subjected to increased workplace discipline; the number of school boards was reduced; and administrators came under increased and contradictory pressures to deal with the results.

While detailing these specific changes, this book has also attempted to situate and explain those changes — their causes and their implications — in both a spatial and a temporal sense. Spatially, we have argued that educational change in Alberta cannot be separated from broader changes occurring throughout the Western industrialized world and, indeed, everywhere under the rubric of globalization. We argue that — more than ever — the meaning and purpose of education is being reduced to that of servant to the economy, in particular, the dominant corporate elite.

At the same time, this book also has tried to identify Alberta in its specificity. While Canada remains on the semi-periphery within global capitalism, so Alberta remains a resource hinterland within Canada and North America. This fact has real consequences for Alberta's class structure, economic development, and the ideas that inform educational debate in the province.

Contrary to some recent theorists, we believe that history matters. The changes that have occurred under the tenure of Ralph Klein are dramatic, but they are not without precedent. These changes are part of the ebb and flow of educational conflict, as noted by Kas Mazurek in chapter one. Nor has the remaking of education in Alberta come to a close. History continues to unfold, albeit in both predictable and unpredictable ways.

It was predictable, for example, that the Klein government would be re-elected on March 11, 1997. Opposition was divided, the economy was booming, and Ralph Klein continued to attract broad support based on personal style. Thus, the Tories captured 63 seats with 51.2 percent of the vote. The Liberals took 18 seats (32.7 percent), the New Democrat's 2 seats

(8.8 percent), and Social Credit no seats (6.8 percent). Since then, the government has pursued — albeit in more subtle ways — the same path of educational restructuring adopted during its first mandate.

It was also predictable that, despite budget surpluses, education in Alberta would continue to be squeezed, with costs continuing to be off-loaded on families and individual schools. Occasionally, the contradictions become obvious. On September 1, 1998, for example, Treasurer Stockwell Day predicted (based on first-quarter figures) a surplus for the year 1998/99 of $277 million. At almost the same time, documents from Alberta Education revealed that school-generated funds (e.g., from raffles, etc.) were $119.4 million for the first quarter, up from a predicted $70.8 million.

The continuation of corporate welfare in Alberta was also predictable. Since April 1997, the Alberta government has written off a $244 million investment in Millar Western Industries; spent $15 million more concluding lawsuits filed on behalf of noteholders in the Principal Group, an Edmonton-based company that filed for bankruptcy in 1987; and, on March 3, 1998, written off $131 million in interest owed from the Al-Pac pulp mill.

Is anyone surprised that the links between corporations and Alberta universities have continued to strengthen? On September 24, 1997, the University of Alberta launched Research and Technology Management Incorporated as a for-profit subsidiary for the commercialization of new technologies developed at the university. The company is owned, operated, and funded by an independent board of directors, but forty percent of its annual $1 million budget is subsidized by the Alberta government. Similarly, on March 26, 1998, forestry giant Weyerhaeuser Canada, along with the Weyerhaeuser Company Foundation, provided $1.05 million to the University of Alberta for forestry research.

But not all of the corporate links have to deal with research. On March 5, 1998, students at the University of Alberta voted to give Coca-Cola an exclusive ten-year-right to sell its product lines of soft drinks on the university campus. In exchange, the company agreed to donate a minimum of $5 million to fund student bursaries and scholarships. The University of Alberta thus joined in the cola wars with the University of Calgary, which signed a similar deal with Pepsi in July 1997.

Finally, it was also predictable that oil prices would remain volatile. On November 1, 1997, the price of oil was $21.08 US per barrel, but thereafter began a steady decline. By March 17, 1998, the price of oil had dropped to $13.23 US per barrel, causing Treasurer Stockwell Day to state that the government might have to revise its budget forecasts downwards. Premier Klein added, however, that, if cuts were necessary, they would not occur in education and health.

Less predictable, and admittedly uneven, has been resistance to the educational change in the province. The bluster of talk radio aside, Albertans are not generally given to protest. Albertans' habitual drive to conformity — "consensus" is the operative word — has been ably reinforced by the government's use of stakeholder forums. Nonetheless, poll after poll since 1993 has shown widespread unease among Albertans regarding these changes. Important concerns remain about the state of health and education in Alberta.

Since the 1997 election, concern has also increasingly translated into action. Teachers have understandably been in the forefront of this unrest. In June 1997, for example, Calgary public teachers took a strike vote which later resulted in job action and work-to-rule, and was only resolved in December 15, 1997 with the acceptance of a new contract with the Calgary Board of Education. Similar kinds of teacher unrest — in both the public and Catholic systems — have occurred in Edmonton, Grande Prairie, and other Alberta locales.

It is not teachers alone, however, who are increasingly speaking out. Students, both at the K-12 and post-secondary levels, and their parents have joined teachers in protesting the changes to education. On October 4, 1997, between 12,000 and 20,000 teachers and their supporters rallied at the provincial legislature condemning provincial budget cuts and demanding more spending on education. This was followed on October 25, 1997 with a march by approximately 1,200 parents, teachers, and students on Premier Klein's Calgary constituency office to protest education cuts and to demand reinvestment.

On January 28, 1998, approximately 150 University of Alberta students marched on the Alberta legislature to protest rising post-secondary tuition fees. On February 13, 1998, the Board of Governors of the University of Alberta announced an increase in tuition fees, from $3,436 in 1997/98 to $3,669 in 1998/99. This increase resulted in further student protests. More recently, on October 13, 1998, twenty student representatives from across Alberta meet with Premier Klein and Advanced Education Minister Clint Dunford to lobby for increased post-secondary funding. The students complained that rising tuition rates and a brain-drain of faculty make it tough for Alberta students to compete.

There are even some signs — though we don't want to overstate this — of resistance growing within the Tory party. Throughout 1997 and 1998, delegates to Alberta Conservative party conventions repeatedly divided on supporting either tax cuts and corporate welfare or increased spending on social programs and education. It will be interesting to see the outcome of these internal divisions within the Tory party on politics and policies in Alberta.

What Can be Done? Public Policy Recommendations

This book describes some of the key changes to education in Alberta since 1993, and the political, economic, and ideological factors underlying those changes. But no book directed at public policy should stop at merely describing. The task is also to prescribe policies and initiatives to deal with practical problems. With this in mind, the contributors to this book recommend the following:

Education and Social Spending

• That public education funding be immediately increased to a level above the average of provincial spending across Canada on education, and that public funding of private schools be eliminated.

• That governments at all levels make increased efforts at redressing the inequities of wealth and income that result in unequal educational outcomes.

• That a serious review be conducted of Alberta's corporate and personal tax structures with an eye to ensuring stable long-term funding for the key programs of health, social welfare, and education.

• That there be increased transparency in the Public Accounts and other government documentation regarding expenditures. At a minimum, all government expenditures should be reported both in actual and real dollars. Additionally, expenditures should be reported in both per-capita and (in the case of education) per-student ratios.

• That funding structures and levels for special needs students be modified.

• That immediate and increased expenditures be made on school infrastructure.

• That all user fees be eliminated immediately at the K-12 levels and that tuition fees be gradually eliminated at the post-secondary level.

Teaching and Teachers

• That real class sizes be limited to twenty students at the elementary level and twenty-five students at the secondary levels in order to provide a better environment for learning, more opportunity for individual student-teacher interaction (enabling teachers to better know their students), and better quality student-teacher interaction in general.

• That barriers to hiring in education, based on sex, religion, ethnicity, race, culture, and class, be eliminated and encouragement be given to the hiring of teachers reflective of the growing diversity of cultures within Alberta and Canada.

• That teachers and their bargaining unit, the Alberta Teachers' Association, be actively consulted and involved in the implementation of changes to primary and secondary education.

• That Alberta legislation governing the employment of part-time teachers (Section 84) be subsumed under a general section regarding contracts of employment, as it is in most other Canadian provinces.

Administration and Curriculum

• That the role of principal be clarified and training for the job designed accordingly.

• That the administrative chain of command be more clearly defined.

• That Alberta Education introduce a universal core curriculum for students in early childhood and elementary education, minimizing diversity and choice until later grades. Where diversity or choice is required — as in the case of Catholic schooling — and to reduce the potential for educational and social inequalities, there should be easy transference of credits from one program to another.

Technology

• That a complete and independent study be conducted on the implications for educational institutions, teaching, and society at large of the increased use of technology at both the K-12 and post-secondary levels.

Alternative Schooling

• That there be a full and broad public consultation about the kind of alternative school programs Albertans are prepared to support.

• That all private schools receiving government funding be promoted to charter school status, with all chartered school corporations being subordinated to democratically elected public boards.

Program Evaluation and Measurement

• That the Alberta government and Alberta Education develop performance measures that provide evidence of the impacts of educational reforms thus far implemented, and that the range of impacts be broadly conceptualized to include social and individual outcomes.

• That the Alberta government, Alberta Labour, and Alberta Economic Development implement measures dealing with the short-term and long-term impact of educational reforms on the teaching profession.

• That expenditures be increased on educational research and data collection within the departments of Advanced Education and Career Development and of Education.[2]

■ ■ ■

Our final recommendation — really, an admonition — is directed at Albertans at large. A battle for education in Alberta, Canada, and the world is raging. Who will run our schools? How will they be funded?

What is education for? Indeed, what is "education"? We cannot shirk from engaging in the contest for our classrooms to answer these questions. We owe it to ourselves and to our children to enter the fray.

Notes

1 "Reading the world and reading the word: An interview with Paulo Freire" in *Language Arts* 62(1) (1985): 17.

2 In the course of conducting research for this book, it became known to the editors that Alberta Education could not provide basic statistics beyond 1994/95, and Advanced Education and Career Development beyond 1991/92. The reason in both cases, we were informed, was because research services had been cut to the bone. Proper planning and assessment is impossible without accurate and up-to-date statistical information.

Appendices

Appendix A: The Alberta Budget, 1998/99 The budget at a glance

$million	Actual	Forecast in 1997 budget	1998 budget	Forecast
Fiscal year ending March 31	1996/97	1997/98	1997/98	1998/99
Revenue	16,747	14,710	17,089	15,159
Total Spending	14,220	14,556	14,890	14,994
– Program Spending	12,892	13,358	13,722	13,901
– Interest on public debt	1,328	1,198	1,168	1,093
Budgetary Surplus	2,527	154	2,199	165
Net New Debt*	-2,527	-450	-2,199	-585
Net Debt Outstanding+	3,743	3,293	1,544	959

* A minus sign indicates the province is paying down debt.
+ Excludes unfunded pension liabilities and is net of Heritage Fund and other financial assets. Numbers may not add due to rounding.
Source: *Globe and Mail*, 13 February 1998.

Alberta revenue sources and expenditures, 1998/99, in percentages

Sources		Expenditures	
Personal Income Taxes	25.3	Education	29.1
Corporate Income Tax	9.7	Health	28.1
Other taxes	15.2	Social Services.	9.2
Resources	15.2	Interest	7.3
Investments	9.3	Transportation/Public Works	6.8
Fees	8.1	Development	5.5
Other Revenue	8.7	Other	14.0
Total:	**$15.2 billion**	**Total:**	**$15.0 billion**

Source: *Edmonton Journal*, 13 February 1998.

Appendix B: Provincial Comparisons of Per-Student Spending, 1985/86 to 1996/97

Province	1985/86	1992/93	1993/94	1994/95	1995/96	1996/97
Newfoundland	3,381	5,306	5,247	5,100	5,040	5,108
Prince Edward Island	3,321	5,226	5,467	5,250	4,901	5,148
Nova Scotia	3,851	5,241	5,635	5,648	5,480	5,366
New Brunswick	3,992	5,784	5,842	5,940	5,973	6,156
Quebec	5,175	6,745	6,946	7,078	7,129	7,032
Ontario	4,552	6,886	7,050	6,857	6,833	6,649
Manitoba	4,615	6,344	6,472	6,481	6,546	6,620
Saskatchewan	4,328	5,474	5,399	5,515	5,653	5,637
Alberta	**4,804**	**5,861**	**5,998**	**5,845**	**5,826**	**5,848**
British Columbia	4,139	6,284	6,509	6,504	6,817	6,882
Canadian Average	4,216	5,915	6,066	6,022	6,020	6,045

Source: Statistics Canada publications, *Education Quarterly Review* 3(2) (cited in the *92nd Annual Report of Alberta Education 1996-1997*).

Appendix C: Real Per-Pupil Spending in Public Elementary and Secondary Schools, 1985/86 to 1996/97 (1986 = 100)

Province	1985/86	1990/91	1996/97	% Change
Newfoundland	3,445	4,051	4,019	+16.6
Prince Edward Island	3,436	3,795	3,884	+13.0
Nova Scotia	3,973	4,398	4,118	+3.6
New Brunswick	4,163	4,640	4,732	+13.7
Quebec	5,373	5,374	5,503	+2.4
Ontario	4,746	5,473	4,889	+3.0
Manitoba	4,732	5,498	5,213	+10.2
Saskatchewan	4,491	4,682	4,597	+2.4
Alberta	**4,972**	**4,901**	**4,547**	**-8.5**
British Columbia	4,194	5,072	5,091	+21.4

Source: Statistics Canada publications, *Education Quarterly Review* 3(2) (cited in the *92nd Annual Report of Alberta Education 1996-1997*).

Appendix D: Estimates of Educational Attainment, Labour Force Participation Rate, and Unemployment Rate, Canada and Alberta, December 1996

Education Level	Canada Population 15 years and over (000)	P.R.	U.R.	Alberta Population 15 years and over (000)	P.R.	U.R.
0-8	2,804	25.7	15.4	135	31.8	—
Some Secondary	4,538	50.3	15.8	430	58.1	11.1
High School	4,464	70.1	9.8	444	75.6	4.7
Some Post-Secondary	2,201	67.2	10.0	237	69.6	6.3
Post-Secondary Certificate/Diploma	6,266	75.9	7.6	591	80.4	4.4
University Degree	3,233	82.1	4.6	291	84.0	4.5
Total	23,507	63.9	9.4	2,129	71.1	5.8

* In thousands
Source: Statistics Canada, Table 5, *Estimates by Educational Attainment, Sex and Age, Canada and Provinces*, December 1996. Cat. #71-001-XPB.

Appendix E: Educational Attainment, Total Population, Canada and Alberta, December 1996, in percentages

Education Level	Canada Population 15 years and over (000)	%	Alberta Population 15 years and over (000)	%
0-8	2,804	12	135	6
Some Secondary	4,538	19	430	20
High School	4,464	19	444	21
Some Post-Secondary	2,201	9	237	11
Post-Secondary Certificate/Diploma	6,266	27	591	28
University Degree	3,233	14	291	14
Total	23,507	100	2,119	100

* In thousands
Source: Calculated from Statistics Canada, Table 5, *Estimates by Educational Attainment, Sex and Age, Canada and Provinces*, December 1996. Cat. #71-001-XPB.

Appendix F: Average Earnings in Canada by Age and Education, 1990 and 1995, in Constant 1995 Dollars

	15-24	25-34	35-44	45-54	55-64	65+	Total
Total 1990	10,212	26,519	33,855	35,816	31,249	21,742	27,170
< Grade 9	9,005	17,273	21,661	24,138	23,092	15,547	21,100
Grades 9-13*	7,175	21,936	26,015	28,173	26,047	19,086	19,933
Grades 9-13**	11,136	24,055	28,627	31,347	29,102	21,406	23,655
< University Degree	11,776	26,683	33,021	35,527	32,571	21,936	27,257
University Degree	13,045	34,462	51,100	60,640	60,067	40,960	44,658
Total 1995	8,199	24,689	32,155	35,317	30,448	20,446	26,474
< Grade 9	8,178	16,197	19,416	22,412	21,442	13,696	19,377
Grades 9-13*	5,498	20,001	24,662	26,705	24,301	17,089	18,639
Grades 9-13**	8,938	22,163	27,006	29,434	26,978	19,199	22,846
< University Degree	9,318	24,258	31,039	33,827	30.706	19,936	25,838
University Degree	10,851	31,002	48,140	55,614	54,519	39,334	42,054

* Without degree.
** With degree.
Source: Statistics Canada, as reported in the *Globe and Mail*, 13 May, 1998, A4.

Appendix G: Post-Secondary Expenses and Debts in Canada

Expenses:

Average yearly expenses, full-time undergraduate study, 1983*	$5,665
Average yearly expenses, full-time undergraduate study, 1997*	$10,856

Debt:

Average post-secondary debt upon graduation, per student, 1990	$8,000
Average post-secondary debt upon graduation, per student, 1993	$13,000
Average post-secondary debt upon graduation, per student, 1997	$22,000
Average post-secondary debt upon graduation, per student, 1998 (est.)	$25,000

* Includes tuition, rent, food, books, transportation, and miscellaneous expenses.
Sources: *The Maclean's Guide to Canadian Universities 97* (Toronto: Maclean Hunter, 1997), 48-52; *Edmonton Journal*, 27 September 1997, A7.

Appendix H: Student Enrollment,* by School System, Level of Instruction, and Gender, 1990/91, 1993/94, 1994/95

	1990/91	1993/94	1994/95
By School System+			
Public	395,416	411,687	414,090
Separate	91,196	104,152	99,063
Private	21,311	23,447	26,289
Home education	1,674	5,465	6,303
Total	509,597	544,751	545,745
By Level of Instruction			
ECS			
Public	27,147	26,191	26,525
Separate	7,668	8,352	7,554
Private	6,448	6,183	6,480
Home education	n/a	n/a	n/a
Total	41,263	40,726	40,559
Elementary			
Public	191,949	195,646	196,479
Separate	45,772	52,482	49,594
Private	7,718	8,545	9,696
Home education	994	3,111	3,481
Total	246,433	259,784	259,250
Junior High			
Public	86,380	90,301	93,624
Separate	19,477	22,473	22,091
Private	3,283	3,902	4,281
Home education	504	1,297	1,582
Total	109,644	117,973	125,578
Senior High			
Public	89,940	99,549	97,462
Separate	18,279	20,845	19,824
Private	3,862	4,817	5,832
Home education	176	1,057	1,240
Total	112,257	126,268	124,358
By Gender#			
ECS			
Male	21,443	20,754	21,006
Female	19,820	19,972	19,553
Elementary			
Male	126,843	132,323	131,609
Female	118,596	124,350	124,160
Junior High			
Male	56,241	60,064	61,662
Female	52,899	56,612	58,334
Senior High			
Male	57,206	64,225	62,919
Female	54,875	60,986	60,199
Totals			
Male	261,733	277,366	277,196
Female	246,190	261,920	262,246

* Excludes Lloydminster, where students are enrolled in the Saskatchewan education system.
+Public includes Public Districts, Divisions and Counties, Roman Catholic Public Districts, Protestant Separate Districts, Regional Districts and Divisions, and Francophone Education Regions. Separate refers to Roman Catholic Separate Districts. Private includes ECS Private Operators.
Does not include home education.
Source: Alberta Education, *Education in Alberta: Basic Statistics*, 1995.

Appendix I: Public and Separate School Personnel,* By Function, 1990/91, 1993/94, 1994/95, in percentages

Function	1990/91	1993/94	1994/95
Administration	13.3	12.5	12.1
Teaching	81.0	82.0	81.8
Support Staff	5.6	4.9	4.3
Unknown	0.2	0.6	1.7

* Excludes substitute teachers.
Source: Alberta Education, *Education in Alberta: Basic Statistics*, 1995.

Appendix J: Total School Personnel,* By Gender, 1990/91, 1993/94, 1994/95, in percentages

Gender	1990/91	1993/94	1994/95
Male	11,706	11,674	11,277
Female	19,389	20,486	20,287
Total	31,095	32,160	31,564

* Excludes substitute teachers; includes personnel in public, separate, and private systems.
Source: Alberta Education, *Education in Alberta: Basic Statistics*, 1995.

Appendix K: Quick Facts on Inequality and Education in Alberta and Canada

Economic Inequality: Statistics gathered by Human Resources Development Canada show that market-income inequality has continued to rise with each recession from 1980 to 1994 and that, since 1978, social health no longer increases in step with a rise in GDP. With some variation, this national pattern is reflected in all the provinces. Similarly, Statistics Canada reports that salary and wage inequalities continue to grow in Canada, with Alberta and Newfoundland singled out for having the fastest rate of growth in inequality. A study released by the Centre for Social Justice in October 1998 provides similar data, showing that the gap between the poorest ten percent and the richest ten percent of income earners in Canada has risen steadily since 1993, with the ratio being 1:22 in 1996. In an international comparison of the richest countries, the 1997 United Nations Human Development ranks Canada as having less income disparity between rich and poor than France, New Zealand, the US, or the UK, but more income disparity than Italy, Germany, Sweden, the Netherlands, and Japan. (Note: Education reform in Alberta is based on national models provided by New Zealand, the US, and the UK, the highest income inequality countries.)

Sources: Statistics Canada, *Canadian Economic Observer*, Catalogue 11-010-XPB, February 1998; Canadian Council on Social Development, *The Progress of Canada's Children 1997* (Ottawa: CCSD, 1997), 19; Human Resources Development Canada, Applied Research Branch (ARB) Strategic Policy, "Social policy research at HRDC: the traditional and the transitional"(HRDC, June 1997); Centre for Social Justice, *The Growing Gap*, 1998.

Income Inequality: The gap between rich and poor incomes has widened considerably in the past decade. The income of the poorest fifth of families fell by twenty percent between 1989 and 1995 (before government transfers). In looking at government transfers, the poorest fifth dropped 3.9 per cent; the next poorest fifth dropped 7.6 percent; and the richest fifth dropped 2.8 per cent. But even though the richest fifth has suffered some loss of transfer payments, anyone with investment or retirement income made market gains (on average $530) and was more than compensated for any loss due to reduced transfer payments. By 1995, government transfers made up just 12.1 percent of total family income, down from 12.5 percent in 1994 and 12.9 percent in 1993. In 1995, governments reduced the after-tax income of the Canadian family to $44,286, down 5.4 percent from its peak in 1989. This drop in market income and withdrawal of transfers affected the poor more than the rich.

Sources: Statistics Canada, "Income after tax, distributions by size in Canada," Catalogue 13-210-XPB (Ottawa: Minister of Supply and Services, 1997); Canadian Council on Social Development, *The Progress of Canada's Children 1997*, Ottawa: CCSD, 1997, 19. Also see *Globe and Mail* The Middle Kingdom, Amazing Facts Archive [online], available at http://www.TheGlobeAndMail.com/docs/webextra/middle_kingdom/ama/ MKamadex.html: B. Little, "Nineties take an income bite from the middle," 19 May 1997; "Youth left out, Canada warned," 15 May 1997; "Consulting the Gini on income," 18 August 1997; "How the earnings of the poor have collapsed," 12 February 1996.

Education, Occupation, and Income: The ten highest-paying occupations in 1995 were judges ($128,791 for men, $117,707 for women); specialist physicians, general practitioners and family physicians; dentists; senior managers (in goods production, finances, or trade); lawyers and Quebec notaries; primary production managers; and securities agents/investment dealers/ traders. The ten lowest-paying occupations were sewing-machine operators ($20,664 for men, $17,340 for women); cashiers; ironing/pressing/finishing occupations; artisans/crasftspersons; bartenders; harvesting labourers; service attendants; food-service counter attendants; food/ beverage servers; and babysitters/nannies/parent helpers.

Sources: Statistics Canada, quoted in the *Globe and Mail* 13 May, 1998, A4.

Family and Education: According to Statistics Canada, the number of children living in families increased by 6.3 percent between 1991 and 1996. Almost none of this increase, however, was attributable to married-couple families. Fifty-two percent of the increase resulted from children living with common-law couples, while nineteen percent resulted from children living with a lone parent. Nearly one in every five children in Canada lived with a lone parent in 1996; four-fifths of these parents were female. The National Survey of Children and Youth states that, while the majority of children with behavioral, academic, and social difficulties (seventy-one percent) live in two-parent families, children in lone-parent families are much more likely to experience these difficulties. One-third of the children from lone-parent families had one or more behavioral problems; one in ten had repeated a grade in school; one in twenty had difficulty in relating to others. The NSCY survey highlights family income and level of poverty as a key factor influencing children's school readiness and verbal development.

Sources: Statistics Canada, "1996 Census: marital status, common-law unions and families," in *The Daily*, released Tuesday, October 14, 1997. [online], available at http://www.statcan.ca:80/Daily/English/971014/ d971014.htm; Canadian Council on Social Development, *The Progress of Canada's Children 1997*, 1997, 12-20; Human Resource Development Canada, *Applied Research Bulletin*, Winter-Spring 1997, 4-19.

Educational Assessment: The Third International Math and Science Study (1998) ranks Canada in the middle of American and European countries (Asian countries absent), with three of the four Canadian provinces that participated in the study (Ontario, Alberta, and British Columbia) scoring above the international average. The results are congruent with other examinations (e.g., Canada's School Achievement Indicators Program) conducted during the 1990s showing that Alberta consistently scores at or near the top of Canadian provinces on written assessments in mathematics and science, and well above the Canadian and international averages.

Sources: Canadian Education Statistics Council, *Education Indicators in Canada [for] 1996* (Toronto: CESC, 1997); "Canadian teens get high marks" in the *Globe and Mail*, 25 February 1998, A4.

Education and Employment: Statistics Canada reports that, in 1997, those with more education have a better chance at getting jobs than those with less. The jobless rate from 1990 to 1997 fell for every age and education group except for young people who failed to stay in school beyond high school and earn some extra credentials. For most of the past decade, the youth unemployment rate for the least educated (those who didn't finish high school) was about double that of post-secondary graduates, and the gap is widening. However, the Centre for the Study of Living Standards shows that while more people than ever are getting more credentials, the value of these credentials related to employability has fallen. Job demand has not kept up with the supply of human capital, creating a paradoxical situation: on the one hand, the odds have increased that staying in school gives a student a better chance of getting a job of some sort, but on the other hand, the odds have fallen slightly that a good education will get a student a job.

Sources: *Statistics Canada Labour Force Historical Review*, Catalogue 71F0004XCB, 1995; *Globe and Mail* The Middle Kingdom, Amazing Facts Archive [online], available at http://www.TheGlobeAndMail.com/docs/webextra/middle_kingdom/ama/MKamadex.html: B. Little, "Education's brutal dividing line on jobs," 9 March 1998; "A sharper picture on jobs and learning," 23 March 1998, A7.

Education and Inequality: The effect of factors that influence social stratification in Canada, the UK, and the US can be estimated based on a variety of comprehensive studies. Ignoring interactive effects, the most significant independent effect occurs among two different groups of variables: 1) individual and cultural characteristics, in particular human capital and status attainment variables; and 2) social structural variables, in particular social class (based on property ownership) and gender variables. By contrast, labour-market factors have only about a third as much impact as any one of these three groups of variables. Similarly, ethnicity (as an independent effect) influences occupational status significantly only in the case of a few, mainly racial, groups and even here the relationship can be highly variable. The estimates of effect for the major variable clusters is as follows: 1) Individual and Cultural Characteristics: intelligence (based on test scores) equals five to ten percent; human capital and status attainment variables, including intelligence scores, years of education and experience, father's occupation and such, equals twenty percent (the addition of family origins and cultural environments to the above factors raises the explained variation in economic inequality to about thirty-five percent). 2) Social Structural Characteristics: labour market factors, such as unemployment rates and segmented labour markets, contribute about eight percent or so of the variation; social class (based on property ownership) equals about twenty percent or a little less of the variation; gender equals about twenty percent or a little more of the variation. The remaining — unexplained — variance is usually attributed to some kind of "luck" of birth or the influence of social networks (the latter requiring an alternative kind of research).

Sources: C.S. Fischer et al., *Inequality by Design* (Princeton: Princeton University Press, 1996); R.J. Brym with B.J. Fox, *From Culture to Power* (Toronto: Oxford University Press, 1989), 92-119; A.C. Kerckhoff, *Diverging Pathways* (Cambridge: Cambridge University Press, 1993); Canadian Education Statistics Council, *Education Indicators in Canada [for] 1996* (Toronto: CESC, 1997).

About the editors

Trevor Harrison is a specialist in political sociology and the author of a number of books, including (with Gordon Laxer) *The Trojan Horse: Alberta and the Future of Canada* (1995). Jerrold Kachur is a professor of educational policy studies at the University of Alberta. His interests include the sociology of comparative and international education.

About Parkland Institute

Parkland Institute is a non-profit research network that conducts, promotes, and disseminates research in the broad tradition of Canadian political economy. The Institute operates under the auspices of the Faculty of Arts, University of Alberta, with input from academic members, as well as from church, private sector, union, professional, community, and general members drawn from across Alberta. Contact the Institute at the address listed on the copyright page; on the Internet at www.ualberta.ca/parkland; or by e-mail at parkland@ualberta.ca.